Health Policy
and the Hispanic

Health Policy
and the Hispanic

EDITED BY

Antonio Furino

Westview Press

BOULDER • SAN FRANCISCO • OXFORD

Copyright © 1992 by Antonio Furino

Published in 1992 in the United States of America by Westview Press, Inc., 5500 Central Avenue, Boulder, Colorado 80301-2847, and in the United Kingdom by Westview Press, 36 Lonsdale Road, Summertown, Oxford OX2 7EW

Library of Congress Cataloging-in-Publication Data
Health policy and the Hispanic / edited by Antonio Furino.
    p.   cm.
Includes bibliographical references and index.
ISBN 0-8133-1456-9
1. Hispanic Americans—Medical care—Congresses.   2. Hispanic Americans—Health and hygiene—Congresses.   I. Furino, Antonio.
[DNLM: 1. Health Policy—United States—congresses.   2. Health Services—organization & administration—United States—congresses.
3. Hispanic Americans.   WA 300 H43393]
RA448.5.H57H42   1992
362.1'089'68073—dc20
DNLM/DLC
for Library of Congress   91-44201
                                                                                                              CIP

Printed and bound in the United States of America

The paper used in this publication meets the requirements
of the American National Standard for Permanence of Paper
for Printed Library Materials Z39.48-1984.

10   9   8   7   6   5   4   3   2   1

Contents

Acknowledgments

A National Action Forum to analyze and discuss the impact of health policy on Hispanics was organized in the fall of 1989 by the Center for Health Economics and Policy of The University of Texas Health Science Center at San Antonio (UTHSCSA) and the San Antonio Metropolitan Health District. Many of the papers presented at the forum were revised and expanded for this volume.

We are grateful to the Partnership for Hope program of the Rockefeller Foundation for providing the project's seed money. Also, we are grateful to the Robert Wood Johnson Foundation for their generous contribution and for the financial and in-kind support received by the RGK Foundation, the South Texas Health Research Center of UTHSCSA, the Monsanto Company, the Benedictine Health Resource Center of San Antonio, the Center for Health Policy Development, Inc., of San Antonio, The Latino Health Policy Center of the University of California at Los Angeles, the IC² Institute of The University of Texas at Austin, and the Office for Substance Abuse and Prevention (OSAP) of the Drug Abuse and Mental Health Administration.

Henry G. Cisneros, during his term as mayor of San Antonio, was the single most effective energy source and motivational force in bringing together the unique mix of public policymakers, academicians, large-scale private sector employers, third-party payors, representatives of nonprofit organizations, and user groups that made the meeting a landmark in the development of a Hispanic health agenda and a rich base for this book. He personally participated in and contributed to the proceedings of the forum and, after completing his term in office and choosing to turn his attention to professional endeavors in the private sector, continued to be supportive and instrumental in ensuring the continuation of this discussion about vital public and private health policy issues. As this book is being published, a new round of contributions is being planned to bring the discussion documented in the volume to a greater level of precision for policy guidance. To Henry, a heart felt "thank you" for his support and inspiration.

Assisting Henry Cisneros, a national steering committee, including Eli Ginzberg, John K. Iglehart, Lawrence S. Lewin, Marion Ein Lewin, Lionel Sosa, Ciro V. Sumaya, and T. L. Tolbert, provided guidance in planning the forum and this publication. Among them a very special mention goes to Eli Ginzberg who read and critiqued drafts of this book, offering, whenever needed, important advice. I am grateful to Fernando Guerra who shared with me the many challenges of planning and implementing the forum.

Many colleagues at The University of Texas Health Science Center at San Antonio offered generously their time and advice. Carlos Moreno coauthored a report on the issues that served as a background for the forum participants.

A large debt of gratitude goes to every participant in the forum, and a special recognition is due to the authors of the chapters in this book for maintaining their enthusiasm and commitment after the event.

I am grateful to Mary Jane Bode for her editorial assistance, to Joanne Hayashi and Marie Tysall for attending with creativity and efficiency to the logistics of the forum, and to Marie Tysall for assisting in the typing of the manuscript.

Antonio Furino

Part One

Issues and Value Questions

1

The Issues: An Overview

Antonio Furino and Fernando A. Guerra

As we learn more about the people and their health status, we discover that Hispanic health issues are better understood and more successfully addressed when we take into account the Latino health discourse (see Chapter 12 and Chapter 4): the viewing of evolving health needs in the historical context of the intellectual and socioeconomic experiences of Hispanic people in the United States. We learn, in our culturally diverse society, that the best opportunities for development and growth are captured when cultural differences contribute to common goals. This occurs when we are able to reinforce rather than dilute the unique strengths that each cultural heritage has captured and preserved over time.

Exploring several dimensions of major Hispanic health issues gives a special character to this book. The intent is to update interested readers with recent information and offer a view of the magnitude, scope, and complementarity of the problems.

Because most Hispanics reside in urban areas, before introducing the contributions to this volume, it may be useful to review certain conditions characteristic of metropolitan health service delivery systems that are neither culture- nor race-specific but that act as barriers to the planning and implementation of targeted health services.

First, a critical mass of efforts capable of bringing relief to the numerous and complex health care needs outlined in the following pages will not be generated by federal public policy alone. Unprecedented budget constraints will continue to limit federal public health programs. The Persian Gulf crisis, the savings and loan bail out, and the uncertainties of the national and global economies are pushing permanent solutions to current budget rigidities further into the future. The availability of federal monies for new programs or even continued support for existing ones will depend, in the foreseeable future, on their neutrality relative to the national budget and on a convincing rationale relative to competing initiatives. Grass-root strategies will offer the best hope of bringing about favorable changes in health behavior and a more effective utilization of existing health care services by Hispanics (see Chapter 2). But community activities will need the support of municipalities and the effective use of state budgets. Also, the role of employers, providers, third-party payors, suppliers, and other private sector institutions will be critical to any serious plan aimed at improving the health of the Hispanic work force or at facilitating the delivery of health care to the underserved.

Cooperation and alliances among the public and private sectors will not occur spontaneously. They will require visionary leadership and determination on the part of the Hispanic people, other minorities, and the traditional community. While bridges between cultures and interest group coalitions will be needed for attaining broader consensus and, therefore, political viability, cross-disciplinary and multiple program approaches will be necessary to insure the success of those comparatively fewer health programs that will survive funding cuts. There are regions where clean water is as important as medical care, urban areas where transportation is as critical as affordable clinical services, communities where work conditions and opportunities are preconditions to better health, and neighborhoods where crime and violence produce the major health risks.

A second barrier to achieving health care targets is that improving the health status of Hispanics, who typically have limited or no health insurance (see Chapter 13), is complicated by the "sectoral" character of health service information and policy. For example, the economic costs of decreased access to health care or of preventable health problems are rarely quantified and do not play a decisive role in budget allocations. The consequences of ill health on the ability of being gainfully employed are known but rarely reflected in decisions allocating resources among those programs that historically have focused individually on either employment, economic development, or health. Reasons for the omission are a lack of quantifiable evidence of the spill-over effects (the costs and benefits that interventions in one area of need have on the others), and a traditional emphasis on the clinical rather than the socioeconomic aspects of health care. As an example, the cost of unplanned pregnancies among teenagers is studied independently from the cost of unemployment due to losses in training and education suffered by the single mother. The vicious circle of being poor—and, therefore, medically deprived and ultimately incapable of preserving a health status adequate to improve one's economic condition—is an accepted paradigm in the discussion of the medically needy. But the linkages among the elements of the vicious circle are rarely made explicit and their cost rarely considered in making public budgets or health policy decisions. Therefore, while it is widely recognized that obstacles to improving the health status of the indigent are not just physical or clinical, but economic, social, psychological, and cultural, this knowledge is not sufficiently reflected in the allocation of resources to public health programs at the local, state, and federal levels. And many cost containment measures rather than attempting to maintain health care delivery with an equal or reduced level of spending, through resource sharing and higher productivity, simply shift costs from the federal to the state and local levels and, ultimately, to individuals through higher taxation or lower levels of services. The outcomes are, usually, reduced access to health care for the needy and higher costs for society as a whole.

A third major obstacle to the delivery of adequate care to Hispanics is the acute care orientation of health services. When emphasis on acute care is combined with ignorance by users on how best to access the health system, hospital emergency rooms become options of last resort for desperate social conditions—a way of coping with poverty and survival rather than medical emergencies—and the system, inappropriately employed, becomes overutilized without producing durable positive health outcomes. Every time a preventable illness reaches the acute or life-threatening stage, large sums of money are spent to delay death, often without improvements in the patient's quality of life. But prevention is seldom viewed as a substitute for acute care since its cost effectiveness is not easily documented and, to be successful, it requires coordinated interventions that address, together with clinical needs, nutritional, educational, housing, life-style, employment, family, and community needs as well.

A fourth major shortcoming in providing adequate urban public health services is the lack, at the local level, of emergency funds for events that are difficult to predict or quantify but are likely to challenge the capacity of metropolitan health systems. Trends such as the information explosion, the internationalization of capital, and the world division of labor have no apparent connection with the delivery of health care in an urban environment, but they can produce large and unexpected changes in health care utilization when they increase the isolation of the urban poor from the mainstream economy, or when, threatening local businesses with global competition, they induce relocations overseas and destroy local manufacturing jobs. Municipalities typically have been unprepared to cope with overloads of the public health system caused by epidemics of disease and catastrophic events, but, more recently, they have been facing less obvious health risks, such as sudden loss of employment and health insurance by large groups of citizens, or the increased social isolation of inner-city residents.

The fifth barrier is lack of compliance with treatment and healthy behavior by those targeted to receive assistance. It is sufficient to enter the overcrowded room of a typical inner-city health care program, to observe the inadequacies of the linkage between the health system and those it serves. Men, women, and children are typically packed in small quarters and wait for hours and sometimes days to receive help. They remain idle around old TV sets while nearby playgrounds, covered with broken glass and abandoned, stay deserted. These people are served by a system that "processes" them but rarely "engages" them in caring for themselves. Therefore, it produces large quantities of paperwork but too few changes in health behavior. Access to health care is attained at the cost of a dehumanizing waiting game in overcrowded, understaffed, and often inefficient public health facilities unaided by the necessary complement of education and neighborhood-based activities. Perhaps more personal care and involvement could be achieved through appropriate economic incentives for private practitioners and the assignment of small groups of indigent patients to providers that are especially trained and compensated for this purpose.

This book is organized in four sections. The sections address (1) the conceptual, institutional, and policy elements of the problems and their solutions, (2) the clinical evidence, (3) social and economic considerations affecting the health status of Hispanics, and (4) future policy options.

Throughout the volume, the terms "Hispanics" and "Latinos" are used interchangeably. It has been argued that the latter better describes the peoples of the Americas since the ethnic components of the U.S. population of "Hispanic" origin are mostly Mexicans, Puerto Ricans, Cubans, and Central and South Americans. However, the term "Hispanics" is the one adopted by the Bureau of the Census, and, therefore, it is the one most commonly used and more readily recognized by those who are not conversant with Latino studies and issues.

Issues and Value Questions

Following this overview, Henry G. Cisneros, in Chapter 2, reviews the policy implications of the country's demographic future characterized by an aging, and proportionally faster growing, traditional population and comparatively younger, minority groups. In discussing the economic and clinical challenges of providing adequate care to Hispanics, Cisneros suggests that we must take full advantage of civic action: from the persuasive powers of our churches to motivate the disenfranchised and the underprivileged, to grass-root organizations for penetrating diffidence and hopelessness in poor neighborhoods, and to senior volunteers for increasing the availability of costly skills. To shape the future, Cisneros sees the need for local government initiatives strengthened by alliances with state and federal governments, employers, and third-party payors. To guide our actions, he proposes that the performance of the health care system be made to conform more closely to the essential elements of the American credo.

In Chapter 3, Eli Ginzberg precedes an analysis of health legislation presently debated in Congress with a discussion of the major factors that determine needs and hinder access to health care among Hispanics.

The educational and socioeconomic characteristics of Hispanic population groups, when combined with the demographic and epidemiologic determinants of need, produce serious health care inadequacies. In addition, underrepresentation of Hispanics in the health occupations complicates both problems and solutions. The elements that are favorable or adverse to better access to health care by Hispanics are reviewed by Ginzberg in light of proposed Medicaid reforms, national health insurance programs, employee mandating, state support for providers of charity care, and new proposals for reducing the cost of private insurance. The analysis uncovers a future of limited choices and lack of consensus among decisionmakers.

An encouraging new perspective for health policy designers is offered by David E. Hayes-Bautista in Chapter 4. First, the author addresses an important methodological issue. He argues that using the underclass model—to design health programs for the underserved—is inadequate for blacks and totally inappropriate for Hispanics. The model, based on studies of urban black minorities during the 1970s and early 1980s, explains low socioeconomic status as the combined effect of characteristics consistently and adversely affecting the integration of certain population groups into society. High rates of low birthweights, infant mortality, and low life expectancy are linked to a loss of work ethic, welfare dependency, and hostile attitudes toward society in a reinforcing vicious circle almost impossible to break in the short run.

Recent health data on Hispanics collected in Southern California paint a different picture of the demographic dynamics of that border region. Data suggest that the majority of Hispanics residing in the states bordering Mexico are foreign born and, contrary to stereotypes, potentially healthier and more productive than the underclass profile would indicate. The startling conclusion is that present social policy responses stifle rather than encourage the needed positive contribution of this population group.

It has been said that the most critical independent variable affecting health status once income differences are taken into account is education. In Chapter 5, Ray Marshall forcefully presents education as a necessary springboard or, when deficient, a formidable barrier to national development. In the discussion, he addresses common myths such as the belief that there is a causal relationship between learning and innate ability, that bilingual education has a damaging effect on educational development, and that quality education for everyone is economically unfeasible.

Marshall starts from the basic proposition that to be a high-income country the United States must have world-class learning systems.

The world economy, he explains, has evolved from the natural-resource and national-market based mass production of the 1930s and 1940s to the human-resource based and information technology-assisted model of the 1970s and 1980s. Accordingly, the tolerance for minimal skills allowed by the standardized technologies of mass production has been replaced with the requirements for higher education and problem-solving skills needed by continuous technological change and production flexibility. In reporting the findings of the recent nationwide study on minority education he chaired, Marshall observes that the disadvantaged position of Hispanics in U.S. education not only prevents the Hispanic people from sharing the rewards of our economic system, but stifles our country's growth potential as we fail to take full advantage of this youthful sector of our otherwise aging work force.

Health Risks for Hispanics

In Chapter 6, Michael P. Stern and Steven M. Haffner review most of the recent literature on the prevalence of type II non-insulin dependent diabetes among Hispanics and conclude that this population group (mostly Mexican Americans, slightly fewer Puerto Ricans, and even fewer Cubans) suffers from a two- to three-fold excess prevalence of the illness as well as a higher risk to succumb to traditional diabetic complications such as severe retinopathy and end-stage renal disease than their non-Hispanic white counterparts. The authors' personal experience as principal investigators of some of the more recent cross-cultural epidemiological studies provides a clear sense of the relative importance of genetic (i.e., the degree of Native American ancestry) versus environmental (change from subsistence economic systems to a modernized life-style and resulting socioeconomic status) factors in the prevalence of the disease. While introducing the reader to the best scientific knowledge presently available for designing appropriate public health responses to the disease, the authors make a strong case in support of further epidemiologic research.

The disadvantaged socioeconomic status of the Hispanic population, the special problems of the border states, the documented lesser access to health services (including immunization services), the low level of educational achievement of Mexican Americans and Puerto Ricans are all indications that Hispanics are likely to be at higher risk of contracting infectious diseases than non-Hispanic whites. Ciro V. Sumaya, in Chapter 7, presents the first extensive review of the medical literature relevant to infectious disease risk differentials between Hispanics and non-Hispanic whites. The gap in the literature is both surprising and worrisome since many infectious diseases are effectively abated through immunization and prevention programs and knowledge of morbidity differentials among population groups is needed to guide targeted and cost-effective public health efforts. Sumaya provides the reader with a detailed discussion and a useful chart that summarizes the findings on twenty major infectious diseases, indicates the areas where the diseases were studied, and gives the relevant references in the literature. Also, he discusses, from the fragmentary evidence available, the factors accounting for the disproportionate representation of Hispanics among those contracting the diseases and recommends actions that may be taken to improve those conditions. For example, factors such as cross-the-border mobility and illegal status require international cooperation and interventions at both sides of the border. Others, such as sanitation, immunization, improvement in basic health behavior, and better access to health services, may be addressed by existing health and economic development programs if sufficient guidance, reliable information, and financial support is provided to program administrators.

In Chapter 8, Fernando S. Mendoza and his colleagues examine a public health challenge of particular importance to both the Hispanic community and the nation. Given the higher birthrate of Hispanic women relative to the rest of the population and the aging of the U.S. work force, the health status of Hispanic children may be considered not only an indicator of the socioeconomic viability of Hispanic families but of the potential vigor of our supply of human resources. First, the authors offer an authoritative discussion of the common measures of children's health status (birth outcomes, birthweight, and the level of premature births) and of their main data sources: the National Vital Statistics System and the Hispanic Health and Nutrition Examination Survey (both under the supervision of the National Center for Health Statistics). Then, using birth outcomes as objective indicators of health status and the perceptions of health conditions by the mothers or by the adolescent children themselves as subjective measures, the investigators arrive at the conclusion that Hispanic children are in relatively good health. As observed by Hayes-Bautista in Chapter 4, this finding is in contradiction with the stereotypes of the underclass model but offers hope for the potential human resource contribution of this sector of our population. Another important finding by the authors is that the differences among the three major Hispanic subgroups are considerable and must be taken into account in policy and program design.

The other end of the age spectrum is discussed by David V. Espino and Marta Sotomayor in Chapter 9. The plight of the Hispanic elderly, often overlooked because of the attention given to the larger, younger cohorts and the shield provided by supportive families, rests on their socioeconomic status, language barriers, little or no insurance, inadequate health service utilization skills, and, consequently, reduced access to health care. Stronger community involvement and the extended family protect Hispanic elderly from early institutionalization but produce additional and sometimes unbearable economic hardship on the younger generations while leaving many needs unmet.

Trauma is the fourth most costly health hazard in the United States and accounts for 7 percent of total health care costs. Yet very little data are available on its incidence and prevalence across racial and ethnic boundaries. A study undertaken by Eric Munoz and colleagues of a large regional trauma center is reported in Chapter 10 and reveals a distinctly different pattern of trauma affecting Hispanics when compared to blacks and non-Hispanic whites. Consistent with the information presented by other contributors to this volume, Hispanics ranked low in insurance coverage by private companies as well as by Medicaid and Medicare.

Oral health data from the Hispanic Health and Nutrition Examination Survey of 1982–1984 and the Ten State Nutrition Survey of 1972 are reported by John P. Brown in Chapter 11. A careful analysis of the available evidence is based on an extensive literature review accompanied by a comprehensive bibliography on oral health status among Hispanics. Brown concludes his review with a set of recommendations for addressing oral diseases among minorities in general and Hispanics in particular.

Economic and Social Considerations

In Chapter 12, David E. Hayes-Bautista complements his criticism of looking at Hispanics through the stereotypes of the underclass model he presented earlier (Chapter 4) with a sensitive and erudite discussion of the conceptual and pragmatic challenges confronting policymakers in a culturally diverse society. Using the AIDS epidemic among California Hispanics as a point of departure and a case study, the author traces the evolution of ideas, values, and actions about health through the history of Hispanic people in North America. An awareness of their health-related experiences through adaptation and survival, called by the author the Latino health discourse, is seen as a necessary precondition to the design of effective health care programs.

Chapter 13, authored by Fernando M. Trevino, M. Eugene Moyer, Robert Valdez, and Christine A. Stroup-Benham, follows the Hayes-Bautista assessment of the intellectual preconditions to effective health policy with estimates of the size of the problem. The authors examine the most recent data on access to and utilization and coverage of health care, including the Hispanic Health and Nutrition Examination Survey of 1984 and the March 1989 Current Population Survey by the Department of Labor. Their findings reveal many inadequacies that place Hispanics and particularly their largest population subgroup, Mexican Americans, at a higher risk of receiving inadequate or no health care than any other population group irrespective of minority or socioeconomic status. To make matters worse, trends point toward a worsening of their condition over time. The problems are not only those of lack of employment. In fact, many of the underserved are classified as "working poor": individuals in jobs without benefits receiving wages too low for purchasing private insurance and too high to qualify for public aid. With one out of every three Mexican Americans without adequate financial resources for minimal health care, the size of the challenge is indeed large. Additional insights on the nature of the problem and some solutions are offered by Adela de la Torre and Refugio I. Rochin in Chapter 14. The occupational distribution of Hispanics in the labor force, mostly concentrated in blue-collar, agriculture, and low-pay service jobs, explains the high proportion of working poor among this population group. Also, it accounts for their low bargaining power since an ample labor supply is available for those occupations and workers can be easily substituted. In evaluating possible solutions, the authors review the Massachusetts and Florida experiments, Medicaid expansion, and universal insurance, as possible, if controversial, approaches to addressing indigent care.

In Chapter 15, David C. Warner concludes the section on economic and social considerations with a close examination of health care on both sides of the U.S.–Mexico border. U.S. trade with Mexico has tripled over the past four years to $60 billion. The *maquiladora* plants on the Mexican side where semifinished manufacturing goods from the United States can be sent for assembly and returned to the United States tariff free, have more than doubled the number of employed Mexican workers. Free trade with Mexico appears to be a reality within the decade. Yet the renewed attention to the border has not improved significantly the health hazards suffered by people on both sides of the boundary line. Poverty, pollution, deprivation, inadequate medical assistance, and high prevalence of certain communicable diseases affect the largely Mexican–American population living in the border counties—some of the poorest in the country—of Texas, New Mexico, Arizona, and California. In contrast, favorable data on infant mortality and birthweight confirm the findings reported by David Hayes-Bautista in Chapter 4.

Warner concludes that binational professional cooperation, adoption of higher environmental standards, the convergence of education and standard of care, and binational agreements on the transferability of insurance coverage are the necessary steps for improving health status in the border regions.

In Chapter 16, Antonio Furino and Ciro V. Sumaya, searching for solutions, examine barriers, opportunities, and strategies awaiting those who are seriously committed to improving the health status of this increasingly larger group of Americans.

The Appendix contains abstracts of additional contributions to the general topic of Hispanic health which could not be presented in their entirety but are believed to be of interest to the readers of this volume.

2

Cooperative Action
for Minority Health Policy

Henry G. Cisneros

Two profoundly important demographic changes are shaping the appearance and the character of our nation. One change is the aging of the traditional U.S. population. The other is the growth of ethnic minorities in the younger age groups.

The aging of America has been well documented, but the magnitude of the related changes has not fully reached public awareness or adequately influenced public policy. Every week in the United States, 210 people, on the average, reach 100 years of age. The fastest growing age group in the country is comprised of people entering their eightieth year. Next year's census will tell us that, for the first time in U.S. history, our society will have more people over 65 years of age than teenagers. At the turn of this century, the average American male spent about 3 percent of his adult life in retirement. During the century that lies ahead, the average American male may spend as much as 30 percent of his adult life in retirement. This is not just a U.S. phenomenon. It has even larger dimensions in Japan and in Europe. And in West Germany, where the largest proportion of older citizens among industrialized nations live, it is possible to observe right now the consequences of a graying society on health and other social programs.

The fact that people in their older years will represent a larger part of society has, per se, no policy significance. The United States always has been able to handle large numbers. But in this case, the phenomenon is combined with economic and social dynamics that reduce the rate of growth of the younger population groups. For instance, women are working in larger numbers than ever before; consequently, they not only are postponing childbearing but are also having fewer children. The result is not only greater numbers of older persons but a greater percentage of them relative to the total population.

The challenging question we must address is, in my judgment, how future-oriented U.S. society will be. A nation traditionally viewing its best days as yet ahead, a nation with a history of adopting successfully an investment philosophy, may well find itself facing the political reality of large groups of citizens who, having already paid for education, may choose not to vote for bond issues or for increases in property taxes needed to improve school programs. Last year in the Florida Democratic primaries, 47 percent of the voters were persons over 60 years of age—almost half of the total vote. Older citizens had 75 percent voter turnout rate, while persons in their twenties had 20 percent.

This reality must be seen in the light of the other demographic trend: the growth of ethnic and racial minorities with a demographic profile decidedly younger than that of the country as a whole. While the median age of the U.S. population is 32 years old, that of Hispanics is 23, that of blacks is 25, and other minorities have, collectively, a median age of 26 years.

It is not an accident that the recently elected mayor of New York is African–American. Nor that the mayors of Philadelphia, Baltimore, Atlanta, Birmingham, and Los Angeles are black. It is not an accident that a Cuban American is the mayor of Miami or a Mexican American was the mayor of Denver. Nor is it an accident that women have assembled progressive coalitions including minority groups and have become mayors of Houston, Dallas, San Antonio, and San Diego. All these events are reflective of fundamentally new demographic realities in the nation's cities.

These realities are now transforming some of our most populous states. For example, California, the state with the largest population, is home to 27 million people; the next largest, New York, has a population of 17 million. It is easy to see why California is so important to this country. In addition to its "people power," if it were ranked according to economic indicators as an independent nation, it would be the sixth most powerful country in the world. In the year 2000, less than ten years from now, California will be 46 percent Hispanic, Asian, and black; San Francisco County will be 65 percent Hispanic, Asian, and black; Los Angeles County, 10 million people strong, will be 60 percent Hispanic, Asian, and black; and Orange County, a traditionally conservative population center, will be 40 percent Hispanic, Asian, and black. Among the rural areas, the Imperial Valley will be 73 percent Hispanic, Asian, and black. In the year 2000, fully 92 percent of the people of California will live in a county where at least 30 percent of the population will be made of Hispanics, Asians, and blacks.[1] Thirty percent certainly constitutes a cultural presence, and immigration will have an important impact on these trends. Indeed, projections indicate that a large portion of the overall population growth will be the result of growth among non-native citizens and undocumented persons, a fact which simply accentuates the diversity of needs to be addressed.

These statistics leave many people perplexed. Some individuals even suggest that action should be taken to curb those trends. But the numbers cannot be easily regulated. In fact, injections of younger persons into an aging labor force may be considered, given adequate training, a source of competitive advantage and, therefore, a favorable phenomenon. However, if the figures are not something to worry about, these figures are something for which to prepare. They represent the mathematically predictable demographic future of our nation. And they have major implications for public health care policy.

For example, Hispanics, projected to become the largest population group in several of our key states, will experience three to five times the incidence of diabetes compared to non-Hispanic whites. This fact in itself calls for a health policy response of a different scale than what we have relied on in the past.

The incidence of cervical cancer among Puerto Rican women in New York is three times that of the general population of women. The expected dramatic growth of the Puerto Rican population will amplify an already significant health issue.

Among pregnant black women, only 60.6 percent receive early prenatal care compared to 81.6 percent of women in the white population.[2] When the higher fertility rate of ethnic minorities is taken into account, one can easily predict that the provision of early prenatal care will emerge in the near future as a key health issue.

Hispanic children ages 5–11 years are twice as likely as non-Hispanic white children to never visit a dentist. Again, we can easily predict that future oral health and dental policies need to be different than in the past.

The Task Force on Black and Minority Health of the Secretary of Health and Human Services has identified specific health problems that place minorities disproportionally at risk relative to the rest of the population. Each one of these problems will become a major challenge for policymaking as minorities increase in number and relative importance in our multicultural society. The challenge is clear. It becomes even greater as we look at the financing of health care and health surveillance and discover how many people in the minority communities have no health insurance. Fully 33 percent of Hispanics and 20 percent of blacks are covered neither by private health insurance nor by a governmental program such as Medicare or Medicaid (see Chapter 13). These statistics compare with only 11 percent of persons who are not covered by insurance in the nation as a whole. Again, our nation is facing a predictable hardening of certain financing and surveillance issues.

We have just looked at a dimension of our future produced by the convergence of two massive demographic trends. Another dimension is created by economic forces which have implications for the distribution of income and, therefore, the distribution of access to health care and health services. We are witnessing the transition of a natural-resource-based economy needing large numbers of blue-collar workers, into an economic system depending on information technologies, automated systems, and fewer production workers. The economy that once required strong arms and strong backs, today needs higher levels of education. The supremacy gained by this country amid limited international competition has been chipped away by strong global challengers that have taken advantage of the information explosion, the opening of new markets, and the shrinking diffusion time of knowledge and technology.

Decisions made about the introduction of a new technology in Japan can result in job losses within the United States. Decisions made about the price of oil and gas in the Middle East decimate, almost instantaneously, the economies of Texas, New Mexico, Louisiana, and Oklahoma. Decisions made about a bad harvest in Argentina affect grain prices, commodities, and jobs in the Plains states. Wealth and jobs originally anchored to mass production in large domestic industries today are created by small businesses in dynamic entrepreneurial settings.

This global reality worsens the effect of the structural demographic changes we discussed earlier. The dislocation of our urban minorities from the vanishing blue-collar jobs to the low-wage service jobs, such as those in fast-food restaurants with few opportunities and no fringe benefits, is well documented. These trends produce widening differences in the distributions of income and a most un-American phenomenon, that of a permanent underclass.

In 1987, the top one-fifth of Americans ranked by income—the top 20 percent—received fully 43 percent of the nation's total income: the largest percentage received by the top 20 percent of the population since the end of World War II. The bottom 20 percent received only 4.7 percent of our national income, the smallest percentage in twenty-five years. In the mid–1970s, the ratio between the top 20 percent and the bottom 20 percent of the population, relative to earnings, was 7 to 1. Last year it was 9 to 1, and it is growing larger.[3]

We are witnessing the solidification of an underclass. From 1974 to 1987, a thirteen-year span from the mid–1970s to the mid–1980s, the number of households with income below $5,000 a year increased from 4.7 million people to 7.2 million people.[4] As one might expect, the number of persons unable to be covered by health insurance has been increasing. Concurrently, traditional health insurance has had dramatic increases in premiums, has been screening out the poorest risks, and is progressively abandoning the coverage of individuals and small employee groups. The relationship between the structural changes in our economy, the widening gaps in the distribution of income, and the hardening of an underclass with decreasing access to medical services is clear.

A third dimension of the future is related to the actions of governments. The federal government has chosen to withdraw from many areas of domestic responsibility. When I became mayor of San Antonio, in 1981, the federal budget for cities included some $69 billion in emergency programs. In 1989, the federal budget allocated approximately $17 billion for similar types of programs—a decrease of 75 percent.

In 1979, $31 billion was earmarked for urban housing initiatives. In 1989, that number was $6.9 billion despite the fact that over the ten-year period, the number of homeless persons had increased.

In the health arena, the federal government relies on Medicaid as the bedrock of health services for poor America. Yet only 45 percent of the poor are covered because of the program's ties with welfare and AFDC income thresholds and cost-shifting strategies at the state level. Due to the continuous retrenchments in our domestic agenda one-half of poor children under the age of 18 are left uninsured.

This erosion of insurance coverage is a serious problem indeed. Some have suggested mandating coverage from the federal level, but I do not believe that this is a feasible remedy. Others propose better insurance coverage for more employees through business tax incentives; but tax incentives are also tax expenditures and it is unlikely that this type of additional federal expenditures will find sufficient support in a political climate predisposed to reject any financial outlay not balanced by a counteracting revenue. With the dominant mood in the nation's capital driven by the federal deficit, it is doubtful that over the next several years major federal initiatives will be directed to increasing health services.

The mixture of demographic changes, economic trends, and the current political climate will shape the health care environment for the 1990s and beyond. Sadly, one-third of the children born over the next decade will live, at best temporarily, below the poverty level. And due to the worsening of non-disease-specific factors, such as real earnings and illiteracy, it is likely that drug abuse and AIDS become increasingly critical. I regret the gloomy nature of the picture I have drawn, but it is a worrisome reality. Our task now is to suggest local models of response to the health care needs of our communities. Ultimately, it is at the local level that public health policies can be made effective. The strategic importance of this fact has increased because, for the time being, federal initiatives are not likely to play a major role in improving health care.

Let us begin by looking at just a slice of the problem such as maternal, infant, and children's care. Children born under weight and malnourished are likely to have a problematic life. When malnutrition continues during early childhood, brain growth is severely compromised. If the condition continues over a two-year period, the chances for remediation diminish drastically and permanent brain injury occurs. The magnitude of the problem is highlighted by the fact that maternal and newborn services make up 25 percent of the uncompensated care of hospitals, and that 35 percent of the uninsured hospital discharges are maternal and newborn. This means that a large portion of the new additions to our population, the children who will inherit and shape our future, are having difficulty in gaining access to basic health care services.

Among the emerging urban pathologies are malnutrition in children, chemical dependency in mothers and youths, and child abuse which can most adequately be diagnosed by health care providers. These morbidities are followed by anxieties of shortened childhood due to early encounters with the traumas of urban survival, by stress reactions to these traumatic experiences such as depression usually left undetected in younger persons because of inadequate health monitoring, neuropsychiatric problems without access to remedial education, sexually transmitted diseases among adolescents, teenage pregnancies, and AIDS.

Recognizing the urgency of the problems, the U.S. Public Health Service, in the recently released *Healthy People 2000* sets forth some important objectives for the nation.[5] Under the title "Reduced Infant Mortality," the goal is to reduce deaths among children under one year from the current 10.4 deaths per 1,000 births to no more than 7. For the black population, the target is to try to bring the number down from 18 births per 1,000, which is the current baseline, to 11 per 1,000 births. Observing these numbers carefully, one realizes that the goal for the black community of 11 per 1,000 births is higher in the year 2000 than the baseline of 10.4 per 1,000 births for the general population today.

Another goal, that of reducing low birthweight (that is, newborns weighing less than 2,500 grams at birth), would attempt to ensure that only 5 percent of all births are characterized by low weight as opposed to the 1986 baseline of 6.8 percent. Again, for the black community, the target is 9 percent from an unacceptably high present level of 12.5 percent.

Under the title "Increasing the Proportion of All Pregnant Women Receiving Prenatal Care in the First Trimester," the goal is to provide prenatal care to 90 percent of U.S. women at the early stage of pregnancy from a baseline of 75 percent in the general population. The corresponding baseline statistics are 61 percent for black women, 60.3 percent for the Hispanic community, and 60.7 percent for Native Americans.

How does one translate goals into services that reduce infant mortality and low weight births or increase the number of women receiving prenatal care in the first trimester? I have already asserted that many of the strategies need to be local. What are the major elements of the approach?

The approach must involve a comprehensive system of clinics reaching the higher need areas of central cities. This requires city/county cooperation and the negotiation of strategies for delivering and financing the services on a scale that we have not seen before now. That is, sharing the burden of programs so that county-wide hospitals will accept the responsibility of central-city obligations. Clinics must be complemented by multiservice centers characterized by holistic approaches to family needs. These are counseling services, educational assistance, job assistance, and other non-disease-specific assistance addressing both health and socioeconomic needs. These services must be physically accessible—near public housing projects, for example—or include a transportation network. Other important components of these multiservice centers are parenting programs where young mothers are taught the basics of nutrition, hygiene, and child care, and mental health programs offering counseling, crisis management, and problem-solving skills in a manner that addresses the unique needs of a multicultural and often bilingual population.

The centers must be linked to other public systems, such as the schools, in order to provide health monitoring of school children and, after hours, utilization of the facilities for health education and other social services that involve the whole community.

In addition to accessible multiservice centers, those who live at the margin of urban communities must be reached. This means reaching addicts and the homeless where they are, frequently in the streets or in specialized centers. It also involves making special efforts to reach those who are most vulnerable to the risks of alcohol, drugs, and poor nutrition. The challenges are staggering. But there are underutilized areas of strength. Our nation has been failing to take full advantage of civic action in the design of local strategies. Churches, for example, can use their persuasive power to motivate the poor and the handicapped. Grass roots community organizations can literally go house to house and bring people together at meetings, and senior citizens groups, continuously growing in size and availability of skills, can play important roles in counseling and technical assistance. On a personal note, I see my own parents involved in this way. My father suffered a stroke in 1976 and, after a life as a civil servant and a colonel in the Army Reserves, was unable to continue working in his profession. Today, my father sits with first- and second-grade special education children at the local Hispanic neighborhood elementary school, providing them with a male role model and him a productive and fulfilling way of using his talents. My mother serves as a board member and volunteer at an organization named ADVANCE, a center dedicated to teaching parenting skills to poor mothers. She dedicated her life to be the best mother in the world and is ready to share her experience and insights with other young women. My parents are an example of what people in their sixties and seventies are available to do. They are a resource that we have not sufficiently tapped.

Any model of access requires funding and to meet that challenge several levels of partnership must be put in place. There needs to be increased funding at the local level even though local governments have limited resources. I feel strongly that we must appeal to metropolitan-wide strategies. It is neither possible nor equitable to place the entire burden for effective health services on central-city governments while the benefits of the services are shared with a surrounding region.

In Hartford, Connecticut, for example, 92 percent of the children in the city's school system are black and Hispanic. But Hartford is a city of only 195,000 people. Therefore, the school system is very small, and its re-sources are a fraction of what they could be if the system were supported by the larger metropolitan area that has a population approaching 800,000. Hartford, the capital of Connecticut, is the economic and governmental center of the richest state, in per capita income, in the United States.

It is critical to fuse metropolitan and regional strategies. One approach might be that of creating incentives by the federal government for area-wide funding mechanisms, for example, block grant programs similar to the Community Development Block Grant Program used for housing and physical development, where area-wide strategies would be a prerequisite to higher levels of federal funding. The approach would target matching funds to communities that have negotiated area-wide strategies for health services cooperation between counties and cities, or between outlying suburbs and central cities.

At this point, one might raise the question as to what is to be the federal government's role. I will not claim originality for my ideas on what the federal government ought to do, but I take my cue from the National Leadership Commission on Health Care, a distinguished group of Americans who recently published recommendations for public and private action relative to three critical issues: access, cost, and quality.[6] The recommendation on the question of access is that the United States should commit itself to a national basic package of health services to be financed by employers in the form of standard health benefits, by employees who desire and can purchase additional coverage, and by individuals who can buy personal insurance. For the 31 million Americans presently without any coverage, the group suggested universal access financed with premium payments from those with incomes of 150 percent or more above the poverty line. To reduce the number of persons depending on the universal access budget, the commission recommended that employers be induced to extend coverage to more employees through special incentives. To avoid creating additional bureaucratic layers, the commission recommended that the program be administered by existing state agencies and that the authority of increasing benefits to address special needs, establishing payment policies, and negotiating with local providers be left with the states. The emphasis is on cooperation across sectors, payors, providers, and users.

Combining the proposal of the National Commission with what was suggested earlier for delivering health services at the local level produces a national access strategy that leaves guidance and some funding support at the national level, assigns fiscal responsibilities mostly at the state level, and creates effective delivery mechanisms as a result of local initiatives. The key elements of this approach are:

1. Universal access to a basic package of health care with optional state enhancements above that level.
2. A combination of individual choices and responsibilities for maintaining acceptable levels of care.
3. Expansion of the existing insurance systems through incentives and disincentives to employers.
4. Recognition that, in addition to apportioning the universal access costs among those who can pay, to raise the health status of those left out by the present system will require new revenues: a necessary and important investment in our future.
5. Reduction of inappropriate care and a focus on quality and effectiveness.

6. An enhanced role for the states in operating and monitoring programs for the uninsured and in negotiating fair compensations with providers.
7. Creation of a system of shared responsibilities at the local level for effective metropolitan health services promoted through guidelines and incentives from the federal government.
8. Establishment and institutionalization of linkages between the health system and other public programs, such as education and social services, and between the public and private sectors.
9. A role for civic action, including the systematic involvement of senior citizens, churches, and grass-roots organizations.
10. Recognition of the fact that since the problems to be addressed are multidimensional, responses must be comprehensive. There must also be a focus on recreating the sense of community life whose disruption has resulted in many of the urban pathologies directly and indirectly related to health status.
11. Accountability at the local level built upon a rational planning process, measurable goals, and concrete rewards to those communities capable of designing, implementing, and evaluating the delivery of effective health services.
12. Emphasis on building from the bottom up, beginning at the grass roots of the system and creating strength through partnerships, alliances, and cooperation. The guiding philosophy must be one of shared roles and responsibilities, an understanding that everyone has a role and a stake in the solution of health problems. Such philosophy must fuel a system that is pragmatic, integrated, and cohesive.

In conclusion, as we think about access to health care and social services, it would serve us well if we would allow ourselves to be guided by the essential elements of the American credo, those we teach to five- and six-year-old children when they first come to school. Since they cannot understand the full meaning of the words, we tell them to just learn them and trust us: "One nation under God, indivisible, with liberty and justice for all." "One nation," we tell them, not islands of privilege, detached from the trauma of a permanent underclass, not groups separated by indices of morbidity or degrees of suffering, not special classes defined by drug use, teenage pregnancy, or violence.

"One nation under God": A God who can see into the "shooting galleries" where young people die in agony, who can see into the home of the battered spouse or the bedroom of the abused child, who can see the anguish of the 14-year-old mother of an undernourished child. "One nation, under God, indivisible": Not divided into black and white, not rendered asunder by fear and hatred, not polarized by race, ethnicity, geography, or income, not battling over a shrinking pie or paralyzed by the complexity and the inertia of the system we have created.

"One nation, under God, indivisible, with liberty and justice for all": Not just for those who were born in richer states, or better neighborhoods. Not just those who went to the best schools, have the right name or a preferred skin color. That is not what we teach. In addressing one of the more complex challenges of our time, we will do best to reach back to the essence of our roots. There is nothing more basic in approaching access to health care than applying in all its strength, all its power, that American ideal.

Given the changes that are upon us, given the waves of demographic, economic, and political change that sweep across our land, we would do well to keep a steady eye on those basic and powerful tenets.

Notes

The material in this chapter has been updated and edited from an earlier version, "Health Policy at the Local Level," The Richard and Hinda Rosenthal Lectures (November 13, 1989). Copyright © 1989 by the Institute of Medicine. Printed with permission from Henry G. Cisneros and the publisher.

1. Los Angeles County. 1989. *Vital Statistics of Los Angeles County.* Department of Health Services, Data Collection and Analysis Division.

2. Jaynes GD, Williams Jr. RM (eds.). 1989. *A Common Destiny: Blacks and American Society.* Washington DC: National Academy Press, pp. 402–403.

3. US Bureau of the Census. 1991. *Statistical Abstract of the United States: 1991.* Washington DC, pp. 421–464.

4. US Bureau of the Census. 1991.

5. US Public Health Service. 1990. *Healthy People 2000: National Health Promotion and Disease Prevention Objective.* Washington DC: Department of Health and Human Services.

6. Report of the National Leadership Commission on Health Care. 1989. *For the Health of a Nation: A Shared Responsibility.* Ann Arbor: Health Administration Press Perspectives.

3

Access to Health Care
for Hispanics

Eli Ginzberg

The conventional population paradigm in the United States has distinguished between the white majority and the sizable and easily identified black minority. Until recently, much less attention has been paid to Hispanics (or Latinos), currently 20 million, whose number the Census Bureau projects will rise to 31 million of a total population of 283 million by the year 2010.[1] In the next two decades, Hispanics will account for one of every three net additions to the U.S. population.[2]

The following analysis considers the critical factors that collectively will determine the access of Hispanics to the health care system and illuminates the changes that, if introduced, will contribute to its improvement. These issues include: the homogeneity or heterogeneity of the Hispanic population; the extent to which socioeconomic status adversely affects Hispanics' access to health care; the influence of demographic and epidemiological factors on their need for care; the role of neighborhood factors in determining their access to the health and medical infrastructures; the paucity of Hispanic health professionals; and, finally, the major reform proposals currently on the nation's health agenda as they relate to the issue of improved access to care for Hispanics.

The Hispanic Population

Over the years, the Census Bureau has used a variety of classification schemes to determine who should be designated a Hispanic. Reliance on a single criterion, such as self-designation, or multiple criteria, such as language and country of origin, yields ambiguous results. In current practice, the 20 million Hispanics in the United States are classified by country of origin. The subgroups of the Hispanic population and their proportional representation are: Mexican Americans, 62 percent; Puerto Ricans, 13 percent; Cubans, 5 percent; Central and South Americans, 12

22

percent; other Hispanics (the Spanish–Mexican–Indian population in the Southwest), 8 percent.[3]

Although every state contains some Hispanics, the vast majority, over 70 percent, reside in six of the nation's most populous states—California, Texas, New York, Florida, New Jersey, and Illinois.[4] Compared to the non-Hispanic white majority, Hispanics are more heavily concentrated in metropolitan centers, particularly in the inner cities.

Several linkages can be made between these geographic-locational characteristics and the growing needs and pressures among Hispanics for improved access to health care services. Their concentration in six states implies that the health policies of these states are first-order determinants of the availability of health care to the Hispanic poor through their Medicaid programs, public hospitals, and special programs, such as compensatory reimbursement to providers for the delivery of uncompensated care.

The overrepresentation of Hispanics within the inner cities of metropolitan areas suggests that most of them live relatively close to hospitals and clinics. The critical question of the ease or difficulty with which low-income Hispanics obtain treatment in such facilities will be assessed below.

Socioeconomic Status

Health care analysts have long understood that the quality of health care available to different groups is influenced by their socioeconomic status, specifically their level of education, occupational achievement, and income. Persons with low income frequently have greater than average need for health care because of the differentially high birthrates, below-par health status, and above-average prevalence of specific diseases associated with these populations.[5] Let us examine the major Hispanic groups to assess the extent to which socioeconomic status influences their access to health services.

A particular disadvantage of the Hispanic population, many of whom are first generation, is the large gap between their level of educational achievement and that of the white majority. See Table 3.1. It is noteworthy that the Cubans and "other" Hispanics (Central and South Americans as well as the Spanish–Mexican–Indian subgroup) approximate most closely the educational levels of the white majority.[6]

Below-average educational achievement is reflected in less favorable occupational status and lower incomes. Among the total population, 56 percent of all employed persons fall into the two highest categories of the occupational ladder, professional and technical[7]; among the Hispanic population, the proportion is 38 percent, except for Cubans, 57 percent of whose working members are classified in these two top categories. Mexican Americans are disadvantaged by virtue of the fact that about 9 percent are still employed in farming, a predominantly seasonal, low-wage sector.

TABLE 3.1   Years of School Completed by Whites and Hispanics,
25 Years and Older, 1987 (in percentages)

	Less Than 5 Years of School	4 Years of High School or More
White (non-Hispanic)	2.0	77.0
Hispanic	11.9	50.9
Mexican	15.4	44.8
Puerto Rican	10.3	53.8
Cuban	6.1	61.6
Other	5.7	61.5

Source: US Bureau of the Census. 1989. *Statistical Abstract of the United States 1989.*
Washington DC: US Government Printing Office, Table 215, p. 133

In comparison, only 1 to 2 percent of other groups of Hispanics are agricultural workers.[8]

The relationship between occupational status and income is confirmed by data for 1988 showing that the median family income of all Hispanics amounted to $21,800, lagging by some 35 percent of the median for whites, $33,900.[9]

In addition to their low family incomes, Hispanics face additional difficulties in accessing the health care system due to the fact that a large proportion of them are employed in low-wage sectors of the economy where employers fail to provide health insurance benefits.[10] Hispanics have lower rates of coverage by private or government health insurance than do whites or blacks. In 1987, 30.1 percent of Hispanics were not covered as opposed to 20.4 percent of blacks and 12.6 percent of whites.[11] Medicaid coverage varies widely by state of residence. As a result, Hispanics in New York and California are more likely to be enrolled in Medicaid than Hispanics in Texas or Florida, a reflection of differential eligibility criteria and administrative practices in these states.[12]

In sum, many Hispanics are poorly positioned to access the health care system by virtue of below-average family income, above-average employment in establishments that do not regularly provide private health insurance, and sizable numbers who live in states with low Medicaid enrollments.

Demographic and Epidemiologic Determinants of Need

The influence of demographic and epidemiologic factors on Hispanics' need and demand for health care services must also be assessed. On the favorable side, Hispanics, other than Cubans, have a younger age profile than the population at large; this means that they are concentrated in age groups that characteristically need and use fewer health care services. Alternatively, their disproportionate representation in the lower income brackets points to an above-average need for health care services because of the association of lower socioeconomic status with poor health status.

A similar favorable/unfavorable balance is suggested by the differentially high birthrates of Mexican Americans, indicating the need for greater access to prenatal and postnatal care for women and children.[13] On the favorable side, it should be noted that the birthweight pattern of Mexican Americans resembles that of upper-income, non-Hispanic whites, rather than that of comparable lower income blacks. Distinctive cultural factors, such as less frequent smoking and lower alcohol intake by Hispanic women, probably contribute to this counterintuitive finding.[14]

For their part, Mexican Americans and Puerto Ricans have a much higher incidence of type II diabetes (adult onset diabetes), approximately two to three times that of the non-Hispanic population. Moreover, this disease strikes a younger age group and often leads to complications that have been attributed in part to the difficulties encountered in obtaining adequate health care.[15]

Although the health status of Hispanics, by subgroup and by gender, has thus far been insufficiently analyzed because of the late start of federal and state bureaucracies in collecting health data based on ethnic background, there is evidence that a considerable number of Hispanic women are obese, perhaps as many as one-third of all Mexican Americans and Puerto Ricans.[16] Other data point to differentially high rates of cervical cancer among Hispanic women, which may be referable in part to their inadequate access to and use of preventive services.[17] On the positive side, many Hispanics have lower than average rates of other varieties of cancer.

Recent data released by the Centers for Disease Control reveal that of the 15,763 reported AIDS cases among Hispanic adults and adolescents, 50 percent are directly or indirectly related to IV drug use; of the 419 reported Hispanic pediatric AIDS patients, 72 percent are children of mothers who had been infected by sexual partners who were drug users.[18] Among selected groups of Hispanics who are heavily addicted to IV drug use, the rising trend of AIDS cases is a serious threat. In New York, this threat is compounded by the fact that the state is seriously lagging in its addiction treatment capacity.[19]

Obviously, the foregoing does not provide a comprehensive view of the morbidity trends of different Hispanic groups; rather, it is a reminder that, in addition to problems of access to the health care system that result from low income and lack of insurance, epidemiological factors underlie the needs of some Hispanics for above-average utilization of health care services.

Locational and Institutional Factors

Locational and institutional factors also influence the ease or difficulty that Hispanic groups experience in obtaining access to health care. Since Mexican Americans constitute the largest group, about three out of every five, we will turn to their problems first.

The Mexican Americans that are most at risk are the close-to-a-million farm workers who have both above-average accident rates and the most limited access to health care providers. A second subgroup is the large number who live along the U.S.–Mexico border stretching from Southern California to Brownsville, Texas. The population on both sides of the border is estimated to approach 10 million this year. In Texas alone, over 110,000 persons live in *colonias* or unincorporated areas. These settlements often lack septic tanks, sewers, and running water.[20]

Water and air pollution threaten residents on both sides of the border as does the dumping of hazardous waste. In Chapter 15, David Warner points out that health care entitlements are extremely thin and that along the entire border, there is only one fully supported public hospital (in El Paso) that serves as a facility of last resort for the poor. Many Mexican Americans cross back into Mexico when they have to buy pharmaceuticals or obtain health or dental care.

Another view of how Hispanics fare in the Texas health care system is had from Harris County (Houston). A recent draft report from the School of Public Health of The University of Texas Health Science Center at Houston states:

> Chronic illness as a health problem is less important than are the problems of younger people: poor pregnancy outcomes, growth and development of children, drug abuse, AIDS, and other infectious diseases. The proportion of users of the district (public) services that are Hispanic has been steadily growing during this decade . . . a high proportion have low incomes. Overcrowding of patients stresses this system . . . a disproportionately large amount of resources is directed to emergency or otherwise delayed and serious admissions. Elective or tardy admissions are crowded out.[21]

Paradoxically, Houston has the greatest concentration of health care facilities of any metropolitan center in Texas.

One more reference to the Mexican–American population, this time to the immigrants in Southern California who are the largest group of Hispanics involved in the amnesty program. For the most part, this population consists of younger people, a great many of whom are classified as "working poor" which implies that most of them do not have private insurance. The Immigration Reform and Control Act of 1989 has placed constraints on their ready access to need-based health service programs. Many new aliens will not be eligible for Medicaid services until 1992 even during the period when they become permanent residents.

If we shift our focus from the West to the East Coast, the situation in New York City clearly illustrates the influence of location upon the health care services that are available to different Hispanic groups in the metropolis. For the most part, Hispanics are dependent in the first instance on the clinics and emergency rooms of public hospitals that are operated by the New York City Health and Hospitals Corporation (HHC); secondarily on the ambulatory care services of selected voluntary hospitals; in some neighborhoods they have access to local community health centers; they also obtain care from group practices and private practitioners. Since there are substantial differences in the availability and quality of ambulatory care or of inpatient care among the hospitals that Hispanics use, any overall generalization about the health services available to them would be unjustified. However, their concentration in low-income areas of the city carries a presumption of a lower quality of care than that available to persons living in higher income neighborhoods.[22]

The Paucity of Hispanic Health Professionals

One of the reasons for the difficulties Hispanics experience in obtaining adequate health care is the fact that they are seriously underrepresented in the health occupations, particularly those requiring higher levels of skill. The complements of Hispanic dentists, registered nurses, pharmacists, and therapists accounted in 1989 for between 2.2 percent and 3 percent of the totals in these professions. The proportion of physicians is somewhat higher, about 5.4 percent; this reflects the considerable number who were trained abroad and subsequently immigrated to the United States.[23]

According to the most recent data from the Association of American Medical Colleges, Hispanics comprise the following proportions of the current student enrollment in U.S. medical schools: Mexican Americans, 1.7 percent; Puerto Ricans, 2 percent; other Hispanics, 1.7 percent. The trend in first-year matriculants in 1989 showed no increase.[24]

Since Hispanics will soon exceed 10 percent of the total population, a continuing gross deficiency of Hispanic health professionals threatens the level of access of this large and growing minority to the health care system. However, to increase significantly the flow of Hispanics into health professional schools is not an easy undertaking and the resources required far exceed those currently available. Such an effort requires early interventions to direct capable students to precollege programs which offer special educational guidance, counseling, and tutoring; the availability of financial assistance; and the provision of a variety of other supports. Effective efforts that might contribute more immediately to reducing the present and prospective gap between the needs of Hispanic users and the availability of Hispanic health care providers include intensive health educational programs by community groups, using oral and written techniques, particularly the preparation and dissemination of preventive health materials in Spanish.

Implications of Major Health Reform Proposals for Improved Access for Hispanics

This section considers the strengths and weaknesses of some of the nation's major health reform proposals from the vantage of their probable impact on access to health care for the large, growing, and highly diversified Hispanic population.

Currently, the only measure with a probability of early action is the further extension of recent federal legislation to improve Medicaid coverage by mandating or permitting the states to liberalize eligibility requirements for women and children. Despite the fact that the federal government funds from 50 to 83 percent of the costs of state Medicaid programs, forty-eight of the nation's fifty governors recently requested the Congress to slow the pace of its liberalization efforts because of the strain that expanded eligibility and service provisions impose on their states' finances. Given the larger proportion of Hispanic women who are of childbearing age than among the population at large and their above-average birthrate, the proposed Medicaid reforms cannot have anything but a positive impact.

As has been noted earlier, two facets of health and medical care for Hispanics warrant the special attention of the federal government. The Mexico–U.S. border creates distinct health problems that exceed the obligations and capabilities of local and state agencies to respond. This is also true for the large number of aliens included in the amnesty program who face barriers in seeking to qualify for Medicaid services. With respect to both, modest actions by the federal government could measurably improve access to health care for particular groups of low-income Hispanics.

Turning to more fundamental reform, the overreaching policy issues that affect Hispanics involve national health insurance, employer-mandating, new approaches aimed at reducing the costs of private health insurance, and state support to compensate providers of disproportionate amounts of charity care. Each will be discussed in turn, from the least to the most radical.

Several states, among them New York, New Jersey, Florida, and California, have had some success in establishing a state financing pool for redistribution among hospitals and other providers that furnish large amounts of uncompensated care. There is considerable potential for extending this strategy, including recourse to "sin taxes" following the recent initiative of California. Greater state support for public hospitals directed to sustaining the extant health care system is a variant of this approach. Since a high proportion of Hispanics lack any, or adequate, insurance, such efforts, if aggressively pursued, should facilitate their access and improve the level of care they obtain.

If the private insurance industry, with the assistance of state and/or federal support, addressed the issue of providing catastrophic insurance to individuals, directly or through intermediaries, a considerable proportion of the presently uninsured Hispanic population could obtain coverage. This proposal reflects the fact that in 1987 over one-quarter of all uninsured Hispanics had incomes that exceeded 200 percent of the poverty level.[25]

Currently, the most widely debated health reform proposal is employer mandating, either by the federal government or by the states. It should be noted, however, that except for Hawaii and the abortive effort in Massachusetts, employer-mandating initiatives are still in the planning stage.

There are good reasons, however, for Hispanics to be cautious of mandating proposals because of the potential disruption they can cause in coverage for dependents, many of whom are now included under so-called "rich" policies of another member of the family. Moreover, faced with a cost that they cannot absorb, many employers would seek to escape the obligation to provide health coverage by hiring part-time employees. Worse, there is a distinct likelihood that a considerable number of employers would be forced to close down their establishments, jeopardizing the jobs of many Hispanics.

Given the many complexities and potentially adverse consequences of employer mandating, it is not surprising that a growing number of Hispanics favor a federal or federal/state system of national health insurance (NHI). In principle, it looks extremely attractive to draw all of the presently uninsured into a system that promises greater equity as well as the potential for effective cost control.

However, there are important negatives that cannot be ignored. So far there is no political consensus for national health insurance; the likelihood of excluding private health insurance companies from the financing of the nation's health care system is problematic; the ability to devise a national system flexible enough to be responsive to the distinctive conditions in each of the fifty states is questionable, the more so in light of the history of declining Medicaid coverage between the mid–1970s and the mid–1980s. Furthermore, there is little reason for confidence that federal or federal–state funded NHI would not run into a financial-service squeeze that would lead to early and probably ever tighter rationing of health care services.

Nevertheless, proposals for NHI as they develop in the years ahead, warrant the serious consideration of Hispanics. If NHI were to move to the top of the health policy agenda, it would be responsive to many of the health and medical needs of the Hispanic population. At the same time, it would carry a great many concomitant and congruent costs that need to be assessed.

Concluding Observations

We know less than we should about the present and emerging health care needs of the different Hispanic populations. Nevertheless, we know enough to understand that Hispanics with below-average education, skill levels, and income are at risk and will remain at risk until all U.S. residents have coverage for essential health services.

We also know that broadened and improved health care services for Hispanics depend in large measure on increases in the number of Hispanics interested in and prepared to enter the health care professions.

Finally, a strengthened economy with associated improvements in family income, housing, and educational services would contribute significantly to the future health and well-being of the large and growing Hispanic minority.

Notes

Reprinted with permission from Eli Ginzberg, "Access to Health Care for Hispanics," *Journal of the American Medical Association* (January 9, 1991), vol. 265, pp. 238–241. Copyright © 1991, American Medical Association.

1. US Bureau of the Census. 1990. *Statistical Abstract of the United States: 1990.* Washington, DC: US Government Printing Office, Table 15 and Table 16.

2. US Bureau of the Census. 1990, Table 15 and Table 17.

3. US Bureau of the Census. 1990, Table 45.

4. US Bureau of the Census. 1989. *Statistical Abstract of the United States: 1989.* Washington, DC: US Government Printing Office, Table 28.

5. Bunker JP, Gomby DS, Kehrer BH. 1989. *Pathways to Health: The Role of Social Factors.* Menlo Park, CA: The Henry J. Kaiser Family Foundation; and US Bureau of the Census. 1989, Table 215.

6. US Bureau of the Census. 1990, Table 645.

7. US Bureau of the Census. 1990, Table 645.

8. US Bureau of the Census. 1990, Table 626.

9. US Bureau of the Census. 1990, Table 716; and US Bureau of the Census. 1990, Table 726.

10. Trevino FM, Moyer ME, Valdez RB. Health Insurance Coverage and Utilization of Health Services by Mexican Americans, Puerto Ricans and Cuban Americans. Chapter 13 in this volume.

11. US Bureau of the Census. 1990, Table 152.

12. US Bureau of the Census. 1990, Table 146.

13. Stroup-Benham CA, Trevino FM. 1991. Reproductive Characteristics of Mexican–American, Puerto Rican and Cuban–Origin Women. *Journal of the American Medical Association* 265(2):222–26.

14. Hayes-Bautista DE. Latino Health Indicators and the Underclass Model: From Paradox to New Policy Models. Chapter 4 in this volume.

15. Stern MP, Haffner SM. 1990. Type II Diabetes in Mexican Americans: A Public Health Challenge. Chapter 6 in this volume.

16. Dawson DA. 1988. Economic Differences in Female Overweight: Data from the 1985 National Health Interview Survey. *American Journal of Public Health* 78:1326–29.

17. National Cancer Institute. 1988. *Cancer in Hispanics.* Bethesda, MD: National Institutes of Health.

18. Estrada AL, Erichson JR, et al. In press. Risk Reduction Among Hispanic IV Drug Users and Receptivity to Community AIDS Education. In Furino A (ed.). *Hispanic Health Policy Issues from Recent Research.* San Antonio, TX: Center for Health Economics and Policy and South Texas Health Research Center, The University of Texas Health Science Center.

19. Joseph SC. 1988. Combatting IV Drug Use. In Rogers DE, Ginzberg E (eds.). *The AIDS Patient: An Action Agenda.* Boulder, CO: Westview Press.

20. Warner DC. Health Care on the U.S.-Mexico Border. Chapter 15 in this volume.

21. Loe H. 1991. *Final Report: Monitoring and Assessment of the Health Delivery System in Harris County, Texas.* Prepared for The Eisenhower Center for the Conservation of Human Resources. New York, NY: Columbia University.

22. United Hospital Fund. 1989. *New York City Health Facts, 1989.* New York, NY.

23. Institute of Medicine. 1989. *Allied Health Services: Avoiding Crises.* Report of the Committee to Study the Role of Allied Health Personnel. Washington, DC: National Academy Press.

24. Jonas HS, Etzel SI, Barzansky B. 1989. Undergraduate Medical Education. *Journal of the American Medical Association* 262:1011–19.

25. Trevino FM, et al.

4

Latino Health Indicators and the Underclass Model: From Paradox to New Policy Models

David E. Hayes-Bautista

Since the 1960s, the country's attention has occasionally focused on the plight of "minorities" in society. Rooted in concern for the plight of blacks in society, the issues of low income, poverty, and low educational attainment begged for some explanation. A model was developed to explain these outcomes, and to provide a basis for social policy. This model was that of the urban underclass.

While there are many variants of the model, most analysts[1] agree on the following characteristics of the underclass:

- High rate of welfare dependence
- High rate of female-headed households
- High rate of male unemployment
- Loss of work ethic, expressed by leaving the work force
- High rate of substance abuse
- High rate of infant mortality
- High rate of low birthweight babies
- Low life expectancy
- Overall high mortality

In some of the more popular presentations of the underclass model, such as that provided by Auletta,[2] the underclass is characterized at the psychosocial level as hostile, fearful, belligerent, excluded from society, and rejecting society's values.

The Underclass Model and Latino Policy

Most of the national level policy debate about minorities has concentrated on blacks and black issues. Thus, the most recent Department of

Health and Human Services publication on the health of non-Anglos is tellingly titled *Report of the Secretary's Task Force on Black and Minority Health*.[3] The model of the urban underclass was developed to undergird policy directed at black concerns. The model has been extended, without much thought, to other minorities, on the assumption that one model fits all. Latinos are among the groups to which the underclass model has been applied.

At first glance, this might seem appropriate. After all, Latinos, like blacks, have low income and low levels of educational attainment. However, we will argue in this chapter that the underclass model is very inappropriate for Latino policy. Its inability to provide a proper basis for Latino policy that fits Latino demographic data further suggests that it might not be an appropriate model for black policy either.

Immigration and the Underclass Model

The Latino population, fueled by immigration and fertility, is growing rapidly. In California, it grew from barely 1.5 million in 1960 to over 7 million in 1990, and is projected to grow to at least 10–12 million by 2000. Nationally, the Latino population stands at about 21 million, and should grow to around 30 million by 2000.[4] This growth is not viewed positively by some Anglos. A quote from a *Los Angeles Times* article on Anglo anti-immigrant groups provides an example of commonly published perceptions of Latinos, and especially immigrants: "The protesters . . . struck a responsive and provocative chord in Southern California, drawing mostly non-Latinos who say they are fed up with illegal immigration and what they view as its corollary evils—drug trafficking, the spread of disease, terrorism, traffic congestion and environmental degradation among others."[5]

A portion of the non-Latino population sees Latino growth as a source of unending social pathology and, thus, as a threat. More Latinos are equated with more social problems. A common reaction, then, is a desire to limit the growth and participation of Latinos, especially immigrants. These policies suggest a desire for a social quarantine.

Such an approach is driven by an application of the underclass model to Latinos in general, and immigrants in particular. Our research has led us to believe that the underclass model is completely inappropriate for Latino policy. As a result of following Latino health indicators since they first became available, we have unravelled the underclass model, and found it to be seriously flawed both in its conception and in its application. We propose to use health indicators as a basis for developing Latino social policy.

Overall Health Indicators: The First Clues

Health data for Latinos in California have not been long available. Up until the 1970s, Latinos were categorized as "white," and their statistics

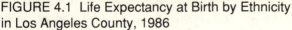

FIGURE 4.1 Life Expectancy at Birth by Ethnicity
in Los Angeles County, 1986

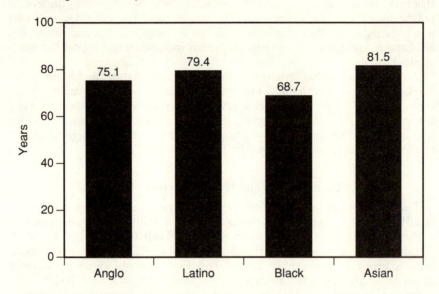

Source: Los Angeles County Data Collection & Analysis, 1989:X.

were combined with Anglos. While data for blacks and Asians have been
used for decades, the compilation of Latino data is fairly recent. Because
Latino and black income levels were both dismally poor, it was common
to assume that Latino health profiles were similar to black. Hence, even
though data were not available, many health and other policy areas were
developed on this assumption. As we shall see, once the data are examined,
that assumption is hopelessly mistaken.

It was not until the late 1970s that some state and county agencies
began using Latino identifiers. Los Angeles County was one of the first to
do so. Given the size of the Latino population residing in the county, over
3 million (more than half the total Latino population of the state), county
data may be generalized to the rest of the state with a fair degree of
confidence. We shall consider data for Los Angeles County for the year
1986, which is the most recent year for which complete data were available
as of this writing.[6]

Overall life expectancy and mortality indicators provide the first clue
that Latinos may not fit the underclass model. In 1986, Latinos had 79.4
years of life expectancy at birth. This was 4.3 years longer than Anglo life
expectancy (75.1 years) and 10.7 years longer than black (68.7 years). Only
Asians had a longer life expectancy—81.5 years—than Latinos.[7] See
Figure 4.1.

FIGURE 4.2 Age-adjusted Death Rate by Ethnicity
in Los Angeles County, 1986

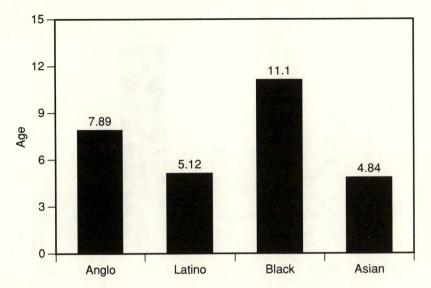

Source: Los Angeles County Data Collection & Analysis, 1989:29.

The age-adjusted death rate shows a similar discrepancy. The Latino age-adjusted death rate for 1986 was 5.12, much lower than the Anglo rate of 7.89, and less than half the black rate of 11.1. Only Asians had a lower age-adjusted death rate than Latinos—4.84.[8] See Figure 4.2.

For most causes of death, Latinos had a significantly lower death rate than Anglos and blacks. For example, the Anglo death rate for circulatory system of 558.4 was over five times the Latino rate of 96.0; blacks had a death rate of 176.5 and Asians, 128.8.[9] One cause of death that is most associated with an underclass style of life is external causes. These are deaths due to violence, homicide, and accident. In Los Angeles County for 1986, the Latino death rate of 56.0[10] was over 20 percent lower than the Anglo rate of 69.7, and was almost exactly one-half the black death rate of 111.4. Asians had the lowest rate, 32.4. See Figure 4.3.

State-level data, although not yet as complete as county data, show similar trends. Clearly, these differences are not flukes, nor are they products of glitches in start-up efforts to identify Latinos. These trends have been noted by demographers,[11] but they have not been noted by general policymakers, health planners, and health providers.

Healthy Babies: Towards a Non-Underclass Model

The data that argue most persuasively against a simple application of the underclass model to Latinos are the birth outcome data. For a number

FIGURE 4.3 Death Rates Due to External Causes,
by Ethnicity in Los Angeles County, 1986

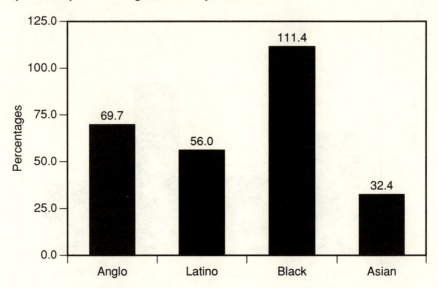

Source: Los Angeles County Data Collection & Analysis, 1989:56.

of reasons, Latinos are the most prolific group in California.[12] In Los Angeles County in 1986, Latinos accounted for 49.7 percent of all births.[13] The Latino birthrate of 32.5 per 1,000 is higher than either Anglo (11.2), black (23.1), or Asian (19.0).[14]

The standard risk-factor model posits that mothers of low income, low education, and limited access to health care run the risk of negative birth outcomes: low birthweight babies, high neonatal and infant mortality. Although income data for Latinas giving birth in the county are not available, from statewide census data it is evident that Latinas have a much lower level of education—an average of 8.9 years—than Anglo (12.5 years) or black (11.8 years) women.[15] Latinas also have a much lower annual income ($7,330 in 1980) than Anglos ($9,900), blacks ($10,110), and Asians ($9,720). Latinas also access health care at much lower levels than Anglo or black women.[16]

Given the lower education, lower income, and limited access to health care of Latinas, one would expect that Latina birth outcomes would be substantially more negative than black or Anglo. In fact, just the opposite has been consistently observed. Latinas have the lowest incidence of low birthweight babies in Los Angeles County: 5.32 percent.[17] This is lower than the Anglo rate of 5.51. Although the difference may seem small, one should remember that Anglo women have much higher income, education, and access to care. The most telling argument against the application of

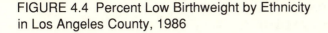

FIGURE 4.4 Percent Low Birthweight by Ethnicity in Los Angeles County, 1986

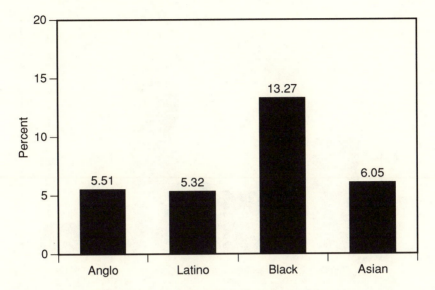

Source: Los Angeles County Data Collection & Analysis, 1989:89.

the underclass model to Latinos is seen in the contrast with black low birthweight: 13.27 percent of births to black mothers were low birthweight, over twice the rate of Latinos, a group with much lower income and education. The rate for Asians was 6.05 percent. See Figure 4.4.

The discrepancy between the expected and the observed is continued in neonatal mortality. The Latino rate of 4.0 was nearly half the Anglo rate of 7.3, and nearly one-third the black rate of 11.0.[18] Asians did have a lower rate—1.9. See Figure 4.5.

This discrepancy is repeated in the infant mortality rate, where again the Latino rate of 5.7 was nearly half the Anglo rate of 11.3 and less than one-third the black rate of 17.7.[19] Because Los Angeles County has longitudinal data, we can appreciate that this is a consistent trend. Figure 4.6, which provides infant mortality rates for the 1974–1986 period, shows that for every year for which data are available, Latino infant mortality has been consistently and substantially lower than Anglo and black infant mortality. See Figure 4.6.

These outcomes are truly surprising, and they lead us to question strongly the wisdom of applying the underclass model to the Latino population. There is no ready, proven explanation for these unexpected, but now often observed, outcomes. We are beginning a research project at the Chicano Studies Research Center to discover the protective mechanisms that cushion Latina mothers against the effects of low income, low

FIGURE 4.5 Death Rates, Neonatal (1,000) by Ethnicity
in Los Angeles County, 1986

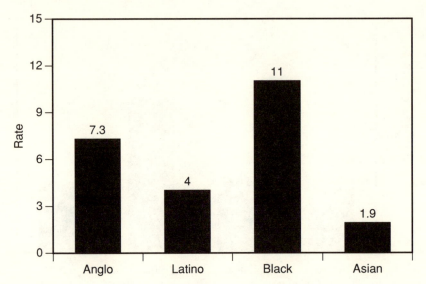

Source: Los Angeles County Data Collection & Analysis, 1989:61.

education, and low access to care. From other research, we may be able
to suggest that there are some inherently very healthy behaviors at work.

Maternal drinking is bound to have an effect on birth outcome. Female
drinking is a commonly reported trait of underclass women. However,
many studies of Latino drinking patterns have repeatedly shown that
Latina females drink much less than Anglo and black women. Indeed,
Latinas are the group most likely to be abstainers.[20] Similarly, Latinas are
much less likely than blacks or Anglos to smoke[21] and much less likely to
use drugs.[22] Latino male patterns are somewhat different, but their effect
on birth outcome is not direct. The healthy behavior of Latinas seems to
indicate that some sort of cultural vitality is overlooked when the underclass model is used.

Our curiosity piqued by these unexpected health data, we turned to
other areas of social life to see how this healthy vitality is expressed in
other areas of Latino life. The picture we developed runs very counter to
the underclass model.

Healthy Families

The gradual erosion and disintegration of the American family has
been noted recently.[23] A virtual lack of family life has long been considered
a hallmark of the urban underclass.[24] Amidst all these jeremiads about

FIGURE 4.6 Infant Mortality Rate by Ethnicity
Los Angeles County, 1974 – 1986

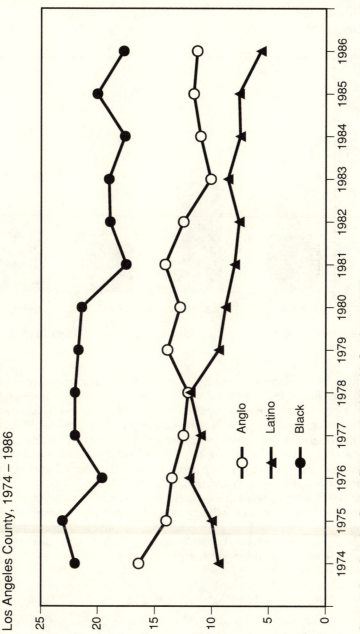

Anglo

Latino

Black

Source: Los Angeles County Department of Health Services, 1987.

FIGURE 4.7 Family Type by Ethnicity, Couples with Children
California, 1980

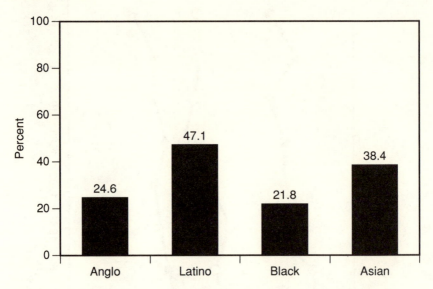

Source: California Employment Development Department, 1986:18-20.

the future of the American family, Latinos have maintained a very healthy family life. From 1980 census data for California, we see that Latinos are nearly twice as likely as Anglos or blacks to have a family consisting of the classical nuclear family of a married couple with children.[25] See Figure 4.7. This is also a consistent trend. Recently published Public Use Micro Sample (PUMS) data covering the 1940–1980 period show that Latinos have consistently been the group most likely to be married and to maintain families of couples with children.[26]

And, of course, when Latinos form households, they tend to be larger than those formed by any other group. The average household size for Latinos in California was 3.74 members in 1980, larger than Anglo households of 2.46 or black households of 2.78.[27] Certainly, the intact family is alive and well among Latinos.

Healthy Work Ethic

Another hallmark of the underclass is a loss of the work ethic and an increasing reliance on welfare and other unearned transfer payments as a source of income. As may be suspected from the above data, Latinos do not fit this model of income generation. To begin with, in California in 1980, Latinos had the highest rate of male labor force participation: 80.6

FIGURE 4.8 Male Labor Force Participation Rates by Ethnicity
California, 1980

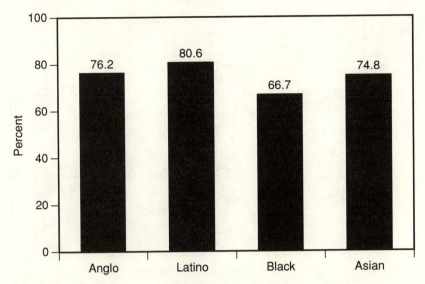

Source: California Employment Development Department, 1986:33-34.

of Latino males were participating in the work force, compared to 76.2
percent of Anglos, 74.8 percent of Asians, and 66.7 percent of blacks.[28]
See Figure 4.8.

This trend is consistently observed in the PUMS data, with Latinos the
most active group in the labor force from 1940 to 1980. By 1980, Latina
females also had surpassed Anglo females in labor force participation
rates.[29]

By a very significant factor, Latinos are more active than any group
working in the private sector: 82.4 percent of Latino males work in the
private sector, compared to only 70.3 percent of Anglos, 62.5 percent of
blacks, and 72.3 percent of Asians.[30] See Figure 4.9.

In contrast, Latinos are the least likely to be employed in government
jobs: only 12.1 percent were so employed, compared to 15.6 percent of
Anglos, 27.6 percent of blacks, and 16.05 of Asians.[31]

The image of a single mother living off welfare also does not hold for
Latinas. In spite of having the lowest income and education of any group,
Latinas participate disproportionately less frequently in government sub-
sidy programs and receive remarkably little unearned income. In 1985,
Latinas age 20 to 24 (the age group most likely to be single mothers)
received an average of $524 in unearned income, only slightly more than
Anglo females ($504), slightly less than Asian females ($535), and nearly
two-thirds less than black females ($1,680).[32] See Figure 4.10.

FIGURE 4.9 Percent Employed in Private Sector by Ethnicity
California, 1980

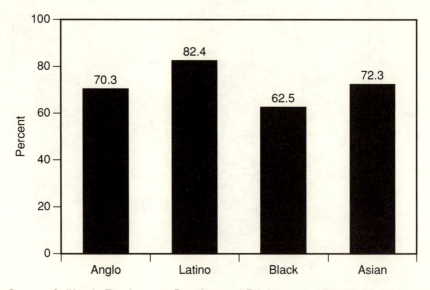

Source: California Employment Development Department, 1986:33-34.

Interestingly, and in contradistinction to the image of Latinas immi-
grating to the United States for the purposes of receiving welfare benefits,
foreign-born Latinas received only $387 in unearned income, the least
amount of any group.

Latinos: The Underclass Model Does Not Fit

It is clear that the underclass model does not fit Latinos. Far from being
a population of unemployed males and disintegrated female-headed
households dependent upon welfare and exhibiting a variety of unhealthy
outcomes, Latinos present a very different picture: strong families, healthy
babies, and a vigorous work ethic.

Yet, Latinos also have the lowest income and educational level of any
group in California. By far the common policy mistake of the past has
been to focus only on income and education, and then assume that low
levels of income and education must be the outcome of some internal
social pathology so often described in the underclass model. Again, by
using health data, we can begin to develop a policy model that might be
more appropriate.

FIGURE 4.10 Per-capita Unearned Income, Female,
Age 20-24, by Ethnicity — California, 1985

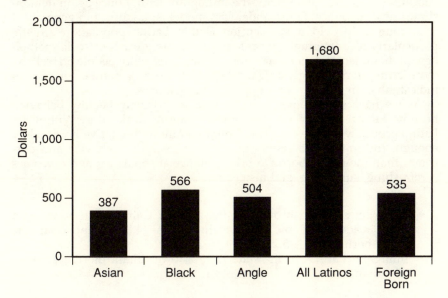

Source: Hayes-Bautista, Schink & Chapa, 1988:166.

Latino Immigrants:
Healthier Behavior, Anemic Results

Currently, much policy debate about Latinos revolves around the issue of immigration. This is a recent development, and one that appears to be very misunderstood. As recently as 1960, immigrant Latinos were rare: only 19.4 percent of the Latino population was foreign born–over 80 percent was native born.[33] However, since 1960 this proportion has reversed. We may adumbrate the findings of the 1990 census by observing the ratio of immigrants to native born we found in a recent survey, the California Identity Project, conducted by the Chicano Studies Research Center at UCLA. In a statewide sampling, we found a population that is nearly 60 percent immigrant and 40 percent native born. Some market researchers would put the ratio as high as 80 percent immigrant and 20 percent native born, although we are not confident of such figures.[34] Nonetheless, it is quite evident that the majority of the Latino population in 1990 is immigrant.

Immigrant Latinos have much lower income and education than the native born. In our recently conducted survey, immigrants had a median income of $19,433, while the native born had $24,057. Likewise, the immigrants had a mean educational level of 7.8 years, while the native born had 11.3 years. Yet, in spite of having much lower income and education than the native born, the immigrant Latino once again demonstrates how inapplicable the underclass model is to Latinos in general.

A commonly held misperception is that Latino population growth, particularly of immigrants, means an inevitable growth of social pathology: higher unemployment, more broken families, more people on welfare, more crime, more drugs, and the like. Data from a number of sources indicate that, in fact, the very opposite may be true.

As we have seen above, Latinos have surprisingly healthy behavior, healthy babies, healthy families, and a healthy work ethic. Within the Latino group, when we compare the immigrant to the native born, oddly enough, the immigrant demonstrates even healthier behavior and outcomes than the native born. To briefly glance at some data and outcomes is refreshing, surprising, and instructive.

- Latina immigrants throughout the state of California have a much lower incidence of low birthweight babies—4.3 percent—than the native-born Latina—5.2 percent.[35]
- Immigrant Latinas in the state have a lower infant mortality rate—7.7—than native-born Latinas—8.1.[36]

Although Latinas in general had healthy habits and family life, the immigrant is slightly ahead of the native born in these areas:

- Immigrant Latinas giving birth in California were more likely to be married—77.4 percent—than native-born Latinas—68.2 percent.[37]
- Immigrant Latinas are much more likely to abstain from alcohol—76.0 percent—than native-born Latinas—48.0 percent.[38]
- The less acculturated Latina (usually, the immigrant) is much less likely to smoke—12.5 percent—than the more acculturated (usually, the native born)—18.9 percent.[39]

From initial analysis of our recently completed California Identity Project Survey,[40] it is evident that the general strengths of the Latino population are emphasized in the immigrant portion:

- Immigrants are slightly more likely than native born to be married—68 percent versus 65 percent.
- Immigrants hold family values a bit more strongly than the native born—a score of 21 out of 40 on a composite scale of family engagement, compared to a score of 19 out of 40 for native born.
- Immigrants are a bit more active in the labor force than the native born—86.5 percent to 84 percent.

- Immigrants are a bit more active religiously than the native born—
68.9 percent of immigrants attend church regularly compared to 61.6
of the native born.

The picture that emerges of the Latino immigrant is rather at odds with
the popular image. Far from being an endless source of social pathology,
the immigrant portion of the Latino population is reinforcing basic social
values of health, family, and the workplace.

The disturbing picture that is emerging is that the Latino population
begins its sojourn in the United States as a fairly active, healthy, vigorous
group. Over time, we notice that these traits seem to erode somewhat, by
generation and assimilation. While there is still enough left of these traits
to lift the Latino population head and shoulders above other populations
in terms of health, family, and work, we are very disturbed by the constant
erosion and loss of strengths. Rather than being a source of pathology,
Latino immigrants from Mexico are in fact maintaining and reinforcing
values of health, family, and work. However, the policy response to Latino
immigration does not recognize the reinforcement, nor build upon it.

Obstructing the Contribution

The social policy response to immigrants, particularly to those from
Mexico and Latin America, is extremely negative. Driven by an image of
a growing underclass, obstacles are purposely placed in the path of Latino
immigrants, criminalizing the very act of seeking work and forming a
family. The Immigration Reform and Control Act has probably done more
to erode Latino families and work ethic than any other policy development.
Other policy initiatives, such as the English Only movement, while seen
as a means to retain American values, only serve to erode Latino values.
And, as we have seen, Latino values in themselves provide a reinforcement
of American values about health, family, and work.

Our policy framework continues to view Latinos as an underclass. In
so doing, our policymakers have not seen the strength and vigor that
Latinos bring to the U.S. economy and society. Our policies are designed
to limit an imagined pernicious influence of Latinos upon society, when
in reality Latinos are contributing much, and have the desire to contribute
more. In essence, our policies, based on an erroneous application of the
underclass model, serve to limit the contributions that Latinos are poised
to make.

Our policies should be reoriented to maintaining and building upon
the strengths that Latinos bring to the economy. It should be our policy
objective to unleash the creative potential that Latinos have, not to obstruct
it. This will mean a reworking not only of the underclass model but also
of the assimilation model. In our data, we consistently note that the more
assimilated Latinos become, the more the key values of health, work, and
the family are eroded. If our society and economy truly desire those

values, and if they are most present in the least assimilated groups, then we will need new models for a multicultural society that does not require that one give up one's ethnic values. This will be a sea change in North American policy discourse, but it is one that the data lead us to argue for.

We recognize that this policy portrait of Latinos is different, and flies in the face of conventional wisdom. However, the health data are extremely compelling and undeniable. Coupled with data on families and labor force participation, it is clear that the underclass model is not appropriate for viewing the Latino population, and provides an erroneous base for public policy. It is the health data that began to help us unravel the underclass model, and it is our sincere hope that policymakers will take advantage of the tremendous opportunity offered the society and economy by the growing Latino population, rather than obstruct those contributions because of the fear of an imagined social pathology.

Notes

1. Wilson WJ. 1987. *The Truly Disadvantaged: The Inner City, the Underclass and Public Policy*. Chicago, IL: University of Chicago Press; Murray C. 1984. *Losing Ground: American Social Policy 1950–1980*. New York, NY: Basic Books; Moynihan DP. 1965. *The Negro Family: The Case for National Action*. Washington, DC: US Department of Labor, Office of Planning and Research; Lewis O. 1968. The Culture of Poverty. In Moynihan DP (ed.). *On Understanding Poverty: Perspectives from the Social Sciences*. New York, NY: Basic Books; Wilson JQ. 1975. *Thinking About Crime*. New York, NY: Basic Books; Glasgow DG. 1980. *The Black Underclass: Poverty, Unemployment and Entrapment of Ghetto Youth*. New York, NY: Random House; and Nathan R. 1987. Will the Underclass Always Be With Us? *Society* 24:57–62.

2. Auletta K. 1982. *The Underclass*. New York, NY: Vantage.

3. US Department of Health and Human Services. 1985. *Report of the Secretary's Task Force on Black and Minority Health*. Washington, DC.

4. Hayes-Bautista DE, Schink W, Chapa J. 1988. *The Burden of Support: Young Latinos in an Aging Society*. Stanford, CA: Stanford University Press.

5. *Los Angeles Times*. 1990. Tactic of Lighting Up Border Raises Tensions. May 26.

6. Los Angeles County. 1989. *Vital Statistics of Los Angeles County*. Department of Health Services, Data Collection and Analysis Division.

7. Los Angeles County. 1989, p. 25.

8. Los Angeles County. 1989, p. 29.

9. Los Angeles County. 1989, p. 54.

10. Los Angeles County. 1989, p. 56.

11. Hayes-Bautista DE, et al. 1988, p. 101; and California Department of Health Services, Center for Health Statistics. 1984. *Public Health Dateline*. Sacramento, p. 4.

12. Hayes-Bautista DE, et al. 1988, pp. 19–21.

13. Los Angeles County. 1989, p. 67.

14. Los Angeles County. 1989, p. 66.

15. California Employment Development Department. 1986. *Socio-Economic Trends in California, 1940–1980*. Sacramento, p. 30.

16. Williams R, et al. 1987. Pregnancy Outcomes Among Spanish Surname Women in California. *American Journal of Public Health* 77(1–6):387–91.

17. Los Angeles County. 1989, p. 89.

18. Los Angeles County. 1989, p. 61.

19. Los Angeles County. 1987. *A Report on Selected Health Status Indicators.* Department of Health Services, Data Collection and Analysis Division, p. 164.

20. Gilbert MJ. 1987. Alcohol Consumption Patterns in Immigrant and Later Generations. *Hispanic Journal of Behavioral Sciences* 9(3):299–314; and Caetano R. 1988. Alcohol Use Among Mexican Americans and in the U.S. Population. In Gilbert MJ (ed.). *Alcohol Consumption Among Mexicans and Mexican Americans: A Binational Perspective.* Los Angeles, CA: UCLA Spanish Speaking Mental Health Research Center.

21. Marin G, Perez-Stable E, Marin BV. 1989. Cigarette Smoking Among San Francisco Hispanics: The Role of Acculturation and Gender. *American Journal of Public Health* 79(2):196–98; and Marin G, et al. 1986. *Cultural Values and Acculturation Among Hispanics.* Technical Report. San Francisco Hispanic Smoking Cessation Project.

22. Smith-Peterson C. 1983. Substance Abuse Treatment and Cultural Diversity. In Bennet G, et al. (eds.). *Substance Abuse: Pharmacological Development and Clinical Perspectives.* New York, NY: John Wiley & Sons, pp. 370–82; and Santisteban D, Szapocznik J. 1982. *The Hispanic Substance Abuser: The Search for Prevention Strategies.* New York, NY: Grune & Stratton.

23. Zimmeister K. 1990. Growing Up Scared. *The Atlantic Monthly* June:49–66; and Axinn J, Stern MJ. 1988. *Dependency and Poverty.* Lexington, MA: Lexington Books, pp. 52–58.

24. Wilson WJ. 1987, pp. 63–93; and Murray C. 1984, pp. 124–34.

25. California Employment Development Department. 1986, pp. 18–20.

26. California Employment Development Department. 1986, pp. 18–20.

27. California Employment Development Department. 1986, p. 16.

28. California Employment Development Department. 1986, pp. 33–34.

29. California Employment Development Department. 1986, pp. 33–34.

30. California Employment Development Department. 1986, pp. 47–48.

31. California Employment Development Department. 1986, pp. 47–48.

32. Hayes-Bautista DE, et al. 1988, p. 166.

33. California Employment Development Department. 1986, p. 10.

34. Strategy Research Corporation. 1988. *The 1988 Los Angeles Hispanic Market* (3):107.

35. Williams R, et al. 1987, p. 388.

36. Williams R, et al. 1987, p. 389.

37. Williams R, et al. 1987, p. 389.

38. Gilbert MJ. 1987, p. 313.

39. Marin G, et al. 1986.

40. Chicano Studies Research Center. 1990. *California Identity Project, Preliminary Analyses.* Los Angeles, CA: UCLA.

5

Education, Productivity, and the Nation's Future

Ray Marshall

It has been demonstrated that there is a strong correlation between educational achievement and health indicators, as well as between educational achievement and various indicators of social pathology. Andrew Sum and Gordon Berlin offer proof of this in *Toward a More Perfect Union*, a very useful book published by the Ford Foundation.[1]

Because education is often confused with schooling, it is sometimes believed that education has no strategic importance in improving quality of life. But education, not just years of schooling, does improve the thinking and decision-making skills that have become necessary in American society.

Since the oil price shock of the 1970s, we have been competing mainly by cutting our real incomes. For example, full-time working males earned on the average $2,600 a year less in 1987 than in 1979. The decrease for the Hispanic counterpart was $4,200. So the average wage gap for Hispanic males relative to white males in 1979 was 79 percent of white males, and in 1987, it was 68 percent—a tremendous drop in relative position. The United States is competing in the world by lowering wages.

The fundamental proposition seems to be fairly straightforward. Either a nation competes by cutting wages and income or by improving productivity, product quality, and production flexibility.

The wealth of this nation was built upon abundant natural resources and the economies of scale made possible by mass production for a large internal market. The introduction of information technology has made capital and resources mobile and consumers more knowledgeable. With increased resource-output ratios, countries that are poor in natural resources can now compete in global markets by focusing on human resource development.

While the U.S. educational system has done a good job teaching the basics of reading and writing—95 percent of the adult population is "technically speaking" literate—less than 20 percent of our young adults can read a bus schedule, figure out the tip on a restaurant bill, or read a page and tell you what they read, to say nothing of doing complex, higher order thinking. Large numbers of U.S. high school graduates cannot do simple rank ordering of fractions. It is not surprising that in 1990, Korea was at the top of the mathematics and science scores for 13-year-olds, Japan, number two, and the United States, last.

The U.S. educational system has been influenced by the Henry Ford mass-production model. The basic component of this model is that workers do not have to think—they only need to follow instructions. Large output and cost reductions under this model make possible relatively high standards of living without much work because once technology becomes standardized, a good living is attainable with limited education and skills.

By following this assembly-line model, the United States developed a work force that could recognize information but lacked problem-solving skills. Machines now do more of the direct production work, such as putting a bolt on a wheel in an automotive factory, and humans do more of the indirect work, such as analyzing, creatively, the large quantities of data generated by the sophisticated monitoring of production processes and product characteristics. Indirect work is best accomplished through team efforts which also require creative thinking and communication skills.

In contrast with elementary and secondary schools, U.S. institutions of higher education are world-renown. The United States exports annually about $6 billion dollars more in higher education than it imports, and more people come to the United States for higher education than go elsewhere. In addition, the nation has world-class science and technology systems. And because of its preeminence in these areas, the country enjoys high-quality legal immigrants which greatly enrich its human capital pool. But without the necessary ingredients for translating research into products, neither higher education nor leadership in science and technology help the United States in world competitiveness because pure research is like defense spending—it's a free good. More Nobel laureates are found at Berkeley than in all of Japan because the Japanese concentrate on creating economic advantage by transforming research findings into new products.

The problem for the Hispanic population is that they are grossly underrepresented in the better-quality higher education systems. This point is reinforced by fairly consistent findings on minority education, and, recently, in *Education That Works: An Action Plan for the Education of Minorities*,[2] the 1990 report of the Action Council on Minority Education. Only about 25 percent of Hispanic high school graduates in recent years have taken courses that qualify them for college work. Despite some recent progress, the educational achievement gap between minorities and whites remains very wide. In 1988, the proportion of 17-year-olds who scored at the intermediate level in reading proficiency were: whites, 89 percent; blacks, 76 percent; and Hispanics, 73 percent. Scores at the adept level were: whites, 46 percent; blacks, 26 percent; and Hispanics, 24 percent. The proportion of those who could complete moderately complex math problems were: whites, 58 percent; blacks, 22 percent; and Hispanics, 27 percent.

High school completion rates reveal similar patterns. Although the proportion of Hispanics who have completed high school increased from 32 percent in 1970 to 51 percent in 1988, by the latter year 36 percent of Hispanics between the ages of 16 and 24 had not completed high school, compared with 13 percent of blacks and 13 percent of whites. Hispanics also are much more likely than other groups to leave school in the early grades. In 1988, for example, 31.4 percent of Hispanic school-leavers had completed only six or fewer years of school; only 3.1 percent of non-Hispanic school leavers had six or fewer years of schooling. Another disturbing fact is that the Hispanic dropout rate remained at about 36 percent between 1968 and 1988, the rates for whites declined from 15 to 13 percent, and the black rate fell to 14.7 percent from 27.4 percent.

College enrollments and degree attainments reveal the same mixed results: there have been important absolute gains, but wide gaps exist between minorities and whites. The number of Hispanics aged 18–24 in college grew 43 percent between 1976 and 1986, but the total number of Hispanics of that age grew 63 percent. In 1986, 35 percent of white high school graduates went to college compared with only 29 percent of Hispanics; in 1976, 36 percent of Hispanic high school graduates went to college. Hispanics also are much more likely to attend two-year institutions: 55 percent of Hispanic students were enrolled in such institutions in 1987 compared with about one-third of whites and 43 percent of blacks.

Not only do they have lower enrollment rates in higher education, but Hispanics are much less likely to graduate. A study of 1980 high school graduates found that six years later whites had earned bachelor degrees at twice the rate of Hispanics. Minorities also have been particularly underrepresented in science and engineering. Of the more than 73,000 baccalaureates awarded in engineering, math, and science in 1986, for instance, less than 7 percent were earned by minority students.

Table 5.1 shows how minority student participation diminishes at various levels of higher education. Hispanics, for example, are 5 percent of undergraduate enrollment but receive only 3 percent of the baccalaureate degrees and 2 percent of masters and Ph.D. degrees.

Despite the strong learning systems at the higher end of the spectrum, we have more poverty and more poor families than any other industrial country. In fact, according to a recent Urban Institute study, the United States has twice as large a proportion of children in poverty than any European country studied.[3] And, of course, Hispanics are overrepresented in this group.

These are troublesome findings because with a few remarkable exceptions, poor families are not very good learning systems. The remarkable exceptions are due to motivation. Once one controls for income, Hispanic

TABLE 5.1   Minority Share of Degrees Declines Along Pipeline, 1986-87 Data

Group	Undergraduate Enrollment	% of Total	B.A.	% of Total
White	8,552,000	79.0%	841,280	85.0%
Hispanic	569,000	5.0%	26,990	3.0%
Am. Ind./Al.	84,000	1.0%	3,971	0.4%
Black	995,000	9.0%	56,555	6.0%
Asian/Pac. Is	394,000	4.0%	32,618	3.0%
Nonresidents	204,000	2.0%	29,308	3.0%
Total	**10,798,000**		**990,722**	

Group	Graduate Enrollment	% of Total	M.A.	% of Total	Ph.D.	% of Total
White	1,132,000	79.0%	228,870	79.0%	24,435	72.0%
Hispanic	46,000	3.0%	7,044	2.0%	750	2.0%
Am. Ind./Al.	5,000	0.3%	1,104	0.4%	104	0.3%
Black	72,000	5.0%	13,867	5.0%	1,060	3.0%
Asian/Pac. Is	43,000	3.0%	8,558	3.0%	1,097	3.0%
Nonresidents	136,000	9.0%	29,898	10.0%	6,587	19.0%
Total	**1,434,000**		**289,341**		**34,033**	

Source: Reprinted from Quality Education for Minorities Project, *Education that Works: An Action Plan for the Education of Minorities* (Cambridge, Mass: MIT, 1990) p. 22.

families give higher values to education than non-Hispanic white families, and, when income is controlled for, minorities actually have lower dropout rates than whites.[4] This is not surprising. Education is the main route of economic improvement for disadvantaged people. So it is not that they do not value education; it is that they are not able to provide a good learning environment because they have not had a lot of formal learning.

This vicious circle of inhibiting conditions will have a large and negative impact on the future of the United States because of the country's demographic trends. The people who historically have benefitted from our world-class learning systems account for a very small fraction of the growth of our work force. Non-Hispanic white males will account for 8.5 to 10 percent of the growth of the work force between 1990 and 2000. Minorities and women will account for more than 90 percent of this growth. And, in spite of the fact that young women entering the work force are better educated than young men, the largest part of the increase in the number of those employed or actively looking for work will be made of people who are not well served by our learning systems. When this demographic reality is coupled with another demographic trend—the graying of the United States—it forcefully underlines the importance and urgency of dealing with the inequity issue. If access of minorities to educational and health care facilities continues to fall behind the rest of the population, it may produce irreversible damage to American society.

The minorities are keeping us young: The median age of Hispanics is about 23 or 24, while the median age of Anglos is 33 and of blacks, about 26. The median age of West Germans is 45, and that of Mexicans, 15. The relative size of the non-Hispanic white population will peak in the year 2020 in the United States. I estimate that non-Hispanic whites will reach minority status in 2080. By the year 2020, they will be a minority in Texas, California, and New York.

We can see the early signs of the change in our schools right now. In California, the majority of children attending public school are minorities. This will be true for Texas by 2000, if not earlier. On the other end of the demographic spectrum, the baby boomers will begin to retire in the year 2010—more than 77 million of them, mainly non-Hispanic whites, who can rely on their pensions. Again, the importance of the inequity issue must be stressed. Few problems are more devastating to human society than racial, ethnic, and religious conflict. The way to avoid it, of course, is to exploit the tremendous advantages of our multicultural, multiracial society.

What should the United States do about its human resource development problem? First, one needs to recognize that, as much as it is needed, fixing the learning systems alone will not solve the problem. A first step would be the promotion of early childhood development programs such as Head Start. The fact that the United States does not fund high-yield programs such as Head Start is a national disgrace. Much is lost when a program in which you can pay $1 and earn $5 to $7 in direct and indirect benefits is not extended to 100 percent of the eligible population.

Minorities have no greater stake in any other movement than they do in the restructuring of the schools. Because minorities are heavily concentrated in the public schools, restructuring of schools so that minorities have the responsibility to see that children are educated would be beneficial.

However, in order to create world-class schools, we must eliminate some of the myths about learning. One myth is that learning is mainly due to innate ability, of which minorities are deprived. The evidence, of course, is that learning is mainly due to hard work and supportive educational systems.

Another myth is that bilingual education tends to weaken one's ability to learn English. This is untrue. Learning any language helps in learning all other languages. The more of them one learns, the better linguist one is likely to be. Therefore, teaching children in their own language until they can be taught in English does not interfere with their education.

We also perpetuate the myth that providing quality education to everyone costs too much. In fact, it will cost us a great deal more not to have an adequately educated work force. The evidence suggests very strongly that one of the reasons for the decline in black enrollment in colleges and universities is that it is much more difficult for them to finance postsecondary education. One way to address this problem would be to have a youth-service program and attach the GI bill to it. How much has the federal government made on those, including the author, who were educated by the GI bill? The debate is whether it is five or twelve times as much as the government paid out, and not whether the government is making sufficiently large returns on its investment. It is absurd not to make this type of investment in human capital. One could make education a free good at every level, as the Swedes do, simply on the strength of available evidence that education is a national high-yield activity.

Also, half of our young people and more than half of all young Hispanics—from 60 to 75 percent—do not attend college at all and of those who do attend less than 10 percent graduate. More attention needs to be paid to improving the ability of our young people to attend and graduate from college. However, because not everyone will choose a college education, we need to strengthen a second-chance system. Part of the nation's poor performance in attracting and retaining students is because its school-to-work transition system is possibly the worst of any major industrial country. We need to improve it by strengthening the Job Corps, Head Start, and other innovative programs. School-based service programs work well if they are user-driven rather than producer-driven. They must have the flexibility to adapt to the needs of those to be served, rather than just process those individuals who fit certain predetermined categories of needs. In the present system of categorical programs, too many people fall between the cracks. We can easily imagine someone saying, "You are not a drug addict yet, so we cannot help you." Or, "If you had robbed a bank, there would be something we could do. If you're just thinking about robbing a bank, there's not a whole lot we can do."

In conclusion, we need to create a sense of national urgency about our human resource development problem. I don't think we have much time left, possibly twenty years. If we wait until the baby boomers retire, the country may be past the point of no return.

The United States needs national leadership to gather support for programs that work. Leadership requires decisionmakers at every level who will view problems as problems to be solved, not to be sympathized with. In my experience, the closer you get to Washington, the more people think they can solve problems with sympathy. They want to have a thousand points of light, but they fail to provide the batteries.

Human resource problems cannot be solved with sympathy. One must approach them with determination and a commitment to rationality as one would any other tough problem. This book, an initiative to bring national attention to Hispanic problems, will benefit not only Hispanics but the whole country. And given the realities of the national and global trends just reviewed, I cannot think of anything more important to the country than to promote quality education for minorities.

Notes

1. Berlin G, Sum A. 1988. *Toward a More Perfect Union*. New York, NY: Ford Foundation.

2. Quality Education for Minorities Project. 1990. *Education That Works: An Action Plan for the Education of Minorities*. Cambridge, MA: MIT. January.

3. Smeeding T, Torrey B, Rein M. 1988. Patterns of Income and Poverty: The Economic Status of Children and the Elderly in Eight Countries. In Palmer J, Smeeding T, Torrey B (eds.). *The Vulnerable*. Washington, DC: Urban Institute.

4. Quality Education for Minorities Project. 1990.

Part Two

Health Risks for Hispanics

6

Type II Diabetes
in Mexican Americans:
A Public Health Challenge

Michael P. Stern and Steven M. Haffner

The prevalence and incidence of type II diabetes is substantially higher in Mexican Americans than in non-Hispanic whites. This fact—combined with an earlier age of onset and the younger age structure of the Mexican–American population—makes diabetes a major public health problem in this ethnic group and one that to a greater extent than in non-Hispanics strikes individuals in the prime of life.

Recent studies also show Mexican Americans to be in "double jeopardy": Not only do they have a greater chance of developing diabetes, but once having developed it, they are at greater risk of suffering from its many complications.

Although this chapter will focus on the Mexican–American population, it is appropriate to summarize briefly the diabetes experience of the other two major Hispanic subgroups in the United States as documented in the 1982–1984 Hispanic Health and Nutrition Examination Survey (H–HANES):[1] Puerto Ricans, like Mexican Americans, were found to have an approximately two- to three-fold excess prevalence of type II (non-insulin dependent) diabetes mellitus compared to non-Hispanic whites. Cuban Americans were found to have a much lower prevalence, only slightly higher than that of non-Hispanic whites.

This pattern is of interest because Puerto Ricans have significant amounts of Native American ancestry, although less than Mexican Americans. They also have a considerable amount of black ancestry, whereas Mexican Americans have much less.[2] Although estimates of Native American ancestry are not available for Cubans living in south Florida (the H–HANES site for Cuban–American research), ethnohistorical considerations would suggest that they have considerably less Native American ancestry than either of the two other Hispanic subgroups. Native Americans are at exceedingly high risk for type II diabetes, raising the possibility

57

TABLE 6.1   Eight-Year Incidence of Type II Diabetes in
Mexican Americans and Non-Hispanic Whites (in percentages)

Age	Mexican Americans	Non-Hispanic Whites	Relative Risk
25-34	7/171 = 4.1	0/ 67 = 0	—
35-44	11/184 = 6.0	1/ 89 = 1.1	5.5
45-54	11/152 = 7.2	2/ 76 = 2.6	2.8
55-64	10/ 90 = 11.1	3/ 73 = 4.1	2.7
Total	39/597 = 6.5	6/305 = 2.0	3.3

Age-adusted (by the Mantel-Haenszel procedure) incidence ratio = 4.0 (95%
confidence interval = 1.64, 9.76; x^2 = 10.47; p = 0.001)
x^2 for homogeneity across age strata = 1.21, p = 0.751.

Source: Stern MP, Haffner SM. 1990. Type II Diabetes and its complications in Mexican
Americans. *Diabetes/Metabolism Reviews*, 6(1):29-45.

that the high prevalence of this disorder among Mexican Americans and
Puerto Ricans derives from their Native American ancestry.

The high prevalence of type II diabetes in Mexican Americans has now
been documented in several studies including three from Texas,[3] one from
New Mexico,[4] one from Colorado,[5] and the H–HANES, which included
all five southwestern states.[6] In all of these studies, the excess prevalence
over that found in non-Hispanic whites approximated two- to three-fold.

Recent incidence data from the San Antonio Heart Study show the
incidence of type II diabetes to be higher in Mexican Americans than in
non-Hispanic whites in all age decades for which data are available. The
age-specific incidence ratios indicate that the ethnic differences in diabetes
incidence decrease with age, going from "infinite" in the youngest age
decade to 2.7 in the oldest (Table 6.1). These results suggest that the
diabetes excess in Mexican Americans may be—at least in part—the result
of an accelerated onset in addition to an absolute increase in risk. Indeed,
a significantly earlier age of onset has been directly demonstrated in this
ethnic group. This difference can be demonstrated in each age decade
indicating that it is not merely a reflection of the younger age structure of
the Mexican–American population.

The earlier age of onset has major public health significance: It means
diabetes is more likely to afflict Mexican Americans in the prime of life.

Although Mexican Americans constitute only 17.3 percent of the Texas
population, they account for 26.3 percent of the diabetic caseload. This
disparity is even more striking for individuals in the 25- to 44-year-old
age range. Here, Mexican Americans account for nearly half—46.2 percent—of the diabetic caseload, even though they constitute only 19.4
percent of the state's population in this age range.

We will consider three types of risk factors for type II diabetes in
Mexican Americans: physiologic, genetic, and environmental.

Physiologic Risk Factors in Mexican Americans

Although physiologic risk factors have both genetic and environmental determinants, these have not been well-delineated in most cases, so it is convenient to discuss these risk factors as a separate group.

Physiologic risk factors include obesity, body fat distribution, and circulating glucose and insulin concentrations.

Many studies have documented a higher prevalence of obesity in Mexican Americans than in non-Hispanic whites.[7] Most of these studies have relied on various weight-for-height indexes, so that they have, in reality, measured overweight rather than excess adiposity, i.e., "fatness" *per se*. (One study, however, measured total body fat by an isotope dilution technique using deuterium oxide, and confirmed that the excess weight of Mexican Americans relative to non-Hispanic whites is indeed associated with excess adiposity.[8])

There has been a recent resurgence of interest in the role of body fat distribution in the development of various chronic diseases, among them diabetes. A variety of indexes of body fat distribution have been proposed, including the ratio of waist-to-hip circumference, the ratio of subscapular to triceps skinfold (centrality index), and indexes based on intraperitoneal fat as assessed by computerized tomography. The latter technique is rarely feasible in epidemiologic studies because of its relatively high cost. There is still no consensus as to which of the various indexes is best, and, indeed, there is at least some evidence that no single index can capture all of the variance in health outcomes associated with body fat distribution.[9]

A large number of cross-sectional studies show an association between type II diabetes and unfavorable body fat distribution—upper body and/ or centralized or truncal obesity.[10] There are also several prospective studies indicating that an unfavorable body fat distribution is a risk factor for the development of type II diabetes, for example, a study of Caucasians from Sweden which used the ratio of waist circumference to hip circumference as the indicator of fat distribution.[11] We recently confirmed this finding in Mexican Americans, using the centrality index as the indicator of fat distribution.[12]

Plasma glucose concentration—either fasting or following an oral glucose load—has been found to be a risk factor for diabetes in a number of studies.[13] To date, only the San Antonio Heart Study—a two-phase survey of 5,174 Hispanic and non-Hispanic adults in three socioeconomically distinct neighborhoods—has examined this question prospectively in Mexican Americans.

In the San Antonio Study, we found that subjects whose fasting plasma glucose concentration was in the highest quartile of the glucose distribution at their baseline examination had a greater than thirteen-fold increased risk of developing type II diabetes over an eight-year follow-up period compared with individuals in the remaining three quartiles of the glucose distribution.[14] Similarly, individuals with baseline plasma glucose concentrations two hours after a standard oral glucose load that met the World Health Organization definition of impaired glucose tolerance[15] had a six-fold increased risk of developing diabetes over eight years compared to individuals with normal glucose tolerance at baseline.[16]

Perhaps more interesting in the search for cause are the prospective data on serum insulin concentrations. Fasting insulin concentrations have been found to be predictive of the future development of diabetes in Pima Indians[17] and Micronesians from the South Pacific island of Nauru.[18] We recently confirmed these findings in Mexican Americans, where a 6.6-fold relative risk of developing diabetes over eight years was found among individuals whose baseline fasting insulin concentration was in the highest quartile of the insulin distribution relative to individuals who were in the lower three quartiles.[19] The predictive power of insulin concentration was statistically significant independently of other risk factors, including age, body mass index, centrality index, and plasma glucose concentration. Together, these three studies strongly suggest that hyperinsulinemia— and by inference, insulin resistance—is characteristic of the pre-diabetic state. This conclusion is reinforced by the finding that Mexican–American subjects with progressively stronger family histories of diabetes, i.e., progressively more likely to be pre-diabetics, have progressively higher insulin concentrations, both fasting and following an oral glucose load.[20] In multivariate analyses, overall body fat and body fat distribution were no longer statistically significant predictors of future diabetes once the metabolic variables (glucose and insulin) were taken into account. These findings suggest that the above summarized effects of body fat and its distribution on diabetes risk may be mediated by metabolic factors related to insulin resistance.

Because elevated blood insulin levels are usually indicative of insulin resistance,[21] the prospective results summarized above offer support for the "insulin resistance/pancreatic exhaustion" theory of the development of type II diabetes: insulin resistance leads to hypersecretion of insulin to maintain glucose homeostasis; after many years (perhaps decades) of insulin hypersecretion, pancreatic exhaustion supervenes and, with it, the onset of clinical diabetes.

It should be emphasized that this scenario does not preclude the possibility of a beta cell defect in the pathogenesis of diabetes. It is entirely possible, for example, that, regardless of the magnitude and duration of the insulin resistance, a normal pancreas will never become "exhausted" in the absence of a superimposed beta cell defect, metabolically silent during the pre-diabetic phase.

Genetic Factors

There is an extensive literature on the genetic risk factors for type II diabetes, but we will confine ourselves to the genetic question only as it relates to Mexican Americans.

Mexican Americans are a hybrid population with both European (mainly Spanish) and Native American ancestry. Since most Native American populations have very high prevalences of type II diabetes, it is natural to speculate that the predisposition to diabetes observed among Mexican Americans derives from their Native American ancestry and may be in direct proportion to the extent of that ancestry, which can vary widely between different subgroups within the overall Mexican–American population. Empirical evidence for this hypothesis is presented in Figure 6.1.

In recent years, there has been growing interest in the possibility of carrying out a "search for the diabetes gene." The spectacular recent advances in molecular genetics offer encouragement that such a search is now feasible. The likelihood of success would obviously be enhanced if diabetes were heavily influenced by one or a relatively few "major genes," rather than resulting from small, incremental effects of a large number of genes.

Although there is no conclusive evidence of a major gene for diabetes, some encouragement can be derived from the fact that plasma glucose distributions (two hours after an oral glucose load) have been demonstrated to be bimodal in five high-risk populations for diabetes, among them Mexican Americans.[22]

Environmental Factors

Among the most powerful arguments for major environmental influences on the development of type II diabetes are the "epidemics" of this disease which have been documented in several underdeveloped societies throughout the world. These epidemics have typically coincided with a relatively rapid change from a traditional—hunter-gatherer or subsistence farming—life-style to a modernized or westernized life-style. This sequence of events has been observed, for example, in Pima Indians,[23] several populations in the South Pacific,[24] and expatriate South–Asian populations living in Fiji, South Africa, and England.[25]

The elements of the modernization phenomenon that have received the greatest attention as possible diabetes risk factors are increased consumption of total calories, dietary fat, and refined sugars; decreased consumption of dietary fiber and total and complex carbohydrates; and decreased physical activity.

In developed societies, there is evidence for a "descending limb" to the modernization/diabetes curve.[26] An inverse relationship between diabetes prevalence and socioeconomic status has been reported in several developed societies.[27] We have confirmed this relationship in Mexican Americans and have further shown that increasing acculturation of this ethnic group to "mainstream," modernized, U.S. society is inversely related to diabetes prevalence, independently of socioeconomic status[28] (see Figure 6.2). A possible explanation for the so-called "descending limb of the curve" phenomenon is that as people become increasingly affluent they

FIGURE 6.1 Relationship Between Diabetes Prevalence and Percentage
of Native American Genetic Admixture
in Selected Populations*

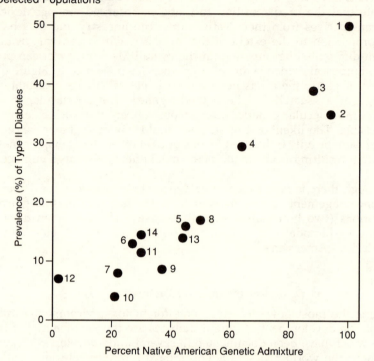

*The populations are as follows: (1) Pima Indians in Arizona; (2)
Seminole Indians in Florida; (3) Seminole Indians in Oklahoma; (4)
Cherokee Indians in North Carolina; (5) Barrio Mexican-American
men; (6) Transitional Mexican-American men; (7) Suburban
Mexican-American men; (8) Barrio Mexican-American women; (9)
Transitional Mexican American women; (10) Suburban
Mexican-American women; (11) Mexican Americans in Starr
County, Texas; (12) non-Hispanic whites from the San Antonio
Heart Study; (13) Hispanics in Colorado; (14) Puerto Ricans in
Puerto Rico.

Source: Stern MP, Haffner SM, 1990. Type II diabetes and
its complications in Mexican Americans.
Diabetes/Metabolism Reviews, 6(1):33.

FIGURE 6.2 Relationship Between Diabetes Prevalence
and Strata of Acculturation*

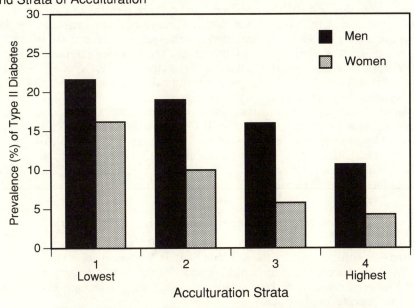

*The development and content of the acculturation scales are
described in Hazuda HP, Haffner SM, Stern MP, Eifler CW. 1988.
Effects of Acculturation and Socioeconomic Status on Obesity and
Diabetes in Mexican Americans: The San Antonio Heart Study.
American Journal of Epidemiology 128:1289–1301.

Source: The San Antonio Heart Study.

become aware of and attempt to reverse what they perceive as negative
consequences of modernization.

In order to translate the diabetes/socioeconomic status/acculturation
relationship into a viable public health strategy, we must identify the
behavioral (and/or other environmental) mediators of this relationship.
In the San Antonio Heart Study, we examined as potential mediators
dietary and exercise concomitants of modernization in three San Antonio
neighborhoods—barrio, transitional, and suburb.

The results indicate that with rising affluence and acculturation both
men and women tend increasingly to avoid both sugar and fat. Unfortunately, these favorable trends were not corroborated by quantitative estimates of nutrient intake assessed by twenty-four-hour dietary recall. These
latter estimates indicate that sucrose consumption declined minimally and
nonsignificantly in women, and not at all in men. Moreover, fat consumption failed to decline in women and actually rose in men. Consumption
of complex carbohydrates declined significantly in both sexes, contrary to

what would be predicted by the "descending limb" of the modernization curve hypothesis.[29] The discrepancies between the results of the dietary behavior scales and the twenty-four-hour dietary recall data could be due to the fact that the "visible" sources of sucrose and fat measured by the two avoidance scales are quantitatively relatively minor and are offset by increases in less visible but quantitatively more major sources of these nutrients. It is also possible that the behavioral scales tend to pick up "wishful thinking," i.e., what people would like to think they are eating rather than what they are actually eating.

Even if this latter explanation is correct, the results are encouraging, since they at least indicate that with rising affluence and acculturation, level of knowledge and attitudes about diet change in a favorable direction which may ultimately result in favorable health effects. The more promising results in women suggest that they may adopt more health-conscious life-styles earlier than men.

Interpretations of Genetic and Environmental Data

A major dilemma in interpreting the genetic and environmental data arises as a consequence of the fact that Native American genetic admixture is inversely correlated with neighborhood[30] (and thus perhaps also with level of acculturation and/or socioeconomic status, although these have not yet been formally tested).

Mexican Americans of low socioeconomic status tend to have a high percentage of Native American admixture and a high risk of diabetes, whereas Mexican Americans of high socioeconomic status tend to have a substantially lower percentage of Native American admixture and a lower risk of diabetes.

Thus, most of the environmental results presented above are potentially confounded by differing degrees of genetic admixture in the various socioeconomic and/or acculturation subgroups. The problem of potential confounding is exacerbated by the fact that most of the key comparisons are ecological in nature. If it were possible to perform analyses in which the individual—rather than a population—was the unit of observation, it might be possible to tease apart the admixture and the environmental effects by some sort of multivariate analysis. Unfortunately, because it is exceedingly difficult, if not impossible, to estimate precisely the admixture of individuals, ecological analyses are forced upon us.

The investigators of the San Antonio study have attempted to circumvent the above problem by extending their study to Mexico itself. They currently are carrying out a replication of the San Antonio Heart Study in a low-income barrio of Mexico City. Preliminary data suggest that Native American admixture (and, hence, we believe, genetic susceptibility to diabetes) is at least as high, if not higher, in a low-income Mexico City barrio than in the San Antonio barrio.[31]

On the other hand, it is expected that the residents of the Mexico City barrio will be found to be less "modernized." For example, preliminary unpublished data suggest Mexico City barrio residents are leaner than their San Antonio counterparts. There also are reasons to believe they consume less fat. The question posed by the new study is: Will the diabetes prevalence in the Mexico City barrio be higher or lower than in the San Antonio barrio? Will it reflect their high genetic susceptibility or their hypothesized lower environmental exposure?

Mexico is thought to have one of the highest per capita sugar consumptions in the world. Thus, if diabetes prevalence is lower than in San Antonio, as hypothesized, it may be possible to distinguish between specific, modernism-related environmental exposures, e.g., fat consumption and sugar consumption.

There are currently three studies of diabetic complications in Mexican Americans: the San Antonio Heart Study, the San Luis Valley Diabetes Study in Southern Colorado, and the Starr County Study in South Texas. Only the first two studies include a concurrent, internal control group of non-Hispanic white diabetics. These two studies, therefore, are most relevant to the question of whether there are ethnic differences in the rates of diabetic complications. Because of the relatively low number of non-Hispanic white diabetics in the San Antonio study, a formal comparison with an external Caucasian control group was also carried out. The external control group was derived from the Wisconsin Epidemiologic Study of Diabetic Retinopathy.[32] In San Antonio, Mexican–American diabetic subjects were found to have higher blood sugars (i.e., worse metabolic control) and a higher prevalence of microvascular complications (diabetic eye and renal disease), but a lower prevalence of myocardial infarction than non-Hispanic white diabetic subjects. In Colorado, on the other hand, the level of blood sugar and the prevalence of microvascular complications were similar in Mexican–American and non-Hispanic white diabetic subjects. No data are currently available on coronary heart disease from the Colorado study. These results will be presented in greater detail below. In the concluding segments of this chapter, we will present possible explanations for the discrepancies between the San Antonio and Colorado results.

Since the San Antonio Heart Study was carried out in two phases involving two independent cohorts, the first enrolled in 1979–1982 and the second in 1984–1988, we had an opportunity to see if the results obtained in the first survey were replicated in the second. For most major study results the replication was excellent.[33]

The results of the two surveys agreed that relative to non-Hispanic white diabetics, Mexican–American diabetics were statistically significantly shifted towards the more severe range of blood sugar level (Table 6.2).[34] In contrast to these results, blood sugar levels were similar in Hispanic and non-Hispanic diabetics in the San Luis Valley Diabetes Study.[35]

Mexican–American diabetics in the San Antonio Heart Study had an increased prevalence of diabetic eye disease compared to non-Hispanic

TABLE 6.2 Distribution of Mexican Americans and Non-Hispanic Whites with Type II Diabetes According to Severity of Glycemia in Two Independent Surveys, 1979-1982 and 1984-1988

	Percent of Mexican American Diabetics		Percent of Non-Hispanic White Diabetics	
Glucose Category	1979-82 (n = 135)	1984-88 (n = 229)	1979-82 (n = 56)	1984-88 (n = 24)
Fasting Plasma Glucose[a]				
Mild (< 140 mg/dl)	40.8	39.6	64.0	72.7
Moderate (140-199 mg/dl)	30.0	29.5	26.0	18.2
Severe (> 200 mg/dl)	29.2	30.9	10.0	9.1
2-Hour Post Load Plasma Glucose[b]				
Mild (< 200 mg/dl)	5.2	3.8	6.4	13.6
Moderate (200-299 mg/dl)	45.7	45.7	70.2	72.7
Severe (> 300 mg/dl)	49.1	50.5	23.4	13.6

[a]Mexican American vs. non-Hispanic white, $p = 0.007$ in the 1979-82 survey and $p = 0.01$ in the 1984-88 survey.

[b]Mexican American vs. non-Hispanic white, $p = 0.0025$ in the 1979-82 survey and $p = 0.002$ in the 1984-88 survey.

Source: Diehl AK, Stern MP. 1989. Special Health Problems of Mexican Americans: Obesity, Gallbladder Disease, Diabetes Mellitus and Cardiovascular Disease. *Advances in Internal Medicine* 34:73-96.

TABLE 6.3 Prevalence and Ethnic Odds Ratios for Diabetic Retinopathy in Mexican-American and Non-Hispanic White Diabetics in San Antonio

	Mexican Americans		Non-Hispanic Whites	
Grade of Retinopathy	n	%	n	%
None	142	55	38	68
Background	50	20	11	20
Preproliferative	50	19	4	7
Proliferative	15	6	3	5
Totals	257	100	56	100

Note: Odds ratio (MA/NHW) for: all grades of retinopathy = 1.71 (95% CI = 0.93, 3.17); severe retinopathy = 2.37 (95% CI = 1.04, 5.39)

Source: Haffner SM, Fong D, Stern MP, Pugh JA, Hazuda HP, Patterson JK, Van Heuven WAJ, Klein R. 1988. Diabetic Retinopathy in Mexican Americans and Non-Hispanic whites. *Diabetes* 37:878-84.

white diabetics (Table 6.3).[36] Ethnic differences were observed both for all grades of retinopathy and for severe retinopathy. For severe retinopathy, the ethnic differences were statistically significant even after adjustment for age, duration of diabetes, level of blood sugar, systolic blood pressure, and type of anti-diabetic therapy. Duration, blood sugar level, and treatment with insulin were themselves significantly related to severe retinopathy.[37]

When Mexican–American diabetics from San Antonio were compared with Caucasian diabetics studied in the Wisconsin Epidemiologic Study of Diabetic Retinopathy, they again displayed a statistically significantly increased prevalence of both all grades of retinopathy and of severe retinopathy.[38] Moreover, the effect of risk factors for retinopathy was similar in both ethnic groups.[39]

A possible explanation for the higher prevalence of retinopathy in Mexican Americans, even after adjusting for diabetes duration, could be that duration is systematically underreported by Mexican–American diabetics (perhaps due to delayed diagnosis). Available data, however, do not support this explanation,[40] suggesting that the greater susceptibility to retinopathy of Mexican–American diabetics in San Antonio is not an artifact.

Mexican–American diabetics in the San Antonio Heart Study had an increased prevalence of clinical proteinuria—excess accumulation of protein in the urine—compared to both non-Hispanic whites in San Antonio and Caucasians in Wisconsin (Table 6.4).[41] After adjusting by multiple logistic regression analysis for insulin use, systolic blood pressure, fasting glucose concentration, and cigarette smoking, Mexican–American diabetics still had an increased prevalence of clinical proteinuria relative to non-Hispanic white diabetics in San Antonio, which was of borderline significance. In the comparison with Caucasians from Wisconsin, however, the excess of clinical proteinuria in Mexican–American diabetics remained statistically significant.

Using a more sensitive indicator of kidney involvement, Mexican Americans also displayed an increased prevalence of minute amounts of albumin excretion (i.e., "microalbuminuria"), compared to non-Hispanic white diabetics (26 percent in Mexican Americans and 9 percent in non-Hispanic whites). There is also evidence that the incidence of diabetes-related, end-stage renal disease is higher in Mexican Americans than in non-Hispanic whites in the state of Texas.[42]

In the San Luis Valley Diabetes Study, no differences were observed in the frequency of clinical proteinuria between Hispanic and non-Hispanic white diabetics.[43]

In the San Antonio Heart Study, Mexican–American diabetics had a significantly decreased prevalence of self-reported myocardial infarction compared to non-Hispanic white diabetics, although this difference was only of borderline significance.[44] On the other hand, their prevalence of peripheral vascular disease as assessed by ankle/arm blood pressure ratios was increased.[45]

TABLE 6.4   Prevalence of Clinical Proteinura (≥ 1 + on Ames Albustix)
According to Ethnicity and Diagnosis Status for Subjects with Type II Diabetes
in San Antonio and Wisconsin

	Mexican Americans		Non-Hispanic Whites		
	Newly Diagnosed	Previously Diagnosed	Newly Diagnosed (SAHS)[a]	Previously Diagnosed (SAHS)[a]	Previously Diagnosed (WESDR)[b]
n	74	243	9	58	476
Negative or Trace	67	197	9	52	413
1+ to 4+	7	46	0	6	63
% with Proteinuria	9.5%	18.9%	0%	10.3%	13.2%

[a]Hazuda HP, Haffner SM, Stern MP, Eifler CW. 1988. Effects of Acculturation and Socioeconomic Status on Obesity and Diabetes in Mexican Americans: The San Antonio Heart Study. *American Journal of Epidemiology* 128:1289-1301.
[b]Wisconsin Epidemiologic Study of Diabetic Retinopathy

Source: Haffner SM, Mitchell BD, Pugh JA, Stern MP, Kozlowski MK, Hazuda HP, Patterson JK, and Klein R. 1989. Proteinuria in Mexican Americans and non-Hispanic Whites with NIDDM. *Diabetes Care* 12:530-536.

Although no data are currently available for macrovascular disease from the San Luis Valley Diabetes Study or the Starr County Study, lower rates of coronary heart disease have been found in several Native American populations including Navajo[46] and Pima Indians.[47] These findings in Native Americans suggest that the unexpectedly low rates of myocardial infarction in Mexican–American diabetics could have a genetic basis.

The lower rate of coronary heart disease in Mexican–American diabetics raises the possibility that their increased prevalence of microvascular complications could be the result of differential survival relative to non-Hispanic white diabetics. Specifically, if non-Hispanic white diabetics are more likely to die of coronary disease, Mexican–American diabetics would presumably survive longer and thus have a greater opportunity to express the microvascular complications of this disease.

In addition to the traditional complications of diabetes, functional status is also an important dimension of the impact of this disease on the daily lives of diabetic patients. We assessed this dimension using the Sickness Impact Profile, a standardized instrument for measuring the degree of functional impairment.[48] Diabetic Mexican Americans had a borderline statistically significant increase in functional impairment compared to diabetic non-Hispanic whites.[49]

Thus, not only do Mexican–American diabetics have higher rates of traditional diabetic complications, but they are also more functionally impaired as a consequence of their disease. This ethnic difference in functional impairment persists even when subjects are stratified by the presence or absence of conventional complications.

The greater severity of hyperglycemia and the excess rate of microvascular complications in Mexican–American diabetics from San Antonio could reflect either an intrinsically more severe biological process in this ethnic group or, alternatively, less satisfactory medical control; the latter could result from some combination of poorer access to or lower quality of medical care or less satisfactory compliance with prescribed antidiabetic regimens.

It is not possible to resolve this dilemma with currently available data, since arguments can be adduced in favor of either explanation.

The discrepancy between the San Antonio and Colorado results can itself be offered as an argument in favor of the "medical care" explanation, i.e., worse outcomes in Mexican–American diabetics are not universal. (It should be noted that the San Antonio population was urban, whereas the Colorado population was rural. Conceivably, differential access to and quality of medical care between the two ethnic groups could be exaggerated in an urban setting.)

Also in support of the medical care explanation is the fact that in San Antonio, Mexican Americans—diabetic and non-diabetic—are less likely to have health insurance and when they do have insurance, their coverage is likely to be less complete, e.g., less likely to cover outpatient medications, etc.[50] Moreover, there is an inverse correlation between the presence and quality of health insurance and the frequency of diabetic complications,[51] although one could question which is cause and which is effect: Diabetics who lack insurance might be more likely to develop complications, or, conversely, diabetics who develop complications could lose their insurance, owing, for example, to loss of employment. Only prospective studies will be able to resolve this ambiguity.

The strongest argument for intrinsic biological differences as the cause of the increased complication rates in Mexican–American diabetics is that in San Antonio, more severe hyperglycemia was observed even among cases that were previously undiagnosed at the time of their survey visit,[52] presumably prior to the time when factors associated with medical care could have had an effect. Also in support of the greater intrinsic severity argument is the observation that various measures of socioeconomic status were not correlated with either degree of blood sugar elevation or severity of diabetic eye disease.[53]

If Mexican Americans had less access to medical care than non-Hispanic whites, one would have predicted that a higher percentage of diabetics from this ethnic group would have been previously undiagnosed at the time of their survey visit. In fact, however, data from the San Antonio Heart Study indicated the opposite: the percentage of diabetics previously undiagnosed was lower among Mexican Americans than among non-Hispanic whites—48 percent vs. 60 percent.[54] Mexican–American diabetics were on average diagnosed at a younger age than non-Hispanic white diabetics, which again argues against a delay in diagnosis such as might result from reduced access to health care.[55]

With respect to the quality of care they receive, data are still sparse, although it is noteworthy that the percentage of previously diagnosed Mexican–American diabetics who reported that they were receiving either insulin or oral anti-diabetic agents was greater than among non-Hispanic white diabetics—68 percent vs. 37 percent.[56] There are as yet no data on possible ethnic differences in compliance, although one study indicated compliance with both insulin and oral anti-diabetic therapy among Mexican–American diabetics was at best fair.[57]

Information on macrovascular complications in Mexican–American diabetics is thus far available only from San Antonio. In contrast to microvascular disease, there is a deficit of coronary heart disease in Mexican–American diabetics. One possible reason for this pattern may be the earlier onset and greater hyperglycemia of Mexican–American diabetics, which would be expected to affect microvascular complications more than macrovascular complications. In contrast, ethnic differences in lipids—water-insoluble fats—and lipoproteins among diabetics are minor[58] and prevalence of hypertension and cigarette consumption are actually lower in Mexican Americans.[59] These latter risk factors would be expected to be relatively more important for coronary heart disease.

Conclusions

The substantially higher prevalence of type II diabetes in Mexican Americans than in non-Hispanic whites poses a major public health problem for this ethnic group.

The environmental factors which appear to contribute to the excess diabetes in Mexican Americans would appear to be those commonly associated with the phenomenon of "modernization" or "westernization," such as dietary change and adoption of sedentary life-styles. They are potentially modifiable and amenable to clinical and public health action. There is as yet no proof from clinical trials that modification of any or all of these environmental factors will in fact prevent diabetes. When clinical trials are performed, high-risk populations, such as Mexican Americans, should be considered as potential target populations, both because of the public health relevance and the lower sample size requirements in such populations.

The increased risk of microvascular complications in Mexican–American diabetics puts this population in "double jeopardy": They have a greater risk of acquiring diabetes in the first instance and once having acquired it, they have a greater risk of suffering from its complications. It is still not clear whether the increased risk of complications in this ethnic group stems from an intrinsically more severe biological process or barriers to adequate medical care and/or poor compliance. Prospective data currently being gathered should help resolve this issue. Assuming medical care plays a role, a major opportunity—and challenge—exists to reduce substantially the morbidity, mortality, and economic burden associated with type II diabetes and its complications in the Mexican–American population.

Notes

The material in this chapter has been updated and edited from an earlier version, "Type II Diabetes and Its Complications in Mexican Americans," *Diabetes/Metabolism Reviews* (1990), vol. 6(1), pp. 29–45. Copyright © 1990 by the John Wiley & Sons, Ltd. Printed with permission from Michael P. Stern and the publisher.

1. Flegal KM, Ezzati TM, Harris MI, Haynes SG, Juarez RZ, Knowler WC, Perez-Stable EJ, Stern MP. In press. Prevalence of Diabetes and Impaired Glucose Tolerance in Mexican–Americans, Cubans, and Puerto Ricans, Ages 20–74, in the Hispanic Health and Nutrition Examination Survey, 1982–1984. *Diabetes Care.*

2. Hanis CL, Hewett-Emmett D, Bertin TK, Schull WJ. In press. The Origins of U.S. Hispanics: Implications for Diabetes. *Diabetes Care.*

3. Stern MP, Gaskill SP, Allen CR, Garza V, Gonzales JL, Waldrop RH. 1981. Cardiovascular Risk Factors in Mexican Americans in Laredo, Texas: I. Prevalence of Overweight and Diabetes and Distribution of Serum Lipids. *American Journal of Epidemiology* 113:546–55; Stern MP, Rosenthal M, Haffner SM, Hazuda HP, Franco LJ. 1984. Sex Difference in the Effects of Sociocultural Status on Diabetes and Cardiovascular Risk Factors in Mexican Americans: The San Antonio Heart Study. *American Journal of Epidemiology* 120:834–51; and Hanis CL, Ferrell RE, Barton SA, et al. 1983. Diabetes Among Mexican Americans in Starr County, Texas. *American Journal of Epidemiology* 118:659–72.

4. Samet JM, Coultas DB, Howard CA, Skipper BJ, Hanis CL. 1988. Diabetes, Gallbladder Disease, Obesity, and Hypertension Among Hispanics in New Mexico. *American Journal of Epidemiology* 128:1302–11.

5. Hamman RF, Marshall JA, Baxter J, Kahn LB, Mayer EJ, Orleans M, Murphy JR, Lezotte DC. 1989. Methods and Prevalence of Non-Insulin-Dependent Diabetes Mellitus in a Biethnic Colorado Population. The San Luis Valley Diabetes Study. *American Journal of Epidemiology* 129:295–311.

6. Flegal KM, et al. In press.

7. Stern MP, Gaskill SP, Allen CR, Garza V, Gonzales JL, Waldrop RH. 1981; Samet JM, Coultas DB, Howard CA, Skipper BJ, Hanis CL. 1988; Stern MP, Haskell WL, Wood PD, Osann KE, King AB, Farquhar JW. 1975. Affluence and Cardiovascular Risk Factors in Mexican–Americans and Other Whites in Three Northern California Communities. *Journal of Chronic Diseases* 28:623–36; Mueller WH, Joos SK, Hanis CL, et al. 1984. The Diabetes Alert Study: Growth, Fatness, and Fat Patterning, Adolescence through Adulthood in Mexican Americans. *American Journal of Physical Anthropology* 64:389–99.

8. Haffner SM, Stern MP, Hazuda HP, Pugh JA, Patterson JK. 1986. Hyperinsulinemia in a Population at High Risk for Non-Insulin Dependent Diabetes Mellitus. *New England Journal of Medicine* 315:220–24.

9. Haffner SM, Stern MP, Hazuda HP, Pugh JA, Patterson JK. 1987. Do Upper Body and Centralized Adiposity Measure Different Aspects of Regional Body Fat Distribution? Relationship to Non-Insulin Dependent Diabetes Mellitus, Lipids and Lipoproteins. *Diabetes* 36:43–51

10. Stern MP, Haffner SM. 1986. Body Fat Distribution and Hyperinsulinemia as Risk Factors for Diabetes and Cardiovascular Disease. *Arteriosclerosis* 6:123–30.

11. Ohlson LO, Larsson B, Svrdsudd K, Welin L, Eriksson H, Wilhelmsen P, Bjrntorp P, Tibblin G. 1985. The Influence of Body Fat Distribution on the Incidence of Diabetes Mellitus: 13.5 Years of Follow-Up of the Participants in the Study of Men Born in 1913. *Diabetes* 34:1055–58.

12. Haffner SM, Stern MP, Mitchell BD, Hazuda HP, Patterson JK. 1990. Incidence of Type II Diabetes in Mexican Americans Predicted by Fasting Insulin and Glucose Levels, Obesity and Body-Fat Distribution. *Diabetes* 39:283–88.

13. Keen H, Jarrett RJ, McCarthey P. 1982. The Ten-year Follow-Up of the Bedford Survey (1962–72): Glucose Intolerance and Diabetes. *Diabetologia* 22:73–78; O'Sullivan JB, Mahan CM. 1968. Prospective Study of 352 Young Patients with Chemical Diabetes. *New England Journal of Medicine* 278:1038–41; Saad MF, Knowler WC, Pettitt DJ, Nelson RG, Mott DM, Bennett PH. 1988. The Natural History of Impaired Glucose Tolerance in Pima Indians. *New England Journal of Medicine* 319:1500–06; and Sicree RA, Zimmet PZ, King HOM, Coventry JS. 1987. Plasma Insulin Response Among Nauruans: Prediction of Deterioration in Glucose Tolerance Over Six Years. *Diabetes* 36:179–86.

14. Haffner SM, Stern MP, Mitchell BD, Hazuda HP, Patterson JK. 1990.

15. World Health Organization Expert Committee. 1980. *Second Report on Diabetes Millitus.* Tech. Rep. Ser. No. 646. Geneva: World Health Organization.

16. Haffner SM, Stern MP, Mitchell BD, Hazuda HP, Patterson JK. 1990.

17. Saad MF, Knowler WC, Pettitt DJ, Nelson RG, Mott DM, Bennett PH. 1988; and Knowler WC, Bennett PH. 1983. Serum Insulin Concentrations Predict Changes in Oral Glucose Tolerance. *Diabetes* 32(Supplement):46A (Abstract).

18. Sicree RA, Zimmet PZ, King HOM, Coventry JS. 1987.

19. Haffner SM, Stern MP, Mitchell BD, Hazuda HP, Patterson JK. 1990.

20. Haffner SM, Stern MP, Hazuda HP, Mitchell BD, Patterson JK. 1988. Increased Insulin Voncentrations in Non-Diabetic Offspring of Diabetic Parents. *New England Journal of Medicine* 319:1297–301.

21. Hollenbeck CB, Chen N, Chen Y-DI, Reaven GM. 1984. Relationship Between Plasma Insulin Response to Oral Glucose and Insulin-Stimulated Glucose Utilization in Normal Subjects. *Diabetes* 33:460–63.

22. Rosenthal M, McMahan CA, Stern MP, Eifler CW, Haffner SM, Hazuda HP, Franco LJ. 1985. Evidence for Bimodality of Two Hour Plasma Glucose Concentrations in Mexican Americans: Results from the San Antonio Heart Study. *Journal of Chronic Diseases* 38:5–16; and Stern MP. 1988. Type II Diabetes Mellitus. Interface Between Clinical and Epidemiological Investigation. *Diabetes Care* 11:119–26.

23. Knowler WC, Pettitt DJ, Savage PJ, Bennett PH. 1981. Diabetes Incidence in Pima Indians: Contributions of Obesity and Parental Diabetes. *American Journal of Epidemiology* 113:144–56.

24. Zimmet P. 1982. Type II (Non-Insulin-Dependent) Diabetes—An Epidemiological Overview. *Diabetologia* 22:399–411; Taylor R, Bennett P, Uili R, Joffres M, Germain R, Levy S, Zimmet P. 1985. Diabetes in Wallis Polynesians: A Comparison of Residents of Wallis Island and First Generation Migrants to Noumea, New Caledonia. *Diabetes Research and Clinical Practice* 1:169–78; Zimmet P, Taft P, Guinea A, Guthrie W, Thoma K. 1977. The High Prevalence of Diabetes Mellitus on a Central Pacific Island. *Diabetologia* 13:111–15; and Zimmet P, Taylor R, Ram P, King H, Sloman G, Raper LR, Hunt D. 1983. Prevalence of Diabetes and Impaired Glucose Tolerance in the Biracial (Melanesian and Indian) Popula-

tions of Fiji: A Rural-Urban Comparison. *American Journal of Epidemiology* 118:673–88.

25. Zimmet P, Taylor R, Ram P, King H, Sloman G, Raper LR, Hunt D. 1983; Jackson WPU. 1978. Epidemiology of Diabetes in South Africa. *Advances in Metabolic Disorders* 9:111–46; and McKeigue PM, Marmot MG, Syndercombe Court YD, Cottier DE, Rahman S, Riemersma RA. 1988. Diabetes, Hyperinsulinemia, and Coronary Risk Factors in Bangladeshis in East London. *British Heart Journal* 60:390–96.

26. Stern MP, Knapp JA, Hazuda HP, Haffner SM, Patterson JK, Mitchell BD. In press. Genetic and Environmental Determinants of Type II Diabetes in Mexican Americans: Is There a "Descending Limb" to the Modernization/Diabetes Relationship? *Diabetes Care.*

27. West KM. 1978. *Epidemiology of Diabetes and Its Vascular Lesions.* New York, NY: Elsevier, pp. 274–77.

28. Hazuda HP, Haffner SM, Stern MP, Eifler CW. 1988. Effects of Acculturation and Socioeconomic Status on Obesity and Diabetes in Mexican Americans: The San Antonio Heart Study. *American Journal of Epidemiology* 128:1289–1301.

29. Stern MP, Knapp JA, Hazuda HP, Haffner SM, Patterson JK, Mitchell BD. In press.

30. Chakraborty R, Ferrell RE, Stern MP, Haffner SM, Hazuda HP, Rosenthal M. 1986. Relationship of Prevalence of Non-Insulin Dependent Mellitus to Amerindian Admixture in the Mexican Americans of San Antonio, Texas. *Genetic Epidemiology* 3:435–54; Relethford JH, Stern MP, Gaskill SP, Hazuda HP. 1983. Social Class, Admixture, and Skin Color Variation in Mexican Americans and Anglo Americans Living in San Antonio, Texas. *American Journal of Physical Anthropology* 61:97–102; and Gardner LI, Stern MP, Haffner SM, Gaskill SP, Hazuda HP, Relethford JH, Eifler CW. 1984. Prevalence of Diabetes in Mexican Americans: Relationship to Percent of Gene Pool Derived from Native American Sources. *Diabetes* 33:86–92.

31. Lisker R, Perez-Briceo R, Granados J, Babinsky V, de Rubens J, Armendares S, Buentello L. 1986. Gene Frequencies and Admixture Estimates in a Mexico City Population. *American Journal of Physical Anthropology* 71:203–7.

32. Klein R, Klein BEK, Moss SE, Davis MD, DeMets DL. 1984. The Wisconsin Epidemiologic Study of Diabetic Retinopathy. III. Prevalence and Risk of Diabetic Retinopathy When Age at Diagnosis is 30 or More Years. *Archives of Ophthalmology* 102:527–32.

33. Diehl AK, Stern MP. 1989. Special Health Problems of Mexican Americans: Obesity, Gallbladder Disease, Diabetes Mellitus and Cardiovascular Disease. *Advances in Internal Medicine* 34:73–96.

34. Diehl AK, Stern MP. 1989; Haffner SM, Rosenthal M, Hazuda HP, Stern MP, Franco LJ. 1984. Evaluation of Three Potential Screening Tests for Diabetes Mellitus in a Biethnic Population. *Diabetes Care* 7:347–53; and Haffner SM, Hazuda HP, Stern MP, Van Heuven WAJ, Patterson JK, Fong D. 1989. The Effect of Socioeconomic Status on Hyperglycemia and Diabetic Retinopathy in Non-Insulin Dependent Diabetes Mellitus. *Diabetes Care* 12:128–34.

35. Hamman RF, Mayer EJ, Moo-Young GA, Hildebrandt W, Marshall JA, Baxter J. 1989. Prevalence and Risk Factors of Diabetic Retinopathy in Non-Hispanic Whites and Hispanics with NIDDM: The San Luis Valley Diabetes Study. *Diabetes* 38:1231–37.

36. Haffner SM, Fong D, Stern MP, Pugh JA, Hazuda HP, Patterson JK, Van Heuven WAJ, Klein R. 1988. Diabetic Retinopathy in Mexican Americans and Non-Hispanic whites. *Diabetes* 37:878–84.

37. Haffner SM, Fong D, Stern MP, Pugh JA, Hazuda HP, Patterson JK, Van Heuven WAJ, Klein R. 1988.

38. Haffner SM, Fong D, Stern MP, Pugh JA, Hazuda HP, Patterson JK, Van Heuven WAJ, Klein R. 1988.

39. Haffner SM, Mitchell BD, Stern MP, Hazuda HP, Moss SE, Patterson JK, Van Heuven WAJ, Klein R. Submitted. Is There an Ethnic Difference in the Effect of Risk Factors for Diabetic Retinopathy?

40. Mitchell BD, Haffner SM, Stern MP. 1989. The Increased Severity of Microvascular Complications in Mexican Americans is not Due to Underreporting of Duration of Diabetes. Presented at the Society for Epidemiologic Research. Birmingham, AL. June 14–16.

41. Haffner SM, Mitchell BD, Pugh JA, Stern MP, Kozlowski K, Hazuda HP, Klein R. 1989. Proteinuria in Mexican Americans and Non-Hispanic Whites with NIDDM. *Diabetes Care* 12:530–36.

42. Pugh JA, Stern MP, Haffner SM, Eifler CW, Zapata M. 1988. Excess Incidence of Treatment of End Stage Renal Disease in Mexican Americans. *American Journal of Epidemiology* 127:135–44.

43. Hamman RF, Franklin GA, Mayer EJ, Marshall SM, Marshall JA, Baxter J, Kahn LB. In press. Microvascular Complications of Non-Insulin Dependent Diabetes Mellitus (NIDDM) in Hispanics and Anglos: The San Luis Valley Diabetes Study. *Diabetes Care.*

44. Mitchell BD, Hazuda HP, Haffner SM, Patterson JK, Stern MP. Submitted. Myocardial Infarction in Mexican Americans and Non-Hispanic Whites: The San Antonio Heart Study; and Haffner SM, Stern MP, Mitchell BD, Hazuda HP. In press. Macrovascular Complications in Mexican Americans with Type II Diabetes. *Diabetes Care.*

45. Haffner SM, Stern MP, Mitchell BD, Hazuda HP. In press.

46. Fulmer HS, Roberts RW. 1963. Coronary Heart Disease Among the Navajo Indians. *Annals of Internal Medicine* 59:740–64; and Coulehan JL, Lerner G, Helzlsouer K, Welty TK, McLaughlin J. 1986. Acute Myocardial Infarction Among Navajo Indians, 1976–83. *American Journal of Public Health* 76:412–14.

47. Ingelfinger JA, Bennett PH, Liebow IM, Miller M. 1976. Coronary Heart Disease in the Pima Indians: Electrocardiographic Findings and Postmortem Evidence of Myocardial Infarction in a Population with a High Prevalence of Diabetes Mellitus. *Diabetes* 25:561–65.

48. Bergner M, Bobbitt RA, Pollard WE, Martin DP, Gilson BS. 1976. The Sickness Impact Profile: Validation of a Health Status Measure. *Medical Care* 14:57–67; and Pollard WE, Bobbitt RA, Bergner M, Martin DP, Gilson BS. 1976. The Sickness Impact Profile: Reliability of a Health Status Measure. *Medical Care* 14:146–55.

49. Mitchell BD, Stern MP, Haffner SM, Hazuda HP, Patterson JK. 1990. Functional Impairment in Mexican Americans and Non-Hispanic Whites with Diabetes. *Journal of Clinical Epidemiology* 43:319–27.

50. Pugh JA, Tuley M, Hazuda HP. 1989. Ethnic Differences in Microvascular Complications: The effect of Health Care Access. *Diabetes* 38 (Supplement 2):39A (Abstract).

51. Pugh JA, Tuley M, Hazuda HP. 1989.

52. Haffner SM, Rosenthal M, Hazuda HP, Stern MP, Franco LJ. 1984.

53. Haffner SM, Hazuda HP, Stern MP, Van Heuven WAJ, Patterson JK, Fong D. 1989.

54. Haffner SM, Rosenthal M, Hazuda HP, Stern MP, Franco LJ. 1984.

55. Haffner SM, Rosenthal M, Hazuda HP, Stern MP, Franco LJ. 1984.

56. Haffner SM, Rosenthal M, Hazuda HP, Stern MP, Franco LJ. 1984.

57. Diehl AK, Bauer RL, Sugarek NJ. 1987. Correlates of Medication Compliance in Non-Insulin-Dependent Diabetes Mellitus. *Southern Medical Journal* 80:322–25.

58. Stern MP, Patterson JK, Haffner SM, Hazuda HP, Mitchell BD. 1989. Lack of Awareness and Treatment of Hyperlipidemia in Type II Diabetes in a Community Survey. *Journal of the American Medical Association* 262:360–64.

59. Haffner SM, Mitchell BD, Stern MP, Hazuda HP, Patterson JK. In press. Decreased Prevalence of Hypertension in Mexican Americans. *Hypertension*; and Mitchell BD, Stern MP, Haffner SM, Hazuda HP, Patterson JK. 1990. Risk Factors for Cardiovascular Mortality in Mexican Americans and Non-Hispanic Whites: The San Antonio Heart Study. *American Journal of Epidemiology* 131:423–33.

7

Major Infectious Diseases Causing Excess Morbidity in the Hispanic Population

Ciro V. Sumaya

Infectious diseases are intimately associated with several general factors such as socioeconomic level, environmental influences (household sanitation, water supply), educational achievement, access to health care, and geographical location, among others.[1] As a group, Hispanics in the United States have a significant proportion of their population living under suboptimal conditions or whose travel to or immigration from countries places them at risk for a greater frequency and severity from infectious diseases.[2]

Sporadic articles or surveillance reports appear in the medical literature noting an increased morbidity or mortality of various infectious diseases in Hispanic populations. Data pertinent to the burden of infectious diseases in Hispanics may be found in published national surveys such as the National Health and Nutrition Examination Survey II (NHANES II),[3] the Hispanic Health and Nutrition Examination Survey (H–HANES),[4] the Epidemiologic Surveillance Project of the Centers for Disease Control,[5] and the Surveillance Summaries or other reports from the Centers for Disease Control. However, the interpretation of findings in the latter instruments is often limited because of a lack of uniformity in racial/ethnic designations, incomplete data, and an insufficient scope in the breadth of infectious diseases and Hispanic population covered.

The current report examined the medical literature for data relevant to infectious diseases in Hispanics, particularly noting disparities in morbidity. To the author's knowledge, this assessment on a national scale is the first undertaken in the recent literature. An evaluation of the impact of infectious diseases on Hispanics should be of major importance in developing appropriate measures to address this health problem.

Methods

A National Library of Medicine MEDLINE search of the literature published from 1980 to 1990 on infectious diseases in Hispanics was conducted. The search was performed on the general terms, communicable disease, infection, and specific infections (bacterial, mycotic, viral, parasitic) and cross-indexed with the term, Hispanic American. Additional terms used for cross-indexes included Chicano, Latin(o), migrant/farm worker, and aliens (undocumented). Existing national surveys since 1980, such as the NHANES,[6] H–HANES,[7] Epidemiologic Surveillance Project of the Centers for Disease Control,[8] and Surveillance Annual Summaries (Centers for Disease Control), were examined for Hispanic-specific data. For two diseases lacking sufficient Hispanic-specific data during this period, the search was extended to 1972. The above sources also served as a guide for additional specific studies or reports. Reports included in the analysis were to contain Hispanic-specific infectious disease data on prevalence, incidence, morbidity, or mortality. Sources outside the search time period that provided other ancillary information on the topic appear as well.

For the purposes of this assessment, Hispanics were defined as persons living in the United States and that are of Spanish descent, origin, or culture. Most persons of Mexican, Puerto Rican, Cuban, and Central or South American culture or origin are Hispanics.[9]

Results of Specific Diseases

Table 7.1 illustrates a summary of major diseases in which there is evidence indicating, or at a minimum suggesting, a disproportionately increased rate and impact among Hispanics. Sources described under the Methods section were used to develop this listing and its content. A more detailed discussion on these diseases follows.

Common Childhood Diseases Preventable by Immunizations

There has been a general waning of the total frequency of immunization-preventable diseases across the country in recent decades, related to widespread routine administration of immunizations. However, as described below, the relatively smaller number of cases currently seen, sometimes in sporadic outbreaks, may still contain a disproportionately increased number of Hispanic patients.

The risk of measles for Hispanics living in Los Angeles County in 1988 was 3.6 times greater than for black non-Hispanics and 12.6 times greater than for white non-Hispanics.[10] An overrepresentation of Hispanics has been well documented in periodic measles outbreaks during the 1980s.[11]

An increased case rate of rubella and congenital rubella syndrome has been reported in Hispanics in New York City,[12] directly related to a lack

TABLE 7.1 Summary of Major Infectious Diseases with Reported Evidence for
Increased Rates in Hispanic Populations

Disease	Evidence	Geographical Area/ Year Described	Reference
Immunizable diseases:			
Measles	Higher case rates	Los Angeles/1988	CDC[10]
	Overrepresentation in outbreaks	New York City/1983	Rutherford et al.[11]
		New York City/1984	CDC[11]
		Los Angeles County/1988	CDC[10]
		New Jersey/1985-86	CDC[11]
Rubella, congenital rubella	Overrepresentation in outbreaks	New York City/ 1985-86	CDC[12]
Tetanus	Higher case rates[a]	U.S. statistics[b]/1987-88, Texas/1982-86	CDC[13] Mendelson[13]
Pertussis	Higher case rates	Texas/1986	Texas Dept. Health[13]
Bacterial gastrointestinal diseases:			
Shigellosis	Higher case rates	U.S.-Mexico border/ 1980	CDC[15]
Salmonellosis			
S. typhi (typhoid fever)	Higher case rates	U.S., mainly South-west/1967-72	Rice[16]
	Large outbreak in migrant camp	Dade County, FL/ 1973	Feldman[17]
Non S. typhi	Higher case rates	Texas/1986	Texas Dept. Health[19]
	Increased multi-drug resistant strains	New Mexico, Texas/1981	Riley et al.[20]
Parasites:			
Soli-transmitted heiminths, Giardia lamblia	Increased rates in Mexican immigrants	Contra Costa County, CA/1980	Arfaa[21]
	Increased rates in Hispanic migrant farm workers	Massachusetts/1979	Ortiz[21]
		Chesapeake Bay area states/1983	Ungar et al.[21]

Amoebic (E. histolytica) dysentery and liver abscess	Increased case rates, usually Mexican immigrant, traveler in Mexico	U.S.-Mexico border: Los Angles Co./ 1975-82	Thompson[22]
		San Diego Co./ 1970-81	Katzenstein[22]
		California statistics/ 1988	Calif. Morb.[22]
Cerebral cysticercosis	Relatively common diagnosis, majority Hispanic recently emigrated	Southwest: Los Angeles Co./1980s	McCormick[23]
		Los Angeles Co./ 1981-86,	Scharf[23]
		San Diego Co./ 1972-81	Grisolia & Wiederholt[23]

Other tropics-endermic diseases:

Leprosy	Disproportionately increased cases, Mexican immigrants more commonly	States bordering Mexico, mainly Texas & California/ cases registered in 1982	World Health Org.[26]
Malaria	Imported cases commonly related to immigrants from Mexico, Central, and South America	Southwest/1979-81	CDC[27]
	Rare clusters of introduced malaria in Mexican migrant workers	Southern California/ 1986, 1988, 1989	CDC[28]
Chagas' Disease	Increased frequency in diagnosis related to Latin American immigration	U.S. statistics/ 1970-80[c]	Kirchhoff and Nova[29]

Sexually transmitted diseases:

Syphilis	Higher case rates, recent increases greater among Hispanics (and blacks)	U.S. statistics/ 1985-88	CDC[30]
Congenital syphilis	Increased case rates, recent increase greater among Hispanics (and blacks)	U.S. statistics/ 1983-85	CDC[30,32]
Chancroid	Recent increased number, outbreaks traced to immigrants	East Coast, West Coast/ 1980s	U.S. Public Health Service[33], Schmid[34]

Chlamydia	Increased infection rates[d]	San Francisco, CA/ 1983/84	Shafer et al.[36]
		Houston, TX/ 1985-86,	Smith et al.[37]
		Denver, CA/1983-84	Eager et al.[38]
Gonococcus	Increased case rates[e]	U.S. statistics/1988	Moran et al.[39]
	Higher case rates in Hispanic males	Denver, CO/1977-78	Judson and Maltz[41]
Hepatitis A	Infection rates increased; relative case rate unclear	U.S.-Mexico border area/1970-80	Chan et al.[43] Sawyer et al.[44]
Tuberculosis	Higher case rates, recent increases in cases disproportion- ately in Hispanics (and blacks)	U.S. statistics/ 1985-87	Rieder et al.[45]
	Nearly one-half of Hispanic cases are foreign born	U.S., mainly Califor- nia, Texas, and New York/1980-87	Snider et al.[45]
	High tuberculin reactor rates	Maricopa Co., AR/1981	Tang[48]
		New York City/ 1980-81	Vennema & Rugiero[48]
		San Francisco, CA/ 1978-83	Perez-Stable et al.[48]
	Higher prevalence of latent tuberculosis infec- tion in HIV infected Hispanics than non- Hispanic whites	New York City/ 1984	Stoneburner & Kristal[50]
		Florida/1981-86	Rieder et al.[50]
AIDS	Disproportionately increased rates in adult/adolescent and childhood cases; females	Mainly in Northeast, Florida/1981-89	CDC[51]
	Higher HIV antibody positivity rates among Hispanic applicants/active duty in U.S. military service	Not given/1985-86, 1988	CDC[54] CDC[55]

Higher HIV antibody positivity rates among intravenous drug abusers	New York City/ 1984-85, 1978-83	Schoenbaum[56] Novick[56]

Note: Reference numbers refer to the Notes section of this chapter.

Abbreviations: CDC = Centers for Disease Control, HIV = Human immunodeficiency virus infection

[a]Hispanics (seven) were placed in "other races combined" category, making an estimated average annual incidence rate of 0.363 cases per million. Whites had a rate of 0.15 per million.
[b]National data with increased rates for Hispanic based over several regions of the country or geographical specialty not given.
[c]Years of study not stated specifically.
[d]Infectious rates comparable to non-Hispanic whites were found in a South Texas study.[36]
[e]Case rates comparable to non-Hispanic whites were found, at least in adolescent females, in two other studies.[37,38]

of rubella immunization among susceptible women in their childbearing age years.

Hispanic patients are overrepresented in the relatively smaller number of cases of tetanus and pertussis that still occur.[13] Fortunately, outbreaks or cases of diphtheria that not uncommonly occurred in Hispanic populations[14] have now become a thing of the past.

Bacterial Gastrointestinal Diseases

Attack rates for the states along the Mexican border and Hispanics in these states have been consistently high for Shigella species.[15] In addition, these border states also have reported an increased isolation of unusual serotypes as *S. dysenteriae type 1* (Shiga bacillus) from travelers from Mexico and other countries further south.

Residents in the United States with Hispanic surnames are at greater risk of contracting typhoid fever (caused by *Salmonella typhi*) than is the rest of the population.[16] The largest outbreak of typhoid fever occurred in a Dade County, Florida, migrant labor camp composed predominantly of Hispanics (most of these were Mexican American).[17] National data do not appear to indicate, although sufficient statistics according to race/ethnicity may be lacking, that Hispanics are at great risk for Salmonella infections (exclusive of *Salmonella typhi*).[18] Regional data, however, may differ with national results. For example, in 1986 the Texas Department of Health reported a Salmonella infection rate of 16.1 cases/100,000 population among Hispanics versus 102 cases for blacks and 8.4 cases for whites in the state.[19] Hispanics also appear to be at greater relative risk, in general, for carriage of multidrug resistant strains of Salmonella isolates.[20]

Parasitosis

Infections with intestinal parasites, especially soil transmitted helminths (roundworm, whipworm, hookworm, Strongyloides, Clonorchis) and protozoa (*Giardia lamblia, Entamoeba histolytica*), are quite prevalent in Mexican immigrants and Hispanic migrant farm workers.[21] Amoebic dysentery and amoebic liver abscess problems are reported along the U.S.–Mexico border (rarely reported elsewhere in the United States) usually in the context of a Mexican immigrant patient or individuals who traveled or lived extensively in Mexico.[22]

Increased immigration from the pandemic regions of Mexico and Central and South America has made cerebral cysticercosis a relatively common disease in the southwestern United States.[23] The incidence of diagnosed cases of cysticercosis at Los Angeles County–University of Southern California Medical Center in the years between 1981 and 1986 nearly doubled.[24] The clinical signs and symptoms seen in patients in the United States may differ from those seen in Third World countries, i.e., milder disease and a lower frequency of arachnoiditis and/or hydrocephalus complications.[25] Some cases, however, are quite severe and manifested by protracted convulsions or acute rises in intracranial pressure.

Other Diseases Endemic in Tropics

An important focus for leprosy cases in the United States is located in the states bordering Mexico, i.e., mainly Texas and California, in addition to the states of Louisiana and Florida.[26] Seventy-six percent of the cases registered between 1967 and 1976 were reported to be born outside of the country, mostly in Mexico and the Philippines.

Imported cases of malaria to the United States are usually related to travelers, military personnel, or immigrants that lived in malaria endemic countries.[27] In the Southwest, this may be related not uncommonly to immigrants from Mexico, Central, and South America. Introduced malaria, i.e., malaria acquired by mosquito transmission in the area in which malaria does not occur regularly, is a rarity in the United States despite the presence of competent anopheline vectors in California (*An. freeborn*), the states that border Mexico, and the entire Southeast (*An. quadrimaculatus*). However, several large outbreaks of introduced malaria have been reported in California among Mexican migrant workers in the 1980s.[28]

Chagas' disease, caused by the protozoan *Trypanosoma cruzi*, is a major public health problem in Latin America, where an estimated 10 to 12 million people are infected. Despite the presence in the United States of several species of redivides bugs (transmit the parasite from sylvatic and domestic mammals to humans) as well as of *T. cruzi*-infected wild mammals, autochthonous Chagas' disease is an extreme rarity. There is evidence, however, that the diagnosis of Chagas' disease is being made with greater frequency related to the markedly increased immigration of Latin Americans from endemic regions.[29]

Syphilis and Other Sexually Transmitted Diseases

A decline in syphilis cases from the early 1980s was reversed in 1987, with the 25 percent increase in cases between 1986 and 1987 being the largest one-year rise in nearly thirty years.[30] These recent increases have been greatest among heterosexual Hispanics (and blacks) in urban areas. From 1986 to 1987, the rate per 100,000 in persons 15–64 years of age increased 7 percent for Hispanic males (66.0 to 70.7) and 24 percent for Hispanic females (17.8 to 22.0) compared to a decrease in white males (6.4 to 5.7) and a minimal change for white females (2.2 to 2.6).

As a direct consequence of the increased case rate of syphilis in women, in the second half of 1987 the rate of congenital syphilis cases increased 21 percent to 10.5 cases per 100,000 live births.[31] Nearly 40 percent of the cases of congenital syphilis in recent years are of Hispanic ethnicity.[32]

Although chancroid was disappearing from the United States during the 1970s, with an average annual number of cases of 877, the 1980s saw a reintroduction of the disease produced principally on the East Coast by immigrants from the Caribbean and on the West Coast by immigrants from Mexico and Southeast Asia.[33] At least nine large outbreaks have occurred in this country over the last decade.[34] These outbreaks shared common epidemiologic features: the preponderance of patients were Hispanics (and blacks), essentially all patients were heterosexual, and prostitutes were quite important in disease transmission in most instances. The largest number of cases was documented in the outbreak in New York (City); smaller outbreaks occurred in Florida, Texas, California, and Massachusetts (Boston).

Surveys performed to determine the prevalence of infections by *Chlamydia trachomatis* in the lower genital tract of various populations of female adolescents and young adults have yielded varying results in rates for Hispanics. A study in South Texas found a similar rate, about 10 percent, in Hispanics and non-Hispanic whites.[35] In contrast, investigations performed at teen clinics in San Francisco[36], Houston[37], and Denver[38] noted rates in Hispanics that were two to three times greater than that found in non-Hispanic whites (23 to 33 percent).

Gonococcal infection rates in Hispanics have been reported to be four times greater than in non-Hispanic whites.[39] However, other studies note rates that approximate those seen in non-Hispanic whites, at least for adolescent females[40] although possibly not for Hispanic men, whether heterosexual or homosexual.[41]

Hepatitis

Although national reporting data may not indicate an overall increased rate of hepatitis A cases in the Hispanic population,[42] prevalence rates for past infection (subclinical and clinical) with this viral agent may yield different results in some Hispanic populations. For instance, a study focused on U.S. counties bordering Mexico often noted an increase rate of hepatitis cases reported between 1970 and 1980.[43] A serologic survey performed in a *colonia* (very impoverished border settlement) near El Paso, Texas, revealed evidence of prior hepatitis A infection in approximately 33 percent of the children and 90 percent of the young adults.[44]

Tuberculosis

The downward trend in the number of tuberculosis cases among the general U.S. population in the early 1980s was reversed in 1986.[45] This was related to the increase in cases produced by individuals with underlying infections with human immunodeficiency virus infections and by the influx of higher risk racial/ethnic minority populations, including Hispanics.

The current overall risk of tuberculosis in U.S. Hispanics in general has been figured to be 4.3 times larger than non-Hispanic whites. (Other minorities may have similar or even greater rates compared to non-Hispanic whites.)[46] The tuberculosis cases among Hispanics, as in other minorities, is concentrated in much younger age groups, 25- to 44-year-olds. Hispanics and other minorities account for 80 percent of cases among children.[47] High tuberculin reactor rates, greater than 1 percent, have been found in schools with significant numbers of Hispanic and other minority childhood populations.[48]

Three states with heavy Hispanic and other minority populations, California, Texas, and New York, contribute three-quarters of the tuberculosis cases in this country.[49] The next three states in rank order include Illinois, Florida, and Arizona. Nearly one-half of the Hispanic cases in recent years were foreign born, with Mexico being the foreign country accounting for most of the cases. About 34 percent of the tuberculosis episodes in foreign-born individuals developed within two years after arrival. In general, foreign-born Hispanic patients are even younger than U.S.–born Hispanics.

It also appeared that because the prevalence of latent tuberculous infection was higher in Hispanics and other racial/ethnic minorities than among non-Hispanic whites,[50] clinical tuberculosis was likely to be more common among HIV-infected non-Hispanic whites.

AIDS

There is a disproportionately increased representation of Hispanics with AIDS, particularly children: 14 percent (9,317 cases) of the adult/adolescent and 23 percent (237 cases) of the childhood cases of AIDS in the United States are of Hispanic ethnicity[51] compared to approximately 5.6 percent and 8.7 percent composition, respectively, of this ethnic group in the general population.[52] Hispanics also are overly represented in the proportion of women with AIDS, 20 percent.[53] HIV antibody positivity rates are higher in Hispanics compared to whites that are applicants for U.S. military service (2.3/1,000 vs. 0.8/1,000, respectively)[54], U.S. active-duty military personnel (2.0/1,000 vs. 0.8/1,000, respectively)[55], and other large screened populations, such as Job Corps entrants and blood donors.

Reports in the Northeast indicate that the antibody prevalence of HIV infections among Hispanic, as well as black, intravenous drug abusers are higher than among non-Hispanic whites, for reasons that are not clear.[56]

An important demographic finding that has received less attention is the pronounced difference in statistics for AIDS and HIV infections that exist among Hispanics according to subgroups or geographic location in the country.[57] In general, the rates of AIDS cases in Hispanics in the Northeastern states, particularly in New York and New Jersey, are particularly high; the rates among Hispanics in Florida are at intermediate levels; while the rates in Hispanics in the Southwestern states are at expected or sometimes underrepresented numbers taking into account the proportion of this ethnic group in the general population.

Other Diseases

In several specific disease states, the available data suggesting a disproportionately increased frequency or severity in Hispanics is less firm because of the small study size or the presence of different findings by other reports. These have not been included in Table 7.1.

The rate of hepatitis B virus infections has been found to be disproportionately increased in some studies (described below) targeting Hispanic populations but not in a national surveillance reporting system.[58] In a community-based, neighborhood health center in Oakland, California, the Hispanic prenatal population surveyed had a slightly greater prevalence (1 percent) of hepatitis B virus carrier state (presence of serum hepatitis B surface antigen) than the general U.S. population (0.2 percent to 0.3 percent).[59] The rate in this Hispanic prenatal population, however, was considerably lower than that for the Asian–American group, approximately 13 percent. A study in a private community teaching hospital in Pasadena, California, found that Hispanic hospital employees had only a slightly greater prevalence (13.7 percent) of antibodies to the hepatitis B virus (the presence of antibodies indicating a prior infection) than whites (10.2 percent). Both these rates were much lower than employees of Asian extraction, 33.3 percent, and blacks, 23.1 percent.

The few cases of murine typhus that occur in the United States are usually in Hispanics along the Mexican border.[60] There is some evidence that other low prevalent diseases, such as brucellosis and botulism, also may be increased in Hispanics.[61] A study in California suggested that Hispanic children may have a higher incidence of infection by *Hemophilus influenzae type b* than white children, particularly when invasive infections other than meningitis produced by this organism were considered.[62] A high rate of asymptomatic Toxocariasis has been reported in Hispanic children surveyed in a hospital-based primary care clinic in Framingham, Massachusetts.[63]

General Reports

The Epidemiologic Project of the Centers for Disease Control noted that significant disparities in the morbidity from some infectious diseases existed between Hispanics and other ethnic groups compared to the non-Hispanic white population, the rates of these diseases being appreciably higher in the former groups.[64] Their findings were relatively consistent with the listing in the Table 7.1. The age distribution of persons with infectious disease cases was often lower among the Hispanics and other minorities compared to non-Hispanic whites. Although the Epidemiologic Project was one of the more complete assessments on racial and ethnic disparities in the rates of selected notifiable infectious disease (for 1987), it lacked specific race-ethnicity data on approximately 40 percent of the case reports, with the incomplete data varying widely by state and disease. The NHANES II conducted between 1976 and 1980 contained too small a sample size of Hispanics to make adequate correlations with the selected infectious diseases evaluated. Aside from tuberculosis, perhaps, the data in the H–HANES pertinent to infectious diseases, particularly acute conditions, were insufficient. A cross-cultural study performed in New Mexico indicated that the case-fatality ratios may be higher in some cases in the Hispanic or minority populations.[65]

Discussion

The data presented indicate that infectious diseases disproportionately affect Hispanics. This is not unexpected since a number of factors attendant to recent or early generation immigrants, as is the case for a large proportion of the Hispanic population, may be particularly influential in increasing the risk for infectious disease susceptibility, transmissibility, and severity. The greater rate of poverty with its associated socioenvironmental problems, language and other increased barriers to health care, less knowledge and utilization of preventive health measures, and importation of infectious diseases endemic in the country of origin are probably some of the major reasons that account for the increase in the above-cited infectious diseases among Hispanics.[66]

It is realized that this assessment may not be exhaustive. Nonetheless, most of the major disease disparities are covered, reflecting the general increased morbidity from these diseases in the Hispanic population. Further discussion on the various factors that could account for these disease disparities follows.

The increased representation of Hispanics in outbreaks of immunization-preventable diseases has been directly related to the lower rates of immunization present in the at-risk population from preschoolers to adults.[67] Indeed, an assessment of diphtheria, tetanus, and pertussis immunizations performed in Mexican–American children living in three large areas of the United States (five southwestern states, New York City, and Dade County in Florida) indicated that the Mexican–American children enrolled in the study were below the immunization levels recommended by the American Academy of Pediatrics.[68] The factors associated with the deficient immunization status in this study, and presumably applicable for other immunizations as well, included a lack of source of medical care, inadequate or absence of insurance coverage, and central-city residency.

Another important consideration responsible for the increased risk for transmission of measles and other immunization-preventable diseases in the inner-city Hispanic community may be their high utilization of hospital emergency rooms for routine medical care.[69] The latter phenomenon with health facility utilization may not only provide an excellent mechanism for person-to-person transmission of these infections but, possibly more importantly, may create an additional barrier for the receipt of routine immunizations.

Significant migration of individuals from countries that have considerable infectious disease problems can have long-standing effects on the endemnicity and continued transmissibility of those health problems in the newly or recently adopted country.[70] The screening process for individuals entering this country may not detect latent or even active infections that were acquired and are endemic in the mother country, only to manifest themselves up to years later. This phenomenon probably accounts for relative increased frequency of various diseases, such as cerebral cysticercosis in the Southwestern United States, tuberculosis, helminthic infestations, amoebic dysentery and amoebic liver abscesses, leprosy, Chagas' disease, and chancroid. Undocumented immigrants that bypass border screening mechanisms may lead to further entry of unsuspected or ongoing infectious diseases. The outbreaks of introduced malaria in California were believed to be associated in part with the importation of malaria by workers, mainly undocumented, who did not receive (or sought) medical treatment for their underlying infection.[71] The full extent of the importation and transmission of infectious diseases in general by undocumented immigrants, who may number in the millions,[72] is obscure.

The frequent interaction of Hispanic residents with relatives and friends from various countries with endemic rates of the disease also may contribute to the excess morbidity of infections such as typhoid fever and tuberculosis in the United States. Since parents and other adult relatives are a likely source of tuberculosis for children, the increased frequency of this disease among Hispanic adults should account for the increased rate among Hispanic children.[73] It has been suggested that Hispanics have a greater frequency of infections with Salmonella strains that are multidrug resistant because these strains were acquired in endemic parts of Central and South America.[74]

Socioenvironmental deficiencies associated with poverty, such as inadequate living conditions and hygiene, may be intimately involved with the increased morbidity from bacterial gastrointestinal diseases, parasitosis, and hepatitis A infections. The fecal-oral transmission routes for these diseases lend themselves to rapid dissemination among households and close community contacts subjected to overcrowding and poor sanitation, as is more commonly present in Hispanics.[75] Moreover, some cases, particularly in rural, poverty areas, may possibly never come to the attention of the health care system and, hence, are never reported.[76] Typhoid fever outbreaks may be related to sewage or fecal contamination of water or food sources as occurred in the Dade County, Florida migrant camp episode.[77] The high hepatitis A infection rates noted in the San Elizario *colonia* near El Paso, Texas, also were likely associated with environmental inadequacies such as sewage-contaminated drinking water.[78] In this impoverished *colonia*, as in the hundreds of others existing along the U.S.–Mexico border, indoor plumbing is characteristically nonexistent; drinking water often is obtained from wells located close to inadequate sewage disposals.[79] The greater infection (prevalence) rates with hepatitis A virus cited here, in contrast to case rates in some reports (see discussion on hepatitis), may be related to the large number of infections occurring in children, an age group in which the infection is commonly subclinical.[80] The most common transmission of *Entameba histolytica* (etiologic agent for amebiasis) in this country is person to person, usually from direct fecal contamination, instead of from ingestion of cysts in contaminated food or water that occurs in more endemic countries.[81]

A variety of barriers in the prevention and management of infectious diseases may exist among Hispanic populations. First, Hispanics at lower income and educational levels may have a minimal understanding of preventive services or are less accustomed to using health care services than the mainstream of society or even other minority groups.[82] In addition, the role that communication difficulty or cultural differences may play in this matter is unclear. Hispanics as a group also have a disproportionately larger number of uninsured or underinsured than the general U.S. population.[83] This, in turn, has a direct effect on obtaining easy access to health care: existing public facilities may be overburdened with patient care responsibilities, inadequate health staff, and insufficient updated diagnostic/management equipment. Migrant farm workers have particular problems with access to health care because of their geographic mobility.[84] Parenthetically, but relevant to this assessment, is the insufficient information available on the number of migrant farm workers and their status on infectious diseases morbidity or other health problems.

The reasons that account for the increased frequency of some sexually transmitted diseases cited above are not clear. The recent increases in syphilis incidence may have been related to the rapid rise in illicit drug use and sexual behaviors, such as prostitution, and possibly relaxation in syphilis control programs.[85] Nonetheless, the implication of the shift to heterosexual transmission in recent years was profound. This epidemiologic change combined with the concentration among urban Hispanics (and blacks) with limited access or less inclination to prenatal care, in turn resulted in the dramatic increases in congenital syphilis.[86] Heterosexuality and prostitution also played a significant role in the outbreaks of chancroid.[87] Although the increased genital infection rates for *Chlamydia trachomatis* in Hispanic females do not appear to be uniformly reported, a greater infection rate could indicate a higher risk for transmission of infection to subsequent newborns with resulting conjunctivitis, trachoma, and pneumonia.[88] The reason for the minor, if any, increase in the rate of gonorrhea in contrast to the much greater rate of syphilis among Hispanics versus non-Hispanic whites is not well-known. Indeed, the data on racial/ ethnic differences in sexual behaviors, health care behaviors, and susceptibility to sexually transmitted diseases that potentially can be related to disease prevalence are meager.[89]

A more precise assessment of the extent of sexually transmitted disease in Hispanic males may be very important in relation to the rates of cervical cancer in Hispanic women. Latin American countries have reported the highest incidence of cervical cancer in the world.[90] A similar increased frequency of this cancer in Hispanic women in the United States has been noted.[91] There is speculation that increased venereal diseases in the male sexual partner may increase the female's risk for cervical cancer.[92]

The increased number of AIDS cases in Hispanics was associated primarily with a high rate of intravenous drug abusers with this disease, a finding of particular note in the northeastern part of the United States.[93] The intravenous drug abuse transmission category comprised approximately one-half of the Hispanic AIDS cases in New York state.[94] The percentage of Hispanic AIDS cases from an intravenous drug abuser transmission category was approximately 4 percent in Texas and 8 percent in Florida (data for California not given).[95]

The high rate of AIDS attributable to the intravenous drug abuser risk category produces other significant epidemiologic consequences. Since the majority of intravenous drug abusers are men with predominantly heterosexual orientation, an increased number of their female sex partners have an HIV infection and AIDS. Moreover, there is an increased rate of Hispanic women who have intravenous drug-abusing habits and have AIDS.[96] Intravenous drug abuse, then, is the principal factor responsible for the increased proportion of heterosexuals of Hispanic ethnicity with AIDS. The overall increased proportion of Hispanic women with AIDS and HIV infections results in an overrepresentation of Hispanic young infants and children with HIV infections and subsequent AIDS.[97]

Conclusions

Despite limitations in information, there are sufficient data currently available in the medical literature, as presented in this chapter, to indicate that Hispanics suffer disproportionately from a number of infectious diseases in comparison to the majority non-Hispanic white population. Unfortunately, the factors that place Hispanics at greater risk for infectious illnesses, such as poverty and lack of assimilation into mainstream society, may continue over several generations.[98]

Several general recommendations and interventions could be considered in reducing this health disparity:

1. Improvement in health education for the individual, family unit, and community. This could include culturally and ethnically sensitive education on preventive measures such as the necessity for recommended immunizations, appropriate nutrition, early medical attention, compliance with treatment, improved food handling or other hygienic practices, and avoidance of high-risk sexual practices.
2. Reduction or elimination of health-related environmental deficiencies associated with infectious diseases. Environmental improvements, such as provision of purified drinking water, satisfactory sewage disposal, and other more sanitary living conditions, should be promoted for all segments of society.
3. Reduction or elimination of barriers to health care management. Improvement in insurance status through expansion of Medicaid eligibility should provide for enhanced health care access to low-income groups.[99] The barrier to health care produced by deficient English-language proficiency of patients and their families should be critically scrutinized.[100] Improved funding for state health departments to carry forth their responsibility satisfactorily needs continued support.
4. Expansion of infectious disease screening programs. Immunization rates need to be well monitored and deficiencies corrected. Programs in tuberculin skin testing, prenatal screening for HB_sAg, and testing for syphilis should be expanded or at least continued, particularly in high-risk populations.
5. Improvements in diagnostic acuity. Health professionals should receive education and training on the types of infectious diseases that are more likely to occur in certain populations or geographical regions.
6. Increased research on other determinants of health disparities. An evaluation of health-related behaviors, such as the use of alternative health care systems, self-coping mechanisms, and sexual life-styles, among others, may shed increased light on infectious disease morbidity.
7. Clearer identification of extent of infectious diseases' morbidity and mortality. National health (infectious disease) assessments are needed that incorporate race/ethnic designations, uniformity in disease reporting, and are broad-based geographically and in disease spectrum. The assessment(s) could identify differences within various

Hispanic or other minority subgroups, regional differences, and other demographic factors.

The recommendations and interventions listed above are not necessarily new. However, a significant expansion in ongoing and future efforts of this type is necessary. The need for a comprehensive national assessment on the impact of infectious diseases on the various race/ethnic populations in the country deserves further emphasis. More precise and comprehensive data are of paramount importance for developing strategies in priorities and the most effective/efficient mechanisms aimed at intervening and reducing infectious disease disparities.

Notes

The material in this chapter has been updated and edited from an earlier version, "Major Infectious Diseases Causing Excess Morbidity in the Hispanic Population," *Archives of Internal Medicine* (August 1991), vol. 151, pp. 1513–1520. Copyright © 1991 by the American Medical Association. Printed with permission from Ciro V. Sumaya and the publisher.

1. Fox JP. 1987. Epidemiology of Infectious Diseases. In Feigin RD, Cherry JD (eds.). *Textbook of Pediatric Infectious Diseases*. Philadelphia, PA: W.B. Saunders, pp. 79–105.
2. Heckler MM. 1986. *Report of the Secretary's Task Force on Black and Minority Health. Vol. VIII. Hispanic Health Issues*. Washington, DC: US Department of Health and Human Services. January.
3. National Center for Health Statistics. 1981. Plan and Operation of the Second National Health and Nutrition Examination Survey, 1976–1980. *Vital and Health Statistics*. Series 1, No. 15. Hyattsville, MD.
4. National Center for Health Statistics. 1985. Plan and Operation of the Hispanic Health and Nutrition Examination Survey. 1982–84. *Vital and Health Statistics*. Series 1, No. 19. Hyattsville, MD.
5. Buehler JW, Stroup DF, Klaucke DN, Berkelman RL. 1989. The Reporting of Race and Ethnicity in the National Notifiable Diseases Surveillance System. *Public Health Reports* 104:457–65.
6. National Center for Health Statistics. 1981.
7. National Center for Health Statistics. 1985.
8. Buehler JW, Stroup DF, Klaucke DN, Berkelman RL. 1989.
9. Heckler MM. 1986.
10. Centers for Disease Control. 1989. Measles–Los Angeles County, California, 1988. *Morbidity and Mortality Weekly Report* 38:49–57.
11. Centers for Disease Control. 1989; Rutherford GW, Desilva JM, et al. 1984. The Epidemiology of Measles in New York City, 1983: The Role of Imported Cases. 19th Annual Immunization Conference. Boston, MA; Centers for Disease Control. 1984. Measles Outbreak–New York City. *Morbidity and Mortality Weekly Report* 33:580–86; Centers for Disease Control. 1986a. Measles Outbreak–New Jersey. *Morbidity and Mortality Weekly Report* 35:213–15.
12. Centers for Disease Control. 1986b. Rubella and Congenital Rubella Syndrome–New York City. *Morbidity and Mortality Weekly Report* 35:770–79.

13. Centers for Disease Control. 1990a. Tetanus–United States, 1987 and 1988. *Morbidity and Mortality Weekly Report* 39:37–41; Mendelson JA. 1987. Tetanus in Texas. *Texas Medicine* 83:7–8; and Bureau of Epidemiology. Texas Department of Health. 1986. Reported Morbidity and Mortality in Texas. *Annual Summary*, pp. 32–33.

14. Brooks GF, Bennett JV, Feldman RA. 1974. Diphtheria in the United States, 1959–1970. *Journal of Infectious Diseases* 129:172–78; and Marcuese EK, Grand MG. 1973. Epidemiology of Diphtheria in San Antonio, Texas, 1970. *Journal of the American Medical Association* 224:305–10.

15. Centers for Disease Control. 1982. Shigellosis in the United States, 1980. *Journal of Infectious Diseases* 125:441–43.

16. Rice PA, Baine WB, Gangarosa EJ. 1977. *Salmonella Typhi* Infections in the United States, 1967–1972: Increasing Importance of International Travelers. *American Journal of Epidemiology* 106:160–66.

17. Feldman RE, Baime WB, Nitzkin JL, Saslaw MS, Pollard RA Jr. 1974. Epidemiology of *Salmonella Typhi* Infection in a Migrant Labor Camp in Dade County, Florida. *Journal of Infectious Diseases* 130:334–42.

18. Buehler JW, Stroup DF, Klaucke DN, Berkelman RL. 1989; and Askerhoff B, Schroeder SA, Brachman PS. 1970. Salmonellosis in the United States—A Five Year Review. *American Journal of Epidemiology* 92:13–24.

19. Bureau of Epidemiology. Texas Department of Health. 1986. Reported Morbidity and Mortality in Texas. *Annual Summary*, pp. 24–25.

20. Riley LW, Cohen ML, Seals JE, Blaser MJ, Birkness KA, Hargrett NT, Martin SM, Feldman RA. 1984. Importance of Host Factors in Human Salmonellosis Caused by Multiresistant Strains of *Salmonella*. *Journal of Infectious Diseases* 149:878–83.

21. Arfaa F. 1981. Intestinal Parasites Among Indochinese Refugees and Mexican Immigrants Resettled in Contra Costa County, California. *Journal of Family Practice* 12:223–26; Ortiz JS. 1980. The Prevalence of Intestinal Parasites in Puerto Rican Farm Workers in Western Massachusetts. *American Journal of Public Health* 70:1103–05; and Ungar BLP, Iscoe E, Cutler J, Bartlett J. 1986. Intestinal Parasites in a Migrant Farmworker Population. *Archives of Internal Medicine* 146:513–15.

22. Thompson JE, Forlenza S, Verma R. 1985. Amebic Liver Abscess: A Therapeutic Approach. *Reviews of Infectious Diseases* 7:171–79; Katzenstein D, Rickerson V, Braude A. 1982. New Concepts of Amebic Liver Abscess Derived from Hepatic Imaging, Serodiagnosis, and Hepatic Enzymes in 67 Consecutive Cases in San Diego. *Medicine* 61:237–46; and California Department of Health Services. 1982. Reported Cases of Selected Notifiable Diseases. *California Morbidity*. December.

23. McCormick GF, Zee C-S, Heiden J. 1982. Cysticercosis Cerebri–Review of 172 Cases. *Archives of Neurology* 39:534–39; Scharf D. Neurocysticercosis. 1988. Two Hundred Thirty-Eight Cases from a California Hospital. *Archives of Neurology* 45:777–80; and Grisolia JS, Wiederholt WC. 1982. CNS Cysticercosis. *Archives of Neurology* 39:540–44.

24. Scharf D. 1988.

25. Mitchell WG, Crawford TO. 1988. Intraparenchyman Cerebral Cysticercosis in Children: Diagnosis and Treatment. *Pediatrics* 82:76–82.

26. World Health Organization. 1984. Leprosy Surveillance in the Americas. *Weekly Epidemiology Record* 59:165–72.

27. Centers for Disease Control. 1979–1981. *Malaria Surveillance Annual Summary*. Atlanta, GA.

28. Centers for Disease Control. 1990b. Transmission of *Plasmodium vivax* Malaria–San Diego County, California, 1988 and 1989. *Morbidity and Mortality Weekly Report* 39:91–94.

29. Kirchhoff LV, Neva FA. 1985. Chagas' Disease in Latin American Immigrants. *Journal of the American Medical Association* 254:3058–60.

30. Centers for Disease Control. 1988a. Syphilis and Congenital Syphilis– United States, 1985–1988. *Morbidity and Mortality Weekly Report* 37:486–89.

31. Centers for Disease Control. 1988a.

32. Centers for Disease Control. 1986c. Congenital Syphilis–United States, 1983–1985. *Morbidity and Mortality Weekly Report* 35:625–28.

33. Centers for Disease Control. 1983. *Sexually Transmitted Disease Statistics* 133:35–36.

34. Schmid GP, Sanders LL Jr, Blount JH, Alexander ER. 1987. Chancroid in the United States. *Journal of the American Medical Association* 258:3265–68.

35. Glenney KF, Glassman DM, Cox SW, Brown HP. 1988. The Prevalence of Positive Test Results for *Chlamydia trachomatis* by Direct Smear for Fluorescent Antibodies in a South Texas Family Planning Population. *Journal of Reproductive Medicine* 33:457–62.

36. Shafer MA, Sweet RL, Ohn-Smith MJ, Shalwitz J, Beck A, Schachter J. 1985. Microbiology of the Lower Genital Tract in Postmenarchal Adolescent Girls: Differences by Sexual Activity, Contraception, and Presence of Nonspecific Vaginitis. *Journal of Pediatrics* 107:974–81.

37. Smith PB, Phillips LE, Faro S, McGill L, Wait RB. 1988. Predominant Sexually Transmitted Diseases Among Different Age and Ethnic Groups of Indigent Sexually Active Adolescents Attending a Family Planning Clinic. *Journal of Adolescent Health Care* 9:291–95.

38. Eagar RM, Beach RK, Davidson AJ, Judson FN. 1985. Epidemiologic and Clinical Factors of *Chlamydia trachomatis* in Black, Hispanic and White Female Adolescents. *Western Journal of Medicine* 143:37–41.

39. Moran JS, Aral SO, Jenkins WC, Peterman TA, Alexander ER. 1989. The Impact of Sexually Transmitted Diseases of Minority Populations. *Public Health Reports* 104:560–65.

40. Shafer MA, Sweet RL, Ohn-Smith MJ, Shalwitz J, Beck A, Schachter J. 1985; and Smith PB, Phillips LE, Faro S, McGill L, Wait RB. 1988.

41. Judson FN, Maltz AB. 1978. A Rational Basis for the Epidemiologic Treatment of Gonorrhea in a Clinic for Sexually Transmitted Diseases. *Sexually Transmitted Diseases* 5:89–92.

42. Alter MJ. 1985. Hepatitis Surveillance, 1982–1983. *Morbidity and Mortality Weekly Report* 34:1SS–10SS.

43. Chan LS, McCandless R, Portnoy B, Stolp C, Warner DC. 1987. *Maternal and Child Health on the U.S.–Mexico Border.* Special Project Report. Austin, TX: LBJ School of Public Affairs, The University of Texas.

44. Sawyer JA, Brown JP, Folke LE, Parra JM, Baez R. 1989. Hepatitis A in a Border Community. *Border Health* 5:2–5.

45. Rieder HL, Cauthen GM, Kelly GD, Bloch AB, Snider DE Jr. 1989. Tuberculosis in the United States. *Journal of the American Medical Association* 262:385–89.

46. Snider DE Jr, Rieder HL, Combs D, et al. 1988. Tuberculosis in Children. *Pediatric Infectious Diseases* 7:271–78.

47. Rieder HL, Cauthen GM, Kelly GD, Bloch AB, Snider DE Jr. 1989.

48. Rieder HL, Cauthen GM, Kelly GD, Bloch AB, Snider DE Jr. 1989.

49. Tang PM. 1983. Tuberculosis Skin Testing Programs in Maricopa County. *Arizona Medicine* 15:16–18; Vennema A, Rugiero D. 1984. Tuberculin-Sensitivity and Risk of Infection in New York City School Children 1980–81. *Bulletin of the International Union Against Tuberculosis and Lung Disease* 59:138–40; and Perez-Stable EJ, Levin R, Pineda A, Slutkin G. 1985. Tuberculin Skin Test Reactivity and Conversions in United States-and Foreign-Born Latino Children. *Pediatric Infectious Diseases* 4:476–79.

50. Snider DE Jr, Salina L, Kelly GD. 1989. Tuberculosis: An Increasing Problem Among Minorities in the United States. *Public Health Reports* 104:646–53.

51. Stoneburner RL, Kristal A. 1985. Increasing Tuberculous Incidence and its Relationship to Acquired Immunodeficiency Syndrome in New York City. Atlanta, GA: International Conference on Acquired Immunodeficiency Syndrome (AIDS). April 14–27; and Rieder HL, Cauthen GM, Bloch AB, et al. 1989. Tuberculosis and Acquired Immunodeficiency Syndrome. *Archives of Internal Medicine* 149:1268–73.

52. Centers for Disease Control. 1990c. *HIV/AIDS Surveillance Report*. May. Atlanta, GA.

53. US Bureau of the Census. 1985. *County and City Data Book*. Washington, DC: US Government Printing Office.

54. Centers for Disease Control. 1987a. Trends in Immunodeficiency Virus Infection Among Civilian Applicants for Military Service–United States. October 1985–December 1986. *Morbidity and Mortality Weekly Report* 36:273–76.

55. Centers for Disease Control. 1988b. Prevalence of Human Immunodeficiency Virus Antibody in U.S. Active-Duty Military Personnel, April 1988. *Morbidity and Mortality Weekly Report* 37:461–63.

56. Schoenbaum EE, Hartel D, Selwyn PA, Klein RS, et al. 1989. Risk Factors for Human Immunodeficiency Virus Infection in Intravenous Drug Abusers. *New England Journal of Medicine* 321:874–79; and Novick DM, Trigg HL, Des Jarlais DC, Friedman SR, Vlahov D, Kreek MJ. 1989. Cocaine Injection and Ethnicity in Parenteral Drug Users During the Early Years of the Human Immunodeficiency Virus (HIV) Epidemic in New York City. *Journal of Medical Virology* 29:181–85.

57. Sumaya CV, Porto MD. 1989. AIDS in Hispanics. *Southern Medical Journal* 72:943–45.

58. Alter MJ. 1985.

59. Arevalo JA, Arevalo M. 1989. Prevalence of Hepatitis B in an Indigent, Multi-Ethnic Community Clinic Prenatal Population. *Journal of Family Practice* 29:615–19.

60. Buehler JW, Stroup DF, Klaucke DN, Berkelman RL. 1989; and Texas Department of Health. 1987.

61. Buehler JW, Stroup DF, Klaucke DN, Berkelman RL. 1989.

62. Granoff DM, Basden M. 1980. *Hemophilus Influenzae Infections* in Fresno County, California: A Prospective Study of the Effects of Age, Race, and Contact with a Case on Incidence of Disease. *Journal of Infectious Diseases* 141:40–46.

63. Bass JL, Mehta KA, Glockman LT, Blocker R, Eppes BM, Bass JL, Mekta KA, Glockman LT, Blocker R, Eppes BM. 1987. Asymptomatic Toxocariasis in Children. *Clinical Pediatrics* 26:441–46.

64. Buehler JW, Stroup DF, Klaucke DN, Berkelman RL. 1989.

65. Becker TM, Wiggins C, Peek C, Key CR, Samet JM. 1990. Mortality from Infectious Diseases Among New Mexico's American Indians, Hispanic Whites, and Other Whites, 1958–87. *American Journal of Public Health* 80:320–23.

66. Fox JP. 1987; Heckler MM. 1986; and Schreiber JM, Homiak JP. 1981. Mexican Americans. In Harwood A (ed.). *Ethnicity and Medical Care*. Cambridge, MA: Harvard University Press, pp. 264–336.

67. Rutherford GW, Desilva JM, et al. 1984; Centers for Disease Control. 1984, 1989, 1986a, 1986b, 1990a; Mendelson JA. 1987; Bureau of Epidemiology. 1986; Brooks GF, Bennett JV, Feldman RA. 1974; Marcuese EK, Grand MG. 1973; and Gergen PJ, Ezzati T, Russell H. 1988. DTP Immunization Status and Tetanus Antitoxin Titers of Mexican American Children Ages Six Months Through Eleven Years. *American Journal of Public Health* 78:1446–50.

68. Gergen PJ, Ezzati T, Rusell H. 1988.

69. Centers for Disease Control. 1989a.

70. Fox JP. 1987.

71. Centers for Disease Control. 1990b.

72. Bean FD, King AG, Passell JS. 1986. Estimates of the Size of the Illegal Migrant Population of Mexican Origin in the United States: An Assessment Review and Proposal. In Browning HL, de la Garza RO (eds.). *Mexican Immigrants and Mexican Americans: An Evolving Relation*. Austin, TX: The University of Texas Press, pp. 13–36.

73. Snider DE Jr, Reider HL, Combs D, et al. 1988.

74. Riley LW, Cohen ML, Seals JE, Blaser MJ, Birkness KA, Hargrett NT, Martin SM, Feldman RA. 1984.

75. Rice PA, Baine WB, Gangaros EJ. 1977; Ungar BLP Iscoe E, Cutler J, Bartlett J. 1986; and Sawyer JA, Brown JP, Folke LE, Parra JM, Baez R. 1989.

76. Heckler MM. 1986.

77. Feldman RE, Baime WB, Nitzkin JL, Saslaw MS, Pllard RA Jr. 1974.

78. Sawyer JA, Brown JP, Folke LE, Parra JM, Baez R. 1989.

79. US General Accounting Office. 1988. *Health Care. Availability in the Texas–Mexico Border Area*. Washington, DC: US Government Printing Office.

80. Sawyer JA, Brown JP, Folke LE, Parra JM, Baez R. 1989; and Maynard JE. 1980. Hepatitis. In Last JM (ed.). *Public Health and Preventive Medicine*. New York, NY: Appleton-Century-Crofts, pp. 153–66.

81. Katzenstein D, Rickerson V, Braude A. 1982.

82. Heckler MM. 1986; and Smith LS. 1988. Ethnic Differences in Knowledge of Sexually Transmitted Diseases in North American Black and Mexican–American Migrant Farmworkers. *Research Nursing and Health* 11:51–58.

83. Heckler MM. 1986.

84. Rust GS. 1990. Health Status of Migrant Farmworkers: A Literature Review and Commentary. *American Journal of Public Health* 80:1213–17.

85. Centers for Disease Control. 1988a.

86. Centers for Disease Control. 1986c.

87. Schmid GP, Sanders LL Jr, Blount JH, Alexander ER. 1987.

88. Schachter J, Holt J, Goodner E, et al. 1979. Prospective Study of Chlamydial Infection in Neonates. *Lancet* 2:377–80.

89. Moran JS, Aral SO, Jenkins WC, Peterman TA, Alexander ER. 1989.

90. Waterhouse J, Muir C, Strangmugaratnamk, et al. 1982. *Cancer Incidence in Five Continents*. Vol. IV. Scientific Pub. No. 42. Lyon: IARC Scientific.

91. Austin DF. 1981. Cancer Incidence and Mortality in San Francisco Oakland. In *Surveillance, Epidemiology, and End Results: Incidence and Mortality Data 1973–1977*. National Cancer Institute Monographs 57:661–786; and National Cancer Institute. 1989. Hispanic Cancer Control Program Working Group Meetings. Washington, DC: US Department of Health and Human Services.

92. Zunzunegui MV, King MC, Coria CF, Charlet J. 1986. Male Influences on Cervical Cancer Risk. *American Journal of Epidemiology* 123:302–07.

93. Centers for Disease Control. 1986d. Acquired Immunodeficiency Syndrome (AIDS) Among Blacks and Hispanics–United States. *Morbidity and Mortality Weekly Report* 35:655–66.

94. Novick LF, Truman BI, Lehman JS. 1988. The Epidemiology of HIV in New York State. *NY State Journal of Medicine* 88:242–46.

95. National Coalition of Hispanic Health and Human Services Organization. 1987. *AIDS, The Impact on Hispanics in Selected States*. Washington, DC.

96. Centers for Disease Control. 1988c. Reports on Selected Racial/Ethnic Groups. *Morbidity and Mortality Weekly Report* 37(SS-3):1–10.

97. Centers for Disease Control. 1986c; and Centers for Disease Control. 1987b. Human Immunodeficiency Virus Infection in the United States: A Review of Current Knowledge. *Morbidity and Mortality Weekly Report* 36(S6):1–48.

98. Schreiber JM, Homiak JP. 1981.

99. Proceedings of Sessions on Uninsured and Medically Indigent. 1989. *Tough Choices and New Challenges: Advances to State Health Policy for the 1990s*. Second Annual Policy Conference of the National Academy for State Health Policy. Prepared for the Health Research and Services Administration by Patrician Butler, pg. 9.

100. A Congressional mandated study on this matter is being carried out by the Health Resources and Services Administration of the Department of Health and Human Services. Lewin/ICF. *Health Care for Hispanics*. Washington, DC.

8

The Health Status of
U.S. Hispanic Children

*Fernando S. Mendoza, Stephanie J. Ventura, Laura Saldivar,
Katherine Baisden, and Reynaldo Martorell*

The health status of Hispanic children in the United States has become an important national issue as a result of the rapid growth and persistent poverty of this population.

At present, there is a greater proportion of Hispanics under the age of 18 years than of non-Hispanic whites—35.5 percent versus 25.7 percent.[1] Among Hispanics, Mexican Americans and mainland Puerto Ricans constitute the largest subgroups, comprising 63 percent and 12 percent, respectively, of the total Hispanic population in the United States. In addition, Mexican Americans and mainland Puerto Ricans have the youngest populations of all Hispanic subgroups, with respective median ages of 23.5 and 24.3 years.

Poverty and limited educational attainment are significant problems for both of these groups. Twenty-five percent of Mexican Americans and 38 percent of mainland Puerto Ricans live below the poverty level, compared with only 10 percent of the non-Hispanic population in the United States. Similarly, only 45 percent of Mexican Americans and 54 percent of Puerto Ricans aged 25 and older in 1987 had completed high school, compared with 77 percent of non-Hispanics of the same age.[2] In contrast, Cuban Americans are considerably less likely than Mexican Americans or Puerto Ricans to be living below the poverty level or to have limited educational attainment.

The high rate of poverty among Hispanic children associated with the limited educational attainment of their parents and the increased risk for poor health that these two factors imply makes it imperative that we achieve a better understanding of the health status of Hispanic children. Until recently, there was a dearth of information concerning the health status of this population. Information obtained previously could not be generalized to all Hispanic children because it had been derived from

97

small regional studies with limited analysis of the variability in socioeconomic and acculturation levels. With the recent availability of broad-based governmental data utilizing improved classification of Hispanics and Hispanic subgroups, however, these limitations have been minimized. Our study utilizes two important data sources: the National Vital Statistics System (NVSS) and the Hispanic Health and Nutrition Examination Survey (H–HANES), both conducted by the National Center for Health Statistics.

The health status of children from the three largest Hispanic subgroups in the United States—Mexican Americans, mainland Puerto Ricans, and Cuban Americans—was examined in accordance with three measures: the birth outcomes of low birthweight, very low birthweight, and premature infants from the NVSS; the prevalence of chronic medical conditions from the H–HANES; and the prevalence of poor health ratings of children as assessed by physicians, mothers, and children participating in the H–HANES. These measures were chosen because each has been commonly used to assess the health status of individual populations of children and because in combination, they provided a multifaceted assessment of the health status of the study population.

The NVSS is a national state-based registration system of births and deaths.[3] The data are provided to the National Center for Health Statistics through the Vital Statistics Cooperative Program. Data for 1987 are based on 100 percent of the 2.3 million birth certificates filed in the United States. More than 400,000 births to Hispanic mothers are included in that file.

Data on births by Hispanic origin of the mother are based on a question on the birth certificate. Two basic formats were used by the states to obtain this information. Some state certificates posed an open-ended question designed to obtain the specific origin or descent of each parent. Certificates from other states specifically asked whether the mother and father were of Hispanic origin. If yes, the specific Hispanic origin, such as Mexican, Puerto Rican, or Cuban, was to be indicated. In both formats, the origin is reported directly by the parents.[4]

Data for Hispanic births were collected beginning in 1978. By 1983, the reporting area had expanded to include twenty-three states and the District of Columbia. Because the Hispanic population in the United States is so geographically concentrated, the reporting area includes more than 90 percent of the U.S. Hispanic population, according to population estimates based on a report from the U.S. Bureau of the Census.[5]

The H–HANES—the first large-scale health and nutrition survey that targeted Mexican Americans, mainland Puerto Ricans, and Cuban Americans—was conducted in 1982–1984 by the National Center for Health Statistics, which used 1980 census data to determine the geographic areas in which these Hispanic groups are greatly concentrated.[6] Mexican Americans were sampled from the five Southwestern states—California, Arizona, New Mexico, Colorado, and Texas—while mainland Puerto Ricans were sampled from the New York City area and Cuban Americans from Dade County, Florida.

Among children ages 6 months to 18 years who were examined, 3,622 were Mexican American (representing 3,602,412 children); 1,289 were mainland Puerto Rican (representing 487,168 children); and 387 were Cuban American (representing 112,877 children). Each child had a physical examination performed at a local site by a H–HANES physician who was trained by the National Center for Health Statistics to perform a standardized evaluation. Prior to the physician's examination, health and sociodemographic information pertinent to the child was obtained via a home interview conducted by a bilingual interviewer. All interview questionnaires were translated into Spanish and validated for these Hispanic populations. Information on children was obtained from the children's mothers for children under 12 years of age, and from subjects or their mothers for children aged 12 and older.

Survey physicians used the health information from the home interview together with their physical examination findings to determine whether a child had a chronic medical condition, defined as any medical condition that had caused loss of function or limitation of activity for the previous three months or longer.[7] For this study, conditions involving one organ system were grouped into a single disease category when those conditions were common (i.e., cardiovascular disease) or into combined categories of diseases when individual conditions occurred infrequently. In addition, for the first condition listed, the following information was obtained: the physician's basis for the diagnosis (history or physical examination or both); the physician's degree of confidence in the diagnosis; the severity of the condition; whether the patient had consulted a physician for the condition in the past year; and the urgency of referral for the condition (emergency, within one month or none).

At the end of each examination, the survey physician subjectively rated the child's or adolescent's overall health status as excellent, very good, good, fair, or poor. A subjective health assessment of children's and adolescents' health status was also obtained from the mothers of children 6 months to 12 years of age and from the children themselves for about half of the 6–11-year-olds. Two-thirds of adolescent subjects answered this question for themselves, while the rest had a family member do so, usually the mother. For all raters, assessments were grouped into one of two categories: good health (excellent, very good, and good) and poor health (fair and poor).

The H–HANES data also provided a comprehensive sociodemographic profile of the child's family. Included were the family's socioeconomic and acculturation levels. The family's socioeconomic level was determined by a poverty ratio, which is a ratio of the family's income divided by the poverty level income for a family of similar size. A ratio of one or less indicated the family was at or below the poverty line. The level of acculturation of the child's family was measured by the home language for children ages 6 months to 12 years or language preference for adolescents. Spanish-speaking children and adolescents were considered non-acculturated, while English-speaking children were considered acculturated. Those who were bilingual were considered bicultural. Although other personal and family characteristics have been used to determine a subject's or family's acculturation level, language usage is a primary factor and was used as a proxy measure for acculturation in this study.

The prevalences of chronic medical conditions and poor-health ratings of children and adolescents were compared across the three Hispanic subgroups. In addition, the effects of sex, age, poverty, and level of acculturation on these health measures were evaluated for each Hispanic subgroup.

The incidence of low birthweight by Hispanic origin and maternal age (Table 8.1) shows that among births to mothers younger than 20 years of age, the incidence of low birthweight for Hispanics as a group is similar to that for non-Hispanic whites but considerably lower than for blacks. For births to mothers aged 20 years and older, the rate of low birthweight is slightly higher for Hispanics than for non-Hispanic whites but is still less than half of the prevalence for blacks. In both age groups, Mexican Americans have the lowest incidence among Hispanics, while mainland Puerto Ricans have the highest. Because Mexican Americans account for nearly two-thirds of all Hispanic births, the level of low birthweight for this group has a substantial impact on the level for the Hispanic group as a whole. The incidence of low birthweight for Cuban Americans is similar to that of non-Hispanic whites, but the proportion for mainland Puerto Ricans is considerably higher than that of other whites and second only to blacks.

When data are further examined according to a mother's place of birth, a clear advantage in terms of low birthweight risk was observed for babies born to foreign or Puerto Rican born mothers. In 1987, 56 percent of the Hispanic women giving birth were born outside the United States. Only 5 percent of births to foreign-born Mexican–American mothers were of low birthweight in 1987, compared with 6.7 percent of births to Mexican–American mothers born in the United States. This relationship was observed mostly for births to older mothers in other Hispanic subgroups, not for births to teens except for Mexican Americans.

The incidence of low birthweight was consistently higher for mothers with limited educational attainment. The percentage of low birthweight births to Mexican–American high school graduates was 5.6 percent, compared with 6.2 percent for births to Mexican–American mothers who did not complete high school. Maternal educational attainment was more of a differentiating factor for mainland Puerto Ricans (7.9 percent for high school graduates vs. 11.1 percent among nongraduates); Cuban Americans (5.6 percent vs. 8.6 percent); and non-Hispanic blacks (11.9 percent vs. 15.0 percent) than for Mexican Americans.

When levels of low birthweight by ethnic group are further examined according to trimester of pregnancy in which prenatal care began (Figure

TABLE 8.1 Percent Low Birth Weight and Percent Very Low Birth Weight by Nativity Status and Age of Mother, 1987

Birth Weight Measure, Nativity Status, and Age of Mother	All Origins[a]	Hispanic				Non-Hispanic		
		Total	Mexican American	Mainland Puerto Rican	Cuban American	Total[b]	White	Black
Percent low birth weight[c]:								
All ages	7.0	6.2	5.7	9.3	5.9	7.1	5.6	12.9
U.S. born	—	7.2	6.7	9.8	6.9	—	—	—
Foreign/Puerto Rican born	—	5.5	5.0	8.7	5.7	—	—	—
Under 20 years	9.4	7.7	7.2	9.9	8.1	9.9	7.8	13.2
U.S. born	—	8.1	7.6	9.7	7.4	—	—	—
Foreign/Puerto Rican born	—	7.1	6.6	10.3	8.5	—	—	—
20 years and over	6.6	6.0	5.4	9.1	5.7	6.7	5.4	12.8
U.S. born	—	6.9	6.4	9.8	6.7	—	—	—
Foreign/Puerto Rican born	—	5.3	4.8	8.4	5.6	—	—	—
Percent very low birth weight[d]:								
All ages	1.2	1.1	1.0	1.6	1.0	1.3	0.9	2.7
U.S. born	—	1.1	1.1	1.7	1.1	—	—	—
Foreign/Puerto Rican born	—	1.0	0.9	1.5	1.0	—	—	—
Under 20 years	1.8	1.3	1.2	1.7	0.8	1.9	1.4	2.8
U.S. born	—	1.3	1.3	1.6	0.7	—	—	—
Foreign/Puerto Rican born	—	1.2	1.2	1.9	0.9	—	—	—
20 years and over	1.2	1.0	0.9	1.6	1.0	1.2	0.9	2.7
U.S. born	—	1.1	1.0	1.8	1.1	—	—	—
Foreign/Puerto Rican born	—	0.9	0.8	1.4	1.0	—	—	—

[a]Includes origin not stated.
[b]Includes races other than white and black.
[c]Birth weight of less than 2,500 grams (5 lb., 8 oz.).
[d]Birth weight of less than 1,500 grams (3 lb., 4 oz.).

Source: Mendoza FS, Ventura SJ, Valdez RB, Castillo RO, Saldivar LE, Baisden K, Martorell R. 1991. *Journal of the American Medical Association,* 265(2):229.

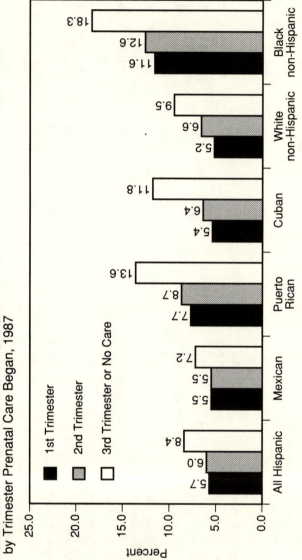

FIGURE 8.1 Percent of Births Weighing Less Than 2,500 Grams, by Trimester Prenatal Care Began, 1987

Legend:
- 1st Trimester
- 2nd Trimester
- 3rd Trimester or No Care

Percent

Group	1st Trimester	2nd Trimester	3rd Trimester or No Care
All Hispanic	5.7	6.0	8.4
Mexican	5.5	5.5	7.2
Puerto Rican	7.7	8.7	13.6
Cuban	5.4	6.4	11.8
White non-Hispanic	5.2	6.6	9.5
Black non-Hispanic	11.6	12.6	18.3

Source: Mendoza FS, Ventura SJ, Valdez RB, Castillo RO, Saldivar LE, Baisden K, Martorell R. 1991. *Journal of the American Medical Association.* 265(2):229.

8.1), the percentage low birthweight babies generally increases as prenatal care is delayed for all ethnic groups. The rate of low birthweight for Hispanic infants compares favorably to that of non-Hispanic white infants in each trimester of prenatal care. The risk of low birthweight is substantially elevated when prenatal care is delayed to the third trimester or when the mother has no care at all. This pattern is observed for Hispanic and non-Hispanic groups alike. Babies born to Mexican–American mothers who had late or no prenatal care, however, were at the lowest relative risk of low birthweight, 7.2 percent, compared with a range of 9.5 to 18.3 percent for other Hispanic and non-Hispanic groups.

Levels of very low birthweight (defined as birthweight of less that 1,500 grams or 3 lb. 4 oz.) are similarly very low for Hispanic infants in general (see Table 8.1). The risk is about the same for Mexican–American, Cuban–American, and non-Hispanic white babies. In 1987, 1 percent of Mexican–American and Cuban–American infants were of very low birthweight, compared with 0.9 percent of non-Hispanic white babies. Very low birthweight was more prevalent among Puerto Rican (1.6 percent) and black non-Hispanic (2.7 percent) infants. There was a tendency in most of the Hispanic groups for the incidence of very low birthweight to be lower for births to mothers who began prenatal care in the second trimester than during the first trimester. Regardless of ethnic origin, however, the risk of very low birthweight was considerably elevated when prenatal care was delayed to the third trimester or when there was no care at all.

The levels of preterm births (babies born prior to thirty-seven weeks of gestation) are not as favorable for Hispanic infants in general or for individual Hispanic groups as are the levels of low birthweight. This is true for teenagers and older mothers (Figure 8.2). Among Hispanic teen groups for example, Cuban–American babies were least likely to be preterm—12.6 percent, followed by Mexican American—13.5 percent, and mainland Puerto Rican infants—14.6 percent. As expected, the incidence of preterm births was directly associated with when prenatal care began in most cases. The earlier care is begun, the less likely the birth will be preterm.

An examination of the prevalence of chronic medical condition for each Hispanic subgroup shows mainland Puerto Rican children have a significantly higher prevalence of chronic medical conditions than Mexican Americans or Cuban Americans (see Table 8.2). However, the population estimate prevalence for Cuban Americans, which is based on nine out of 387 sampled children, is inadequate to provide an accurate prevalence for this group and reflects only the percentage of Cuban–American children with chronic medical conditions who were examined in the H–HANES.

While the three groups did not differ with respect to physicians' confidence in their diagnoses nor in the severity of conditions, Mexican–American children were the group least likely to have had their chronic medical conditions identified by history alone. This suggests that more Mexican–American mothers may be unaware of their children's medical conditions than mothers from the other two groups.

FIGURE 8.2 Percent of Babies Born Before 37 Weeks
of Gestation, by Age, 1987

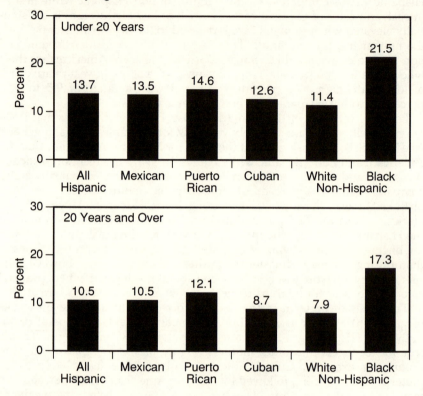

Source: Mendoza FS, Ventura SJ, Valdez RB, Castillo RO,
Saldivar LE, Baisden K, Martorell R. 1991. *Journal of the American
Medical Association*. 265(2):230.

Except for age, none of the other variables examined—sex, poverty
status, level of acculturation (determined by language)—effected the prevalence of chronic medical conditions (see Table 8.3). This suggests that
genetic propensity for the specific condition rather than poverty or cultural
behaviors has a greater effect on the prevalence of chronic medical
conditions for these children.

Among children diagnosed as having cardiovascular disorders, aortic
valve disorders were most common (sixteen of twenty-nine children) (see
Tables 8.4 and 8.5). Elevated blood pressure was found in eight subjects,
and two had rheumatic heart disease. One-third of children with mental/
central nervous system disorders had seizures, and another third had
mental retardation. Six of the twenty children with congenital anomalies

TABLE 8.2   Prevalence and Physician's Assessments of
Chronic Medical Conditions (CMC) Among Hispanic Children[a]

	Mexican-American (n = 3622)	Mainland Puerto Rican (n = 1289)	Cuban-American (n = 387)	Intergroup Difference[b]
Number of children with a CMC:				
	139	81	9	
Prevalence of CMC (Percent ± S.E.P.[c]):				
	3.93 ± .84	6.24 ± .66	2.49 ± 8.6[d]	p < .05
Primary Method of Determining the Presence of a CMC (%)				
History only	19.3	54.5	45.8	p < .01
Exam only	37.8	14.3	13.1	
Both	42.9	31.2	41.1	
Confidence in assessment (%):				
Certain	70.6	59.3	38.3	N.S.
Likely	21.3	29.8	61.7	
Uncertain	8.1	10.8	0	
Severity of condition (%):				
Mild	70.1	69.9	64.5	N.S.
Moderate	27.0	24.7	23.7	
Severe	2.9	5.4	11.8	

[a]Physician assessments based on first CMC listed.
[b]By chi-square or likelihood ratio chi-square adjusted for sample weights and complex sample design.
[c]Percent and standard error of the percent are calculated from sample weights and adjusted by the design effect.
[d]Population estimate does not meet reliability standard and reflects prevalence among sample subjects only.

Source: Mendoza FS, Ventura SJ, Valdez RB, Castillo RO, Saldivar LE, Baisden K, Martorell R. 1991. Journal of the American Medical Association, 265(2):230.

had anomalies of the heart and four of the twenty had Down's Syndrome. The only other common conditions were obesity (twelve cases) and asthma (eleven cases).

Except for respiratory disorders among mainland Puerto Rican children, neither they nor Cuban–American children have a significant number of chronic medical conditions (see Table 8.5). Among the mainland Puerto Rican children with respiratory disorder, forty-nine of fifty had asthma. Table 8.6 shows that H–HANES physicians assessed 1 percent or fewer children examined in each subgroup to be in poor health. Although the proportion was higher for those children with chronic medical conditions, even among this group the majority (88 percent or more) were subjectively

TABLE 8.3 Prevalence of Chronic Medical Conditions (CMC) by Sex, Age, Poverty, and Language Usage (in percentages)

	Percent with CMC[a]		
	Mexican-American	Mainland Puerto Rican	Cuban-American
Total Group	3.9	6.2	2.5[c]
Sex:			
Male	3.9	6.2[b]	2.1[c]
Female	4.0	6.3[b]	2.9[c]
Age:			
0-5 Years	2.3[b]	7.4[b]	0[c]
6-11 Years	4.5	6.8[b]	5.3[c]
12-18 Years	4.9	5.1[b]	1.8[c]
Poverty Status:			
Poor	3.7[b]	6.8[b]	1.7[c]
Not Poor	4.1	5.4[b]	2.8[c]
Home Language (6 mos.-12 yrs.):			
Spanish	3.8[b]	7.2[c]	1.0[c]
English	3.2[b]	7.8[b]	8.3[c]
Both	4.3[c]	3.9[c]	5.0[c]
Language Preference (12-18 yrs.):			
Spanish	1.8[c]	0[c]	0[c]
English	5.2[c]	2.6[c]	3.0[c]
Both	3.7[c]	6.4[c]	0[c]

[a]Percentages calculated from sample weights.
[b]Population estimate does not meet usual reliability standards and can only be used for an approximation of true population estimates.
[c]Population estimate is unreliable and, therefore, estimate only reflects attributes of examined subjects.

Note: Chi-square adjusted for sample weights and design effect [a]$p < .05$

Source: Mendoza FS, Ventura SJ, Valdez RB, Castillo RO, Saldivar LE, Baisden K, Martorell R. 1991. Journal of the American Medical Association, 265(2):231.

assessed to be in good health by survey physicians. This was mirrored in the limited number of children who were referred for medical care by survey physicians. Only Mexican–American children with chronic medical conditions had a rate of referral which would raise concern.

Responses to the question of which children with chronic medical conditions consulted a physician within the previous year reflect the subjects' knowledge of their chronic medical conditions and whether they have access to health care. Mexican Americans have the lowest percentage

TABLE 8.4   Prevalences of Categories of Chronic Medical Conditions
Among Mexican-American Children

Category	Sample Frequency	Weighted Prevalence (per 10[5])	95% Confidence Interval[a] (per 10[5])
Cardiovascular diseases	29	831	± 369
Mental/CNS disorders	23	628	± 313
Endocrine, nutritional metabolic, blood disorders	19	589	± 323
Congenital anomalies	20	524	± 280
Genito-urinary/gastrointestinal diseases	14	426	± 272
Eye and ear disorders	15	425	± 262
Respiratory diseases	14	410	± 262
Musculoskeletal disorders/injuries	11	289	± 208
Miscellaneous[b]	11	260	± 187

[a]Approximate 95% confidence intervals, using Poisson Theory, and a design effect of 1.5.
[b]Infectious/Parasitic/Skin/Hair/Neoplastic Diseases.

Source: Mendoza FS, Ventura SJ, Valdez RB, Castillo RO, Saldivar LE, Baisden K, Martorell R. 1991. *Journal of the American Medical Association,* 265(2):231.

of children with chronic medical conditions who have contacted a physician within the previous year. They are significantly lower than either of the other two subgroups. This coincides with the previous observation that Mexican Americans are least likely to have their chronic medical condition identified by history alone.

A breakdown of percentages of children and adolescents rated in poor health by either their mothers or themselves showed that only among mothers of children ages 6 months to 11 years was there a significant difference between subgroups (see Table 8.7). This demonstrated that mainland Puerto Rican mothers rated a greater proportion of their children in poor health, compared with the other two subgroups. In addition, Mexican–American mothers were twice as likely to rate their children in poor health as Cuban–American mothers. Ratings by mothers of adolescents and by the adolescents themselves show a similar pattern, although these differences were not statistically different.

The maternal poor-health ratings for children ages 6 months to 11 years were further examined by children's sex, age, poverty status, home language or acculturation level, and the presence of a chronic medical condition (see Table 8.8). Both Mexican–American and mainland Puerto

TABLE 8.5   The Distribution of Categories of Chronical Medical Conditions
Among Hispanic Children

Type	Mexican-American		Mainland Puerto Rican		Cuban-American	
	no.	(%)	no.	(%)	no.	(%)
Cardiovascular diseases	29	(18)	7	(9)	1	(10)
Mental/CNS disorder	23	(15)	9	(11)	1	(10)
Endocrine, metabolic nutritional, blood disorders	19	(12)	6	(7)	0	(0)
Congenital anomalies	20	(13)	4	(5)	1	(10)
Genito-urinary/gastrointestinal diseases	14	(9)	0	(0)	1	(10)
Eye and ear disorders	15	(10)	1	(1)	0	(0)
Respiratory disease	14	(9)	50	(62)	3	(30)
Musculoskeletal disorders/injuries	12	(8)	1	(1)	1	(10)
Miscellaneous[a]	11	(7)	3	(4)	2	(20)

[a]Infectious/Parasitic/Skin/Hair/Neoplastic Diseases.

Source: Unpublished report by FS Mendoza.

Rican mothers' poor-health ratings were significantly affected by their child's age, regardless of poverty status, acculturation level, and whether their child had a chronic medical condition. Cuban–American mothers seemed to be most affected in their rating by the presence of a chronic condition. Logistic regression analyses demonstrated that Mexican–American mothers were more likely to rate their children in poor health if they spoke Spanish in the home, had a chronic medical condition, lived in poverty, or were older. Furthermore, those children who were bilingual in the home were more likely to be rated in poor health by their mothers than those children who spoke only English. For mainland Puerto Rican mothers of children ages 6 months to 11 years, the presence of a chronic medical condition, speaking Spanish in the home, and having a older child increased the likelihood of rating the child in poor health. Among Cuban–American mothers, the only predictive variable for a poor-health rating was the presence of a chronic medical condition.

The approach taken in this study to assess the health status of Mexican–American, mainland Puerto Rican, and Cuban–American children involved two objective measures of health status—birth outcomes and chronic medical conditions—and one subjective measure—the perception of children's health status. These indicators of health are commonly used to compare populations and are health measures that are associated with

TABLE 8.6 Survey Physicians' Perception of Subjects' Overall Health Status, Need for Referral for Medical Care, and Use of Medical Care (in percentages)

	Mexican-American	Mainland Puerto Rican	Cuban-American	Intergroup Difference[a]
Percent of all sampled children assessed by MD to be in poor health	1.0[b]	0.4[c]	0.3[c]	NS
Level of referral needed for all children: Medical care needed within one month	1.3[c]	2.1[c]	0.3[c]	NS
No major medical findings	98.7	97.9	99.2	
Percent of children with CMC assessed by MD to be in poor health	11.6[c]	6.4[c]	19.3[c]	NS
Level of referral for children with CMC: Medical care needed within one month	19.2[b]	5.4[c]	11.7[c]	p < .10
No referral needed	80.8	94.6	88.3[b]	
Percent of subjects with a chronic medical condition who have consulted a physician within the last year	58.0	78.6	86.9[b]	p < .001

[a]By chi-square adjusted for sample weights and complex sample design.
[b]Population estimate does not meet usual reliability standards and can only be used for an approximation of true population estimates.
[c]Population estimate is unreliable and, therefore, estimate only reflects attributes of examined subjects.

Source: Partially published in Mendoza FS, Ventura SJ, Valdez RB, Castillo RO, Saldivar LE, Baisden K, Martorell R. 1991. *Journal of the American Medical Association,* 265(2):230. The rest from an unpublished report by FS Mendoza.

significant morbidity for children. Although the perception of the child's health is not as objective a measure as birth outcomes or chronic medical conditions, it does provide unique information about the rater's concern about the child's health. It can be as important as any objective measure since it is highly likely to influence the rater's (physician's or mother's) action towards the child and in the case of the child's self-rating, inform us about the child's sense of well-being.

The evaluation of low birthweight among Hispanics demonstrated an interesting difference among ethnic groups: Hispanic mothers, especially Mexican–American mothers, tend to have limited educational attainment and a higher rate of poverty than non-Hispanic whites. This is true for those born in the United States as well as for those born outside the

TABLE 8.7   Percent of Children and Adolescents Rated in Poor Health

	Mexican-American	Mainland Puerto Rican	Cuban-American	Intergroup Difference[a]
Mother of children 6 mos.-11 yrs.	14.1	19.9	6.7[c]	p < .01
Mother of adolescents 12-18 yrs.	16.9	20.1[b]	8.4[c]	NS
Children, 6-11 yrs.	11.4	15.2[b]	16.5[c]	NS
Adolescents, 12-18 yrs.	18.7	17.0	7.5[c]	NS

[a]By chi-square adjusted for sample weights and complex sample design.
[b]Population estimate does not meet usual reliability standards and can only be used for an approximation of true population estimates.
[c]Population estimate is unreliable and, therefore, estimate only reflects attributes of examined subjects.

Source: Unpublished report by FS Mendoza.

United States or in Puerto Rico, although women born in the United States are somewhat more likely to be high school graduates.

Whereas more than 80 percent of non-Hispanic women giving birth in 1987 were high school graduates, only 57 percent of all Hispanic mothers and 42 percent of Mexican–American mothers had completed high school.[8] Furthermore, maternal educational attainment has been shown to be very closely associated with initiation of prenatal care and with levels of low birthweight.[9] In this study, the incidence of low birthweight was consistently higher for births to mothers with limited education. While this relationship held true for all population groups in this analysis, it was comparatively weak for births to Mexican–American mothers. Levels of low birthweight were relatively low for Mexican Americans, regardless of the mother's educational attainment, age, birthplace, or use of prenatal care. In contrast, maternal educational attainment, age, and use of prenatal care were greater differentiating factors for mainland Puerto Rican, Cuban American, and non-Hispanic birthweight.

Many researchers have tried to account for the relative advantage of Mexican–American and other Hispanic mothers and their babies in terms of low birthweight, given the fact that use of prenatal care is low. It has been reported elsewhere that Hispanic mothers (except Cuban Americans) are substantially less likely to begin prenatal care in the first trimester and considerably more likely to receive delayed or no prenatal care than are white non-Hispanic mothers.[10] In 1987, for example, only 61 percent of Hispanic mothers began care in the first trimester compared with 82 percent of white non-Hispanic mothers.[11] One important factor may be

TABLE 8.8   Percent of Children 6 Months to 11 Years Rated in Poor Health by Mothers According to Demographic Variables and Presence of Chronic Medical Conditions

	Percent Rated in Poor Health[a]		
	Mexican-American	Mainland Puerto Rican	Cuban-American
Total Group	14.1	19.4	6.7[c]
Sex:			
Male	14.6	21.7	6.4[c]
Female	13.7	18.0	7.1[c]
Age:			
6 Mo.-5 Yrs.	11.3[f]	15.7[d]	2.4[c]
6-12 Yrs.	17.0	23.3	9.8[c]
Poverty Status:			
Poor	20.2[f]	22.5[d]	9.3[c]
Not Poor	10.8	14.7[b]	6.0[c]
Home Language:			
Spanish	25.9[f]	27.1[d]	7.1[c]
English	7.6	15.2	3.8[c]
Both	13.5	20.3[b]	12.8[c]
Chronic Medical Condition:			
With	26.6[e]	40.6[e]	31.4[c]
Without	13.7	18.3	6.0[c]

[a]Percentages calculated from sample weight.
[b]Population estimate does not meet usual reliability standards and can only be used for an approximation of true population estimates.
[c]Population estimate is unreliable and, therefore, estimate only reflects attributes of examined subjects.

Note: Chi-square adjusted for sample weights and design effect d = $p<.05$, e = $p<.01$, f = $p<.001$

Source: Unpublished report by FS Mendoza.

the much lower incidence of smoking among Mexican–American compared to non-Hispanic women. Unpublished data from the 1980 National Natality Survey, conducted by the National Center for Health Statistics, showed that only 10 percent of Mexican women smoked during pregnancy, compared with 27 percent of white non-Hispanic women. Information from the 1985 National Health Interview Survey confirms a significantly lower rate of smoking among Hispanic women.[12] Another study of pregnancy among Mexican–American and white and black teenagers also found a much lower rate of smoking among Mexican teens as well as a clear tendency for Mexican teenagers to gain more weight during pregnancy than their white and black peers.[13] It is possible that these behavioral patterns—at least for Mexican–American women—may be more critical in influencing birth outcome than educational attainment or timing of prenatal care.

The prevalence of chronic illness has been used frequently to assess the health of populations because it usually is assumed that those with chronic illnesses will be the most functionally impaired and have the greatest need for health resources. The current study showed that the prevalence of chronic medical conditions—conditions that limited activity for the prior three months—among children surveyed in H–HANES ranged from 2.49 to 6.24 percent. Newacheck et al., utilizing the 1979–1981 National Health Interview Survey found the overall prevalence of activity limiting chronic conditions among U.S. children under 17 years of age was 3.8 percent.[14] A similar examination by Trevino and Moss of the National Health Interview Survey (1978–1980) determined the prevalence of limitation due to chronic conditions in Mexican Americans, mainland Puerto Ricans, Cuban Americans, black and white children to be 3.0, 6.2, 3.5, 3.7, and 4.0 percent, respectively.[15] Both studies used data from the National Health Interview Survey, which assessed the presence of a chronic condition solely from home interview information and without benefit of a physical examination. This required parents to be aware of their children's medical conditions in order to report them.

The advantage of the H–HANES is that the survey physicians had the benefit of a physical examination to determine whether a child had a chronic medical condition. This could theoretically increase the prevalence by detecting those children who would not normally be classified by interview alone. However, without diagnostic testing to validate some of the determined chronic medical conditions such as aortic valve disorders, this methodology could also lead to an overestimation as well.

Unpublished data from our groups show that the prevalence of severe conditions (those most likely to be chronic medical conditions) in U.S. children surveyed in N–HANES II is about 4 percent. Therefore, we conclude that the prevalence of chronic medical conditions for Mexican–American and Cuban–American children are similar to non-Hispanic U.S. children. The prevalence of chronic medical conditions for mainland Puerto Ricans was significantly higher than the other two Hispanic subgroups and appeared to be higher than the national average. However, the high prevalence of asthma among mainland Puerto Rican children, sampled from the New York City area, suggests that possible local environmental factors, such as air pollution, could be affecting the prevalence of some conditions. Otherwise, the prevalence of chronic medical conditions did not seem to be affected by sex, poverty status, or the level of acculturation of the child and family.

In adults, self-reported health status has been predictive of demands for health care services, survival, and many other health status measures.[16] Previous studies of children conducted by the National Center for Health

Statistics have shown positive relationships between parental perception of children's health status and their children's actual health status.[17] However, Eisen et al. found that parental ratings of children's health status were significantly associated with their own self-perceived health status.[18] It has been suggested that this association may be a result of common genetic or environmental factors or the effects of the child's illness on the family. Additionally, children—particularly adolescents—have the ability to rate their own health status, and such ratings have been correlated with their actual health status.[19]

In this study, clear differences were seen in this measure of health status by rater and the group being assessed. Survey physicians rarely rated the children in H–HANES to be in poor health. When they did, it was usually because a chronic medical condition was present. In contrast, a significantly greater proportion of children were rated in poor health when assessed either by their mothers or by themselves. Among mothers of children under the age of 12, all were influenced in their rating of their children's health status by the presence of a chronic medical condition. However, both Mexican–American and mainland Puerto Rican mothers were, in addition, more likely to rate their children in poor health if their children were older or less acculturated, that is, spoke Spanish in the home. Moreover, for Mexican–American mothers, being bilingual also increased the chances of a poor-health rating of their children. Although poverty appeared to affect only the health assessments made by Mexican–American mothers, the assessments of mainland Puerto Ricans probably also were affected because of the association between acculturation and lower socioeconomic status.

These findings suggest that Mexican–American and mainland Puerto Rican mothers are more likely to rate their children in poor health than are non-Hispanic parents, who rate only 5 percent of their children in poor health.[20] Only Cuban–American mothers appear to match the national rate. These differences may be based upon actual differences in health status that are not detectable by cross-sectional health surveys such as the H–HANES or they could also reflect differences in the sociocultural perception of good and poor health.

Utilizing all of the above measures of health status—low birthweight, prematurity, chronic medical conditions, and subjective health ratings—provides a means to begin to define the health status of U.S. Hispanic children. With this approach, we have demonstrated that for the objective health measures, Hispanics appear to be in good health. However, this may be somewhat deceptive because of the significant differences between mainland Puerto Ricans and Mexican Americans and Cuban Americans. The latter two groups appear to have better outcomes in pregnancy and lower prevalences of chronic medical conditions. While this would be expected of Cuban Americans because of their lower rates of poverty, this is quite unexpected for Mexican Americans because they have a similarly high rate of poverty as mainland Puerto Ricans. Furthermore, among

Hispanics, Mexican Americans have the least access to health care, as was suggested in this study by their low levels of physician contact for chronic medical conditions.[21] By contrast, mainland Puerto Ricans reported in the 1978–1980 National Health Interview Survey the highest rate of physician contacts for children under 17 years.[22] Moreover, even though mainland Puerto Ricans and Mexican Americans both have high poverty rates, mainland Puerto Rican families are more likely to be headed by a single parent than Mexican–American families, who have a two-parent percentage similar to non-Hispanic whites.[23] These sociodemographic differences may contribute to some of the differences in health.

The subjective ratings of children's health, particularly by mothers, suggest a different picture of Mexican–American children's health status than that obtained from the more objective measures. It is quite likely these perceptions of health held by mothers may influence their actions toward their children, and it is equally likely that the children's self-perceived health status is also influenced by their mothers' perception of their health. All of these factors could have significant impact on the child's function.

It is clear the Hispanics are not homogeneous, either in their sociodemographic or health characteristics.

Each group should be investigated as a separate entity rather than as a combined whole. Health interventions directed at Hispanics need to take into account these intragroup differences as well as to acknowledge some of the sociocultural characteristics that make them distinctive from the rest of the nation's population.

Notes

The material in this chapter has been updated and edited from an earlier version, "Selected Measures of Health Status for Mexican-American, Mainland Puerto Rican, and Cuban-American Children," *Journal of the American Medical Association* (January 9, 1991), vol. 265(2), pp. 227–232. Copyright © 1991 by the American Medical Association. Printed with permission from Fernando S. Mendoza and the publisher.

1. US Bureau of the Census. 1987. *Current Population Report. The Hispanic Population in the United States: March 1986 and 1987* (Advance Report). Series P-20, No. 416. Washington, DC: US Government Printing Office.

2. US Bureau of the Census. 1987.

3. National Center for Health Statistics. In press. *Vital Statistics of the U.S. 1987.* Vol. 1 (Natality), Technical Appendix and Vol. 2 (Mortality, Part A), Technical Appendix. Hyattsville, MD.

4. National Center for Health Statistics. In press.

5. US Bureau of the Census. 1987.

6. National Center for Health Statistics. 1985. Plan and Operation of the Hispanic Health and Nutrition Examination Study 1982–84. *Vital and Health Statistics.* Series 1, No. 19. Hyattsville, MD.

7. National Center for Health Statistics. 1985.

8. National Center for Health Statistics. 1989. Advance Report of Final Natality Statistics, 1987. *Monthly Vital Statistics Report* 38(3)(Supplement) June 29.

9. Traffel S. 1978. Prenatal care: United States, 1969–75. National Center for Health Statistics. *Vital and Health Statistics*. Series 31, No. 33. Hyattsville, MD.

10. Ventura SJ, Heuser RL. 1981. Births of Hispanic Parentage, 1978. National Center for Health Statistics. *Monthly Vital Statistics Report* 29(12); Ventura SJ. 1982. Births of Hispanic Parentage, 1979. National Center for Health Statistics. *Monthly Vital Statistics Report* 31(2)(Supplement); Ventura SJ. 1983. Births of Hispanic Parentage, 1980. National Center for Health Statistics. *Monthly Vital Statistics Report* 32(6)(Supplement); Ventura SJ. 1984. Births of Hispanic Parentage, 1981. National Center for Health Statistics. *Monthly Vital Statistics Report* 33(8)(Supplement); Ventura SJ. 1985. Births of Hispanic Parentage, 1982. National Center for Health Statistics. *Monthly Vital Statistics Report* 34(4)(Supplement); Ventura SJ. 1987. Births of Hispanic Parentage, 1983 and 1984. National Center for Health Statistics. *Monthly Vital Statistics Report* 36(4)(Supplement); and Ventura SJ. 1988. Births of Hispanic Parentage, 1985. National Center for Health Statistics. *Monthly Vital Statistics Report* 36(11)(Supplement); and National Center for Health Statistics. 1989.

11. National Center for Health Statistics. 1989.

12. Schoenborn C. 1988. Health Promotion and Disease Prevention, United States, 1985. National Center for Health Statistics. *Vital and Health Statistics*. Series 10, No. 163. Hyattsville, MD.

13. Felice ME, Shragg MA, James M, Hollingsworth DR. 1986. Clinical Observations of Mexican American, Caucasian, and Black Pregnant Teenagers. *Journal of Adolescent Health Care* 7:305–10.

14. Newacheck PW, Budetti PD, Halfon N. 1986. Trends in Activity-limiting Chronic Conditions Among Children. *American Journal of Public Health* 76(2):178–84.

15. Trevino FM, Moss AJ. 1984. Health Indicators for Hispanic, Black and White Americans. *Vital and Health Statistics*. Series 10, No. 148. National Center for Health Statistics. Hyattsville, MD.

16. Ware JE, Jr. 1985. Commentary: Monitoring and Evaluating Health Services. *Medical Care* 23(5):705–09; Mossey JM, Shapiro E. 1982. Self-Rated Health: A Predictor of Mortality Among the Elderly. *American Journal of Public Health* 72(8):800–08; and Kaplan GA, Camacho T. 1983. Perceived Health and Mortality: A Nine-Year Follow-Up of the Human Population Laboratory Cohort. *American Journal of Epidemiology* 117(3):292–304.

17. National Center for Health Statistics. 1972. Examination and Health History Finding Among Children and Youth. *Vital and Health Statistics*. Series 2, No. 1A. Hyattsville, MD.

18. Eisen M, Ware JE, Jr., Donald CA, Brook RH. 1979. Measuring Components of Children's Health Status. *Medical Care* 17(9):902–21.

19. Landsberger BH. 1981. Adolescent's Health Status: Sex Differences Among Whites and Nonwhites. *Journal of Adolescent Health Care* 2:9–18.

20.National Center for Health Statistics. 1986. Current Estimates from the National Interview Survey, United States 1985. *Vital and Health Statistics*. Series 10, No. 160. Hyattsville, MD.

21. Californians Without Health Insurance. 1987. *A Report to the California Legislature*. California Policy Seminar, Technical Assistance Project. Berkeley, CA: University of California, September.

22. National Center for Health Statistics. 1984.

23. US Bureau of the Census. 1987.

9

Health Policy
and the Elderly Hispanic

David V. Espino and Marta Sotomayor

Mexican Americans comprise the majority of the Hispanic elderly population—approximately 54 percent. Cubans comprise 13.6 percent; mainland Puerto Ricans, 8.9 percent; Central and South Americans, 6.5 percent; and "other" Hispanics, primarily New Mexicans who identify themselves as "Hispanic" or "Spanish," 16.6 percent.[1]

The ethnic identification of these groups is influenced by the respective country of origin, length of residence or history of the family in the United States, and the cumulative experience of interactions with members of the majority and other minority groups. The effects of historical events, such as migration, acculturation, urbanization, and discrimination, also impact upon the health and well-being of the Hispanic elder.[2]

The majority of research on elderly Hispanics has been conducted by independent investigators with little testing of previously derived hypotheses or findings. This has resulted in controversy and a lack of systematic theories to guide future research.[3] Lack of documentation also has hampered the identification of potential participants in research endeavors. Few elderly Hispanics have birth certificates, marriage certificates, or other legal documents that attest to significant life events.

Despite the problems associated with the heterogeneity of the Hispanic population and the methodology employed, research on the Hispanic elder published to date does provide insights into the challenges of aged Hispanic persons as they interact with mainstream U.S. society.

The Socioeconomic Perspective

Among the Hispanic elderly ages 60 to 64, the ratio of men to women is 86 to 100, with this gender ratio declining to 61 to 100 at age 85.[4]

The ethnic and geographic distribution of the Hispanic elderly follows that of the total Hispanic population. Most urban dwellers whose origins are Mexico and Central America gather primarily in California and Texas.

Most Cuban descents live in Florida, while New York hosts large numbers of Hispanic immigrants from Puerto Rico and the Caribbean Islands.[5]

A large proportion of the Mexican–American elderly come from older families who have lived in the Southwest since the nineteenth century or earlier while elderly Cubans are usually recent immigrants who came to the United States as political refugees.[6]

There are major differences in the median age distribution among Hispanic subgroups: Cubans have relatively older cohorts with a median age in 1987 of 35.8 years, compared to 23.5 for Mexican Americans, 24.3 for Puerto Ricans, and 27.3 for Central and South Americans. The median age for the total U.S. population is 31.9 years of age. Hispanic subgroups continue to grow at rates exceeding those of the general elderly population.

The Hispanic elderly population is more likely to live in the community and less likely to be institutionalized when compared to the non-Hispanic white elderly population.[7] Among the elderly age 85 and older, only 10 percent of the Hispanics are in extended-care facilities, compared to 23 percent of non-Hispanic whites. The Hispanic elderly population also appears to be more likely than other groups to live with their children in multigenerational families.

In 1985, 60.7 percent of Hispanic elderly owned their own homes. This is a lower percentage than that for the non-Hispanic white population. Only 23.6 percent of the Hispanic elderly lived alone; 36.5 percent lived with a spouse or other family members; and 0.7 percent lived with nonrelatives.[8]

The Hispanic elderly have the least number of years of formal education when compared to other minorities and to non-Hispanic whites. According to the Bureau of Census, they run a close second to blacks in illiteracy rates.[9] Up to 56 percent of Hispanic adults are functionally illiterate in English. It also has been estimated that 88 percent of Hispanics who fall in the general category of limited-English proficiency not only are illiterate in English but also in their native language.

Approximately 90 percent of Hispanic elderly speak Spanish at home, with 22 percent reporting that they do not speak English at all. Only 50 percent of them reported in 1987 that they spoke English well or very well.[10]

In 1986, Hispanic men age 65 and older had a median per capita income of $7,369 per year, compared with $4,583 per year for Hispanic women. This compares to $6,757 for black males, $4,508 for black females, $12,131 for white males, and $6,738 for white females, according to a 1987 report by the Bureau of Labor Statistics.[11]

Older Hispanics are more than twice as likely to live in poverty than non-Hispanic whites.[12] In 1988, almost 31 percent of aged Hispanics lived in poverty, compared to 14 percent among aged non-Hispanic whites. And in 1980, nearly 245,000 Hispanic aged sixty or older—approximately 42 percent of all older Hispanics—were classified either as poor or marginally poor, which contrasts with 23 percent of non-Hispanic whites.[13]

Approximately 13 percent of Hispanic elderly were in the labor force—
the same as the non-Hispanic white population, but the percentage of
unemployed elderly Hispanic workers—9 percent—was nearly twice as
great as that found among the non-Hispanic white populations—5 percent.[14]

In summary, the Hispanic elderly are more likely to be poorly educated,
marginally literate, and have poor communication skills in English. Also,
they are more likely to live in poverty and to be unemployed when
compared to non-Hispanic whites of the same age. Finally, a lesser
percentage of them are institutionalized and a greater proportion live in
multigenerational families than non-Hispanic whites.

Other than health-related data collected by the Hispanic Health and
Nutrition Examination Survey (H–HANES) in 1982–1984, objective health-
related information on older Hispanics is sparse. Information collected
primarily through self-identification and self-evaluation questionnaires
administered to a relatively small number of respondents indicates Hispanics view their health as generally poorer than the non-Hispanic white
population.[15]

A 1973 study in San Antonio showed that 46 percent of elderly Hispanic
men and 35 percent of elderly women categorized their health as being
poor or very poor.[16] These findings roughly agree with a study done in
East Los Angeles, which showed that 53 percent of elderly Hispanic men
and 37.5 percent of elderly Hispanic women also considered their overall
health status as being either poor or very poor.[17] The Los Angeles study
also indicates 53 percent of males and 41 percent of females considered
themselves disabled, and a similar number reported that a physician had
categorized them disabled.

Major medical problems reported by elderly Hispanics include arthritis,
diabetes mellitus, cardiovascular disease, hypertension, cognitive impairment, depression, dysphoria (restlessness), and cerebrovascular disease.[18]
Data related to specific medical problems are scarce. Espino and colleagues
recently reported that a greater proportion of older Mexican Americans
had diabetes mellitus than comparable cohorts in the total population
sampled. Arthritis and heart disease were proportionally less prevalent.[19]

While the proportion of older Mexican Americans with hypertension
was smaller than that of the general population, the opposite was true
among more acculturated older Hispanics.[20]

While early researchers found that Mexican Americans generally had
lower levels of stress and stress-related problems that non-Hispanic
whites[21], more recent data—specifically about elderly Hispanics—show
greater prevalence of depression and dysphoria among this group than
among their non-Hispanic white counterparts.

In addition to the scarcity of data, there is disagreement regarding the
health status of Hispanic elderly by gender. An East Los Angeles study
reported a higher degree of disability among retired Hispanic men when
compared to women, while a large-scale survey in Texas found the health

of elderly Mexican–American females to be significantly worse than their male counterparts.[22]

Strong family ties and strong mutual-helping patterns exist among Hispanic families in several cities, with younger Hispanics providing support to older Hispanics within the intergenerational family.[23] The greater prevalence of exchanging aid and services within Hispanic families versus their non-Hispanic white counterparts[24] is based on high expectations that children should provide support for the elderly[25] and a marked preference among the senior members of the family to rely on family for support rather than on friends or more formal sources.[26]

It has been argued that the extended intergenerational support model has been to a certain extent stereotypic.

It may be that the extended intergenerational support system is triggered only at times of family tragedies or for periods of general societal disorganization.[27] During those times, it acts as a cultural holdover—a functional adaptation to stress or a linking mechanism to the formalized health care system.[28]

Also, while the intergenerational family function enhances information processing and dissemination, provides emotional support and care-giving, and can even complement financial assistance, its limited resources cannot offer adequate support for the disabled elderly person who remains dependent on available formalized health care services.

Health Policy

While programs and services have already expanded to meet the needs of the growing number of the elderly in the U.S. population as a whole, the Hispanic elderly have not utilized them in proportion to their need. For example, the White House Conference Report of 1988 indicates that 90 percent of the general population used Social Security as an important source of income.[29] In contrast, only 56 percent of the Hispanic elderly were drawing Social Security benefits. Only 82 percent of Mexican–American males were Social Security insured at age 65, compared to 92 percent of non-Hispanic whites in the same age group.[30] Twenty-eight percent were not receiving Social Security Old Age Social Insurance (OASI) benefits at all compared with only 7 percent of white elderly males. For those who were receiving OASI benefits, the level of benefits was considerably lower than those received by their white counterparts. The percentage (8.1 percent) of Hispanic elderly who received retirement benefits is considerably lower than that in the general population, or 25 percent for unrelated persons and 40 percent for families with heads of households over 65 years of age. Work in noncovered employment, intermittent work patterns, the holding of multiple Social Security numbers, and the nonreporting of contributions by employers are often given as reasons for such low level of benefit eligibility.[31]

Despite the poor health and severe risk factors experienced by this population of elderly, lack of access and low utilization rates of available health care services continues to be an issue for which effective solutions are yet to be found. A number of reports, including those issued by the U.S. Civil Rights Commission and the U.S. General Accounting Office, have identified factors related to issues of access, equity, quality, and cost of health care that contribute to low service utilization rates.[32] The most often mentioned are institutional policies and procedures that discourage their utilization by the Hispanic elderly, lack of bilingual and bicultural health care personnel at all levels of the health care system, location of the health care facility, lack of transportation, and inadequate outreach in the language of their preference. Other reports mention the Hispanic elderly's reluctance to seek health care before it becomes an emergency, strong reliance on alternative health care practices, cultural conflict, discrimination, and lack of information about the various services available. Their limited knowledge of English certainly adds to their lack of understanding of a health care system that in many ways appears to them as uncoordinated, contradictory, and complex.[33]

All of these factors are interdependent and contribute significantly to the Hispanic elderly's poor health status. But, for a population of elderly characterized by limited education that has relegated them to the lowest occupational levels and unskilled occupations resulting in high levels of poverty, none of these factors is as significant as the high cost of health care and the way it is financed.

More than 205 million Americans, 86 percent of the civilian population, have some form of health insurance. Approximately 181 million persons have private health insurance, and approximately 136 million obtain insurance coverage through employment-related plans. Others have health benefits that provide access to health care through the Veterans Administration (VA), the Public Health Service, and the Department of Defense. About 66 percent of all persons with private health insurance and 75 percent of all covered workers obtain their insurance through employer-sponsored group benefit plans. Approximately 147 million Americans have health insurance coverage through an employer-sponsored plan.[34] Data show that the number of uninsured persons rose by over 1 million each year between 1978 and 1986. Although most uninsured persons were in families headed by someone who was fully employed, the wages of these workers were generally low. In 1985, three-quarters of the uninsured workers earned less than $10,000 and nearly 93 percent earned less than $20,000 in 1985.[35] For the most part, Hispanic elderly have not been covered by private health insurance and rates of coverage may vary among the different Hispanic subgroups. For example, over one-third (35 percent) of the Mexican–American population have neither private nor public health insurance compared with 29 percent of Cubans and 22 percent of Puerto Ricans. However, most uninsured Hispanics report that the main reasons for lack of coverage was that they could not afford the cost of health insurance. Consequently, they are considerably less likely to see a physician, and were the least likely to report unemployment as the main reason for noncoverage.[36] Reports support the finding that the low rates of private health insurance coverage among Hispanic population groups is primarily the result of their low income and employment in places where health insurance coverage is not provided as a fringe benefit. Fifty-eight percent of the uninsured Mexican Americans, 40 percent of the uninsured Cuban Americans, and 51 percent of the uninsured Puerto Ricans are living in poverty.[37] Thus, the segment of the population most affected by the cost of medical services is the "working poor Hispanics who are not eligible for government programs and at the same time cannot afford the rising cost of medical services."[38]

In general, total national health care expenditures have risen from $75 billion in 1970 to approximately $600 billion in 1989.[39] While all items included in the consumer price index increased at an average annual rate of 11 percent, health costs increased at an average annual rate of 17 percent from 1970 to 1988, a rate that is rising twice as fast as wages.[40] The total cost for health care administration alone, including multiple public and private insurers and third-party payments, is estimated to be approximately 22 percent of all personal health care spending.[41] Businesses pay 45 percent of their operating profits for health care, and small businesses, where most Hispanics are employed, pay 20 to 35 percent more than large firms for identical health insurance coverage for their workers.[42]

Financial limitations and an increasingly competitive health care environment have forced many hospitals, both for profit and not for profit, to curtail the amount of uncompensated care they provide and to shift uninsured patients to public hospitals. It is estimated that more than 1 million Americans are turned away from hospitals each year because they lack insurance or other means to pay for care, and many of the uninsured who require emergency care are transferred to public hospitals.[43] While there are no figures indicating the proportions of Hispanic elderly that are turned away from hospitals, it is assumed that the proportions are quite high simply because hospital emergency rooms have become the treatment of choice due to lack of resources to pay for private care.

Half of all public hospitals are operating at a loss, with an average deficit of $11 million. Inability to meet operating costs is the main reason given by 40 percent of the nation's hospitals for not meeting health and safety standards required by the Joint Commission on Accreditation of Hospitals. Without a financial base of insured or privately paying patients, public hospitals are finding it increasingly difficult to provide care that is equal in quality to that provided in private hospitals. Yet, it is in these hospitals where most Hispanics are more likely to seek medical care.[44]

Efforts to address the spiraling costs of medical care were initiated in the mid–1960s by the federal government through changes in the Social Security Act that established Medicaid and Medicare. Medicare is presently the major health service provider for the Hispanic elderly as it is for practically all elderly in this country[45] since it was intended to provide medical coverage for short-term acute illness to insured individuals with-

out regard to their incomes or assets. Part A of Medicare, the hospitalization component, requires that the person be 65 years of age or over and
eligible for Social Security OASI. As noted previously, a relatively high
percentage of elderly Mexican Americans are not eligible for OASI, and
thus they are ineligible for Part A of Medicare.[46] While an individual can
participate on a voluntary basis in Part A and Part B of Medicare (the
outpatient component) for a premium, the amount is prohibitive for the
Latino elderly whose income is already below the poverty level. The
deductible which amounts to the first day of hospitalization more often
than not represents another major barrier to seek inpatient treatment.

Medicaid, a federal and state program, was established to provide
assistance to certain categories of low-income people which include the
elderly. However, qualifying for the program is often a function of an
individual's assets and income, for which standards vary widely among
the fifty states and that pose severe barriers to access. As a result of these
variations, in 1989, the national average income threshold for a family of
three to qualify for Medicaid was $4,942, approximately 49 percent of the
federal poverty level of $10,080.[47] Those eligible for OASI may qualify for
the means-tested SSI, and if eligible they also are eligible for Medicaid. In
such situations, the state has the option of enrolling the individual in the
Medicare program and paying the premium, deductible, and co-insurance.
But the cost-shifting and cost-sharing approach is disproportionally adverse for the poor Hispanic elderly whose health tends to be worse than
that of the general population. For this population of poor, out-of-pocket
health care costs can go up to 29 percent of their annual income. Increased
copayment and deductible strategies also increase not only out-of-pocket
payments, but also increase the number of people who cannot buy Part B
Medicare physician coverage, which in turn increase the number who
cannot receive nor purchase medigap insurance.[48] Some states may extend
Medicaid eligibility to persons who fall into the category of "medically
needy," but this practice is not compulsory. Thus, while Medicaid can
provide some options to poor populations, its impact on accessing health
care services by the poor Latino elderly is uncertain. Finally, because
Medicaid payment rates are low, many physicians refuse to treat Medicaid
patients, forcing the poor Latino elderly to use emergency care where
continuity and coordination of care is impossible.

Trevino, in Chapter 13, provides national estimates of access to health
care by Hispanics based on data from the National Health Interview
Survey.

Conclusions

The Hispanic elderly constitute a large and ethnically diverse subgroup
of the Hispanic population of the United States that has been largely
ignored in the development of health programs and policies.

Their growing number and the subsequent disabilities expected of aging
populations, coupled with the neglect by health care and human service

providers, create health service challenges of high urgency. Unfortunately, in the case of the Hispanic minority and the elderly poor, policymakers divert their attention to younger age cohorts.

The unprecedented growth in the number of Hispanic elderly will result in an increased demand for already scarce health care services.

In the long run, alternatives to the present system will be necessary, including some form of a nationwide financing mechanism to ensure access for all. It is quite possible that in the long run nothing short of universal access to a level of basic health care will be fair to the Latino elderly.

Notes

1. US Bureau of the Census. 1987a. *Current Population Reports. The Hispanic Population in the United States: March 1986 and 1987.* Series P–20, No. 416. Washington, DC: US Government Printing Office.

2. Curiel H, Rosenthal JA. 1988. The Influence of Aging on Self-Esteem: A Consideration of Ethnicity, Gender, and Acculturation Level Differences. In Sotomayor M, Curiel H (eds.). *The Hispanic Elderly. A Cultural Signature.* Edinburg, TX: Pan American Press, pp. 11–32.

3. Newton FC. 1980. Issues in Research and Service Delivery Among Mexican American Elderly. A Concise Statement of Recommendations. *Gerontologist* 20(2):208–13.

4. US Bureau of the Census. 1987a.

5. US Bureau of the Census. 1987a.

6. US Bureau of the Census. 1987b. *Statistical Abstract of the United States 1987.* Washington, DC: US Government Printing Office.

7. U.S Bureau of the Census. 1987b.

8. US Bureau of the Census. 1987b.

9. US Bureau of the Census. 1987a.

10. US Bureau of the Census. 1987a.

11. US Bureau of Labor Statistics. 1987. *Current Population Survey.* Washington, DC: US Department of Labor.

12. Agree E. 1986. *The A.A.R.P. Minority Affairs Initiative. A Portrait of Older Minorities.* Washington, DC: The Center for Population Research.

13. US Bureau of the Census. 1987c. *Current Population Reports. Money, Income, and Poverty Status of Families and Persons in the United States, 1986.* Series P–60, No. 157. Washington, DC: US Government Printing Office.

14. US Bureau of Labor Statistics. 1987.

15. Cantor M, Mayer M. 1976. Health and the Inner City Elderly. *Gerontologist* 16(1):17–25; Juarez RZ. 1984. Health Status of Mexican American and Anglo Elderly in South Texas. Paper presented at the Annual Meeting of the American Public Health Association. Anaheim, CA; and Salcido RM. 1979. Problems of the Mexican–American Elderly in an Urban Setting. *Social Caseworker* 612:22–25.

16. Gomez E, Martin H, Gibson G. 1973. Adaptation of Older Mexican Americans. Implications for Social and Health Programs. Unpublished manuscript.

17. Cooper T, Simonin M, Newquist D. 1978. *Project MASP. Health Fact Sheet.* Los Angeles, CA: Andrus Gerontology Center, University of Southern California.

18. Lopez-Aqueres W, Kemp B, Plopper M, et al. 1984. Health Care Needs of the Hispanic Elderly. *Journal of the American Geriatrics Society* 32(3):191–98; and

Lopez-Aqueres W. 1985. An Assessment of the Rehabilitation Physical and Mental Health Status of the Elderly Hispanic. Highlights of Findings. Los Angeles, CA: University of Southern California, Rehabilitation Research and Training Center on Aging, Rancho Los Amigos Hospital.

19. Espino DV, Burge SK, Moreno CA. 1989a. *Chronic Diseases Among Older Mexican–Americans. Data from 1982–84 Hispanic HANES.* XI World Congress of Gerontology. Acapulco, Mexico. June.

20. Espino DV, Maldonado D, Lawler WR. 1989b. *Acculturation and Hypertension in Elderly Mexican Americans. Data from 1982–84 H–HANES.* American Geriatrics Society Scientific Session. May.

21. Atunes G, Gordon C, Gaitz CM, Scott J. 1974. Ethnicity, Socioeconomic Status and the Etiology of Psychological Distress. *Sociology and Social Research* 58:361–68; and Madsen W. 1969. Mexican–Americans and Anglo–Americans. A Comparative Study of Mental Health in Texas. In Plog SC, Edgerton RB (eds.). *Changing Perspectives in Mental Illness.* New York, NY: Holt, Rinehart & Winston.

22. Blau S. 1978. *Aging, Social Class, and Ethnicity.* Ann Arbor, MI: School of Social Work, University of Michigan.

23. Becerra RM, Shaw D. 1984. *The Hispanic Elderly. A Research Reference Guide.* New York: University Press of America.

24. Mindel CH. 1980. Extended Familism Among Urban Mexican Americans, Anglos, and Blacks. *Hispanic Journal of Behavioral Science* 2:21–24; and Wagner RM, Schaefer DM. 1980. Social Networks and Survival Strategies: An Exploratory Study of Mexican American, Black and Anglo Female Family Heads in San Jose, California. In Melville MB (ed.). *Twice a Minority: Mexican American Women.* St. Louis, MO: C.V. Mosby Co.

25. Martinez MZ. 1980. Los Ancianos: A Study of the Attitudes of Mexican Americans Regarding Support of the Elderly. Ph.D. dissertation. Brandeis University.

26. Keefe SE, Padilla AM, Carlos ML. 1979. The Mexican American Extended Family as an Emotional Support System. *Human Organization* 38:144–52; and Starrett RA, Mindel CH, Wright R. 1983. Influence of Support Systems on the Use of Social Services by the Hispanic Elderly. *Social Work Research Abstracts* 19:35–40.

27. Sena-Rivera J. 1979. Extended Kinship in the United States: Competing Models and the Case of La Familia Chicana. *Journal of Marriage and Family* 41:121–29.

28. Starrett RA, Mindel CH, Wright R. 1983.

29. Garcia A. 1988. Social Policy and Elderly Hispanics. In Applewhite S (ed.). *Hispanic Elderly in Transition: Theory, Research, Policy and Practice.* New York, NY: Greenwood Press.

30. Gallego TD. 1988. Income Maintenance and the Hispanic Elderly. In Applewhite S (ed.). *Hispanic Elderly in Transition: Theory, Research, Policy and Practice.* New York, NY: Greenwood Press.

31. Garcia A. 1980. The Contribution of Social Security to the Adequacy of Income of Elderly Chicanos. Ph.D. dissertation. Brandeis University.

32. US Commission on Civil Rights. 1982. *Minority Elderly Services: New Programs, Old Promises (Parts 1 and 11).* Washington, DC: US Government Printing Office; and US General Accounting Office. 1988. *Long-Term Care for the Elderly. Issues of Need, Access and Cost.* GAO/HRD-89-4. Washington, DC: US Government Printing Office.

33. Andrulis D. 1977. Ethnicity as a Variable in the Utilization and Referral Patterns of a Comprehensive Mental Health Center. *Journal of Community Psychology* 5(3):231–37; Kline L. 1986. Some Factors in the Psychiatric Treatment of Spanish Americans. *American Journal of Psychiatry* 125(12):231–35; Morales A. 1978. The Need for Non-Traditional Mental Health Programs in the Barrio. In Casa M, Keefe S (eds.). *Family and Mental Health in the Mexican American Community*. Monograph No. 7. Los Angeles: Spanish Speaking Research Center, University of California; Putsch RW. 1985. Cross-Cultural Communication. The Special Case for Interpreters in Health Care. *Journal of the American Medical Association* 254(23):3344–48; and Sotomayor M, Randolph S. 1988. A Preliminary Review of Caregiving Issues Among Hispanic Elderly. In Sotomayor M, Curiel H (eds.). *The Hispanic Elderly. A Cultural Signature*. Edinburg, TX: Pan American Press.

34. Health Insurance Institute. 1989. *Source Book of Health Insurance Data*. New York.

35. Health Insurance Institute. 1989.

36. Trevino MF. 1989. Health Insurance Coverage of the Mexican American, Puerto Rican and Cuban American Populations. Paper presented at the National Action Forum on Health Policy and the Hispanic. San Antonio, TX.

37. Trevino MF. 1989.

38. Andersen RM, Giachello AL, Aday LA. 1986. Access of Hispanics to Health Care and Cuts in Services. A State-of-the-Art Overview. *Public Health Reports* 101(3):238–52.

39. Letsch SW, Levit KR, Waldo DR. 1988. National Health Expenditures, 1987. Health Care Financing Trends. *Health Care Financing Review* 10:109–29.

40. US Bureau of Labor Statistics. 1990. Consumer Price Index. *Social Security Bulletin* 53:57.

41. Himmelstein DU, Woolhandler S. 1986. Cost Without Benefit. Administrative Waste in US Health Care. *New England Journal of Medicine* 314:441–45.

42. US Senate. Committee on Labor and Human Resources. 1990. *The Health Care Crisis. A Report to the American People*. Document No. S. Print 101–100. Washington, DC: US Government Printing Office.

43. Chollet D. 1987. *Uninsured in the United States. The Nonelderly Population Without Health Insurance*. Washington, DC: Employee Benefit Research Institute.

44. Bureau of Data Management and Strategy. 1989. *1989 HCFA Statistics*. Pub. No. 03294. Baltimore, MD: Health Care Financing Administration.

45. Bureau of Data Management and Strategy. 1989.

46. Garcia A. 1988.

47. National Governors Association. 1989. *State Medicaid Information*. Washington, DC. July.

48. US House of Representatives. Select Committee on Aging. 1984. *Long-Term Care: Need for a National Policy. Hearing before the Subcommittee on Health and Long-Term Care*. 98th Congress, First session. Comm. Pub. No. 98–444. Washington, DC: US Government Printing Office.

10

Traumatic Injury
in Hispanic Americans:
A Distinct Entity

Eric Munoz, Bartholomew J. Tortella, Mary Ann Sakmyster,
Douglas S. Livornese, Maureen McCormac,
John W. Odom, and Ramon Torres

Trauma—the fourth most costly disease in the United States—disproportionately affects minority Americans.

We recently analyzed the experience of a large urban level 1 trauma center, surveying types of trauma by race, and found that although blacks and Hispanics had a disproportional share of admissions relative to non-Hispanic white populations, Hispanics had distinct mechanisms of injury compared to both blacks and whites.

Comparisons of mechanisms of injuries by race demonstrated that Hispanics had a lower rate of penetrating injury, such as stab and gunshot wounds, compared to blacks. However, they had a rate greater than whites. Hispanics had a higher rate of blunt trauma, i.e., motor vehicle accidents (MVA), compared to blacks but a lower rate than whites. These data suggest Hispanics may suffer a distinctly different pattern of trauma compared to other whites and blacks.

Public health policy with initiatives directed at lowering morbidity and mortality from both blunt and penetrating trauma should be sensitive to patterns displayed by Hispanic Americans.

Trauma currently accounts for direct and indirect costs of 2.3 percent of the U.S. Gross National Product and 6.9 percent of all U.S. health care costs.[1] Trauma is the leading cause of death for Americans from 18 to 44 years of age and tends to effect young men.[2]

Minority Americans are disproportionately effected by trauma.[3] Blacks and Hispanics appear to be particularly vulnerable to this health problem. Both blunt and penetrating trauma are, however, costly to the nation.

The distribution of these two types of trauma varies by urban and rural characteristics: Penetrating trauma tends to effect urban populations; blunt trauma is associated with motor vehicle accidents and pedestrian incidents and effects suburban and rural populations.[4] Traditionally, inner-city populations have a high volume of penetrating (gunshot or stab wound) trauma.

Little data of patterns of trauma by race exist. One recent study demonstrated that victims of nonfatal motor vehicle accidents tended to be young, single, employed white males whereas penetrating injuries involved young, single, often unemployed, black males.[5] Another study demonstrated that childhood pedestrian injuries were higher in census tracts with nonwhite populations and lower household incomes.[6] Since minorities are concentrated in cities, it is assumed that minority individuals suffer predominantly from penetrating trauma. Conversely, nonminority individuals who are less concentrated in urban areas suffer more commonly from blunt trauma. This hypothesis is supported by the homicide statistics of minorities and the higher lifetime mortality risk of minorities dying of trauma.[7]

Few data on the dynamics of trauma for Hispanics are available, but there has been some study of trauma rates for Hispanics in New Mexico. One study compared injury mortality rates in American Indian, Hispanic, and non-Hispanic children.[8] While American Indian children had the highest rates in this study, motor vehicle crashes and drowning were the first and second leading causes of death. Homicide rates accounted for twice the proportion of injury death in Hispanics compared with non-Hispanic white males.[9]

The purpose of our study was to characterize the dynamics of trauma for Hispanics and other races at a large urban, level 1 trauma center in the Northeast United States.

The hospital of the University of Medicine and Dentistry of New Jersey, a 508-bed hospital in Newark, New Jersey, is the principle teaching hospital of the New Jersey Medical School.

As the level 1 trauma center for Northern New Jersey, University Hospital is responsible for a large ground Emergency Medical Service (EMS) in the greater Newark metropolitan area as well as the NorthSTAR Aeromedical Helicopter program. The level 1 catchment area for these programs encompasses the northern half of New Jersey (the most densely populated state in the Union) and serves a 4.5 million population. The trauma service had 2,163 admissions in 1989.

We analyzed all admissions (1,093) to University Hospital for the six-month period of July–December 1989. Data were analyzed by race—white (274), black (600), and Hispanic (219)—and included mechanism of injury (penetrating vs. blunt) and was further divided into falls, beatings, motor vehicle accidents, pedestrians struck by automobile, stab wounds, and gunshot wounds.

In addition to patient age, hospital resource consumption data included hospital length of stay in days, total hospital cost, mortality, and the

TABLE 10.1   Mechanism of Injury by Race as a Percentage
of the Total Trauma Population

Mechanism of Injury	Hispanic	Black	White	All Patients
Beating	6.3	8.6	2.1[b]	6.0
Fall	4.9	6.1	11.0[b]	7.5
MVA[a]	46.3	22.4[b]	56.9[b]	35.0
MVA vs. Pedestrian	12.8	8.4	9.2	8.6
Stab Wound	12.9	13.6	6.7[b]	11.2
Gunshot Wound	12.3	37.2	6.9	25.6
Other	5.6	5.2	8.0	6.1

[a]Motor vehicle accident.
[b]Statistically different from all patients, $p < .05$.

Source: University of Medicine and Dentistry of New Jersey-University Hospital Trauma Center, Newark, New Jersey, 1989

number of ICD-9-CMs (International Classification of Diseases-9th Revision-Clinical Modification), diagnosis, and procedure codes. Payor status, such as Medicare, Medicaid, commercial insurance, self-pay, and no pay also was computed for each category.

The mechanism of injury—penetrating vs. blunt—by race differed for the various populations (Table 10.1). Blunt trauma for all patients was 57.1 percent; penetrating trauma for all patients was 36.8 percent; and 6.1 percent of patients had "other" injuries.

The detailed breakdown of mechanism of injury for all patients was beating, 6 percent; falls, 7.5 percent; motor vehicle accidents, 35 percent; pedestrian struck by motor vehicle, 8.6 percent; stab wounds, 11.2 percent; gunshot wounds, 25.6 percent; and other injuries, 6.1 percent.

There were significant differences in these rates by race: Hispanics demonstrated a rate of blunt trauma of 74.8 percent and penetrating trauma of 25.2 percent. Blacks showed a blunt trauma rate of 49.2 percent and a penetrating trauma rate of 50.8 percent. Whites had a blunt trauma rate of 86.7 percent and a penetrating trauma rate of 13.3 percent. Thus, for penetrating trauma, blacks had the highest rate, followed by Hispanics, then whites. For blunt trauma, whites had the highest rate, followed by Hispanics, then blacks. See Figure 10.1.

Hospital resource consumption for trauma patients also varied by race (Table 10.2). For all patients, age was 33.1 years; hospital length of stay per patient was 7.38 days; the total hospital cost per patient was $8,944; the number of diagnosis codes per patient was 3.37; and the number of

FIGURE 10.1 Blunt vs. Penetrating Injury, by Race

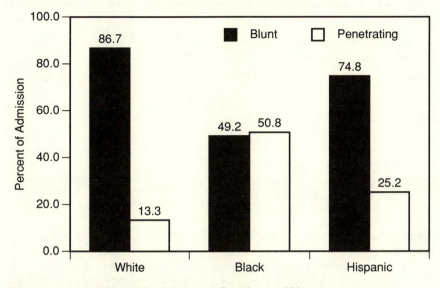

Source: University of Medicine and Dentistry of New
Jersey – University Hospital Trauma Center, Newark, New
Jersey, 1989.

TABLE 10.2   Hospital Resource Parameters by Race

	White	Black	Hispanic	All Patients
Age	36.6	28.3	31.8	33.1
Length of Stay (days)	8.60[d]	6.02[d]	7.30	7.38
Cost[b]	$10,430[d]	$7,283[d]	$8,795	$8,944
Diagnosis[c]	3.72[d]	2.89[d]	3.25	3.37
Procedure[c]	3.38	2.89[d]	3.00	3.23
Mortality (%)	12.8	7.6	6.9	8.9

[a]Mean per patients, divided by DRG weight index.
[b]Mean total cost per patient.
[c]Number of ICD-9-CM codes per patient.
[d]Statistically different from all patients, p < .05.

Source: University of Medicine and Dentistry of New Jersey-University Hospital Trauma
Center, Newark, New Jersey, 1989

TABLE 10.3   Hospital Payor Class by Race (in percentages)

	White	Black	Hispanic	All Patients
Commercial	11.1	8.8	4.0	8.7
Medicaid	1.1[a]	9.0	5.9	6.5
Medicare	2.1	0.3	2.0	1.0
Self-Pay	46.5[a]	59.3	70.3[a]	57.5
No pay	39.1[a]	22.6	17.8	26.3

[a]Statistically different from all patients, p < .05.

Source: University of Medicine and Dentistry of New Jersey-University Hospital Trauma Center, Newark, New Jersey, 1989

average procedure codes was 3.23. Mortality for all patients was 8.9 percent.

The payor status of these trauma patients is shown in Table 10.3. Hispanics constituted the greatest percentage of self-pay patients. For all patients, commercial insurance covered 8.7 percent of the population; Medicaid, 6.5 percent; Medicare, 1 percent; self-pay, 57.5 percent; and no pay, 26.3 percent. There were substantial differences, however, in these rates among the various races. Self-pay or no-pay prevalence was highest for Hispanics, 88.1 percent; followed by whites, 85.6 percent; and then blacks, 81.9 percent.

Our analysis by race of the recent experience of a large urban level 1 trauma center showed blacks and Hispanics comprised the majority of admissions, a proportion greater than their representation in the general population.

Blacks represent 14.8 percent of the population of New Jersey, and Hispanics represent 7.4 percent of the population. Essex County, where the trauma center is located, is 41 percent black and 21.2 percent Hispanic.

The mechanism of injury—blunt vs. penetrating—was substantially different for minority Americans. Traditionally, it has been believed that urban minority populations suffer more commonly from penetrating trauma. This study supports this concept. However, Hispanics had rates of both penetrating and blunt trauma that were substantially different from both non-Hispanic whites and blacks. Hispanics had rates of penetrating trauma between those of blacks and whites. This new finding suggests that the factors that affect the mix of trauma for Hispanics should be studied further.

Trauma is a costly disease to the nation. A number of studies have demonstrated that young males tend to incur the greatest expense from this disease. Although there is evidence to suggest that blacks and Hispanics suffer a greater incidence of trauma, the cost per trauma patient in our study was not substantially different between races.

The policy implications from our study suggest that public policy initiatives directed toward Hispanics should be sensitive to the dynamics of trauma for these patients. Hispanics demonstrated a mix of penetrating and urban trauma that displayed both urban and rural characteristics. Although our findings may be confounded by certain demographic characteristics, Hispanics did not follow the patterns of trauma for other whites or blacks.

The reasons for these findings are likely to be multifactorial: The Hispanic portion of our trauma patients is predominantly urban. Interestingly, Hispanics generated less penetrating trauma. Perhaps rates of handgun and/or other weapons use is lower for Hispanics compared to other groups. This requires further study.

Blunt trauma for Hispanics is higher than for blacks. Perhaps factors relative to automobile safety for this population need to be examined. Mechanisms to improve driver education and safety also may need improvement.

The study suggests that Hispanics have different mechanics of major trauma compared to both blacks and whites. Further study of this finding by race and region will be needed. The nation is in the process of regionalizing and standardizing trauma health care delivery. This involves a number of hospital, prehospital, and other societal issues. The U.S. trauma community and health care delivery systems will need focused efforts to further address the dynamics of trauma for Hispanics.

Notes

1. Munoz E. 1984. Economic Costs of Trauma, United States, 1982. *Journal of Trauma* 24:237–44.

2. Barancik JI, Chatterjee MS, Green YC, et al. 1983. Northeastern Ohio Trauma Study: Magnitude of the Problem. *American Journal of Public Health* 73:746–51.

3. U.S. Department of Health and Human Services. 1989. *Health United States, 1988*. Washington, DC, March.

4. Hartunian NS, Smart CN, Thompson MS. 1981. *The Incidence and Economic Costs of Major Health Impairment*. Lexington, MA: Lexington Books.

5. Cesare J, Morgan AS, Felice PR, Edge V. 1990. Characteristics of Blunt and Personal Violent Injuries. *Journal of Trauma* 30:176–82.

6. Rivara FP, Barber M. 1985. Demographic Analysis of Childhood Pedestrian Injuries. *Pediatrics* 75:375–81.

7. U.S. Department of Health and Human Services. 1989.

8. Olson LM, Becker TM, Wiggins CL, Key CR, Samet JM. 1990. Injury Mortality in American Indian, Hispanic, and Non-Hispanic White Children in New Mexico, 1958–1982. *Social Science and Medicine* 30:479–86.

9. Sewell CM, Becker TM, Wiggins CL, Key CR, Hull HF, Samet JM. 1989. Injury Mortality in New Mexico's American Indians, Hispanics, and Non-Hispanic Whites, 1958 to 1982. *Western Journal of Medicine* 150:708–13.

11

Oral Health of Hispanics: Epidemiology and Risk Factors

John P. Brown

In 1976, the U.S. Congress required federal agencies to collect, analyze, and publish health, social, and economic data on Hispanic Americans, but much of their health status remains largely undefined.

Despite being the fastest growing minority in the United States, Hispanics were not studied separately as part of national health surveys until 1982. Consequently, comparative, supporting, and longitudinal health data are lacking as well as information about health knowledge, attitudes, and practices. Furthermore, available data often overlook the importance of differentiating the national origin of Hispanics, thus ignoring differences in socioeconomic, geographic, and cultural characteristics that often are barriers to health care.

A major study addressing these issues is the Hispanic Health and Nutrition Examination Survey of 1982–84 (H–HANES).[1] The survey includes Hispanics living in five Southwestern states—Texas, New Mexico, Arizona, Colorado, and California, and the Miami area—(Dade County)—and selected areas of New York City, New Jersey, and Connecticut. Mexican Americans in the Southwest are well represented (97 percent) and Cuban Americans, Puerto Ricans, and other Hispanics less so. The H–HANES therefore is not representative of all Hispanics in the United States but of those living in the areas sampled (76 percent of the total Hispanic population).

The H–HANES included a probability sample of persons ages 6 months to 74 years. Equivalent Spanish and English questionnaires and detailed health examinations were used, including an oral examination to assess an index of dental decay or caries; an index of the need for treatment of caries; an index for oral hygiene status; an index of gum or periodontal disease, presence, and adequacy of full dentures for those without natural teeth; and an assessment of severe tooth crowding, alignment, and relationship (malocclusion) and whether orthodontic treatment had been provided.

Nutritional assessments, important to determine causes of caries and periodontal disease, were made and alcohol and tobacco consumption assessed. The latter are known to relate to the risk of oral cancer. Separate attitudinal and dietary questionnaires were administered to children and adults. Oral health services and prevention, eating patterns, and school attendance for children also were surveyed.

Caries and periodontal disease findings from the H–HANES have been analyzed for Mexican Americans, Cuban Americans, and Puerto Ricans, and association of acculturation with these diseases explored.[2] Nutritional and other relationships of preventive and treatment interest are not yet analyzed.

Caries in Children and Adolescents

In considering dental caries, it is usual to differentiate the deciduous—primary or milk teeth—from the permanent ones. It is also necessary to distinguish caries scores obtained at a single examination, known as prevalence, from caries rates determined by two or more examinations over a defined time and known conventionally as caries incidence. Most population-based epidemiologic data are of caries prevalence. The age-specific prevalence of caries in the permanent teeth of Mexican Americans ages 5 to 17 reflects the national decline in caries prevalence over the past two decades.[3] Mexican Americans from the H–HANES tended to have slightly higher caries, when compared with the whole population of the Southwestern states. Texas, Colorado, New Mexico, and Arizona comprised Region V in the National Institute of Dental Research (NIDR) 1979–1980 study, and this was the basis used for comparison.[4] It should be noted that the differences in caries between this nonequivalent geographic grouping of states were not significant. Forty-six percent of young Mexican Americans were caries-free, although only 14.6 percent of 17-year-olds were caries-free, and 19.4 percent of them had between nine and twenty-eight teeth decayed, missing due to caries, or filled. This summation of the outcomes of caries is referred to as the decayed, missed, and filled (DMF) index, and may be based on teeth (DMFT) or surfaces of teeth (DMFS). Overall, one-third of the decay had not been treated by filling the teeth involved.

The occlusal surfaces of molars are those most often decayed. This form of caries on the chewing surfaces of back teeth can be prevented by sealants, which are plastic coatings bonded to the teeth to prevent the growth of bacteria and entry of the fermentable food substrates necessary for caries to develop. Since the rate of increase of filled surfaces by age cohort was three times that of the rate of increase of decayed surfaces, treatment of caries by filling, rather than earlier prevention by sealants, has been the treatment of choice. This is unfortunate because fillings have a limited life and their replacement tends to become evermore costly. Restoration of the tooth by filling is also technically more difficult for dentist and patient.

TABLE 11.1   Caries by Sex and Ethnicity for Adolescents in Texas, 1984-1987

	Population	DMFS[a]		%
Sex/Ethnicity	Represented	(Mean)	(S.D.)	D/DMFS[b]
Male Anglo	88,272	2.1	3.1	19
Female Anglo	88,196	2.4	3.8	16
Male Hispanics	36,736	2.5	3.3	43
Female Hispanics	40,048	3.1	4.3	35
Male Blacks	19,247	2.9	5.0	46
Female Blacks	19,946	3.1	4.6	40

[a]DMFS = sum of the decayed, missing and filled permanent tooth surfaces.
[b]D/DMFS = the proportion of the total caries experienced which has not been treated by filling.

Note: Differences in means and proportions are statistically significant: $p < .01$.

Source: Killian K, Crow D, Kapadia AS, Brown JP. 1989. The Prevalence of Dental Caries in Texas Adolescents 1984-87. Report of the Texas Department of Health, Bureau of Dental and Chronic Disease Prevention.

Family income is negatively correlated with caries experience and positively correlated with completeness of treatment. These results are largely comparable to what was reported for the population of this region in the NIDR survey.[5]

Children in the Southwest have long had somewhat lower caries prevalence than children in the rest of the United States. This is largely attributed to the many communities with natural optimal levels of water fluoridation and its adjustment to optimal levels in many other cities over the past forty years. The optimal level is approximately one part per million of the fluoride ion in solution and varies slightly with climate. Seventy percent of Texans drink fluoridated water and more than 50 percent of the people using reticulated water in the states of New Mexico and Colorado also use it. The observance of the caries-preventive effects of naturally fluoridated water led to community fluoridation by addition to the water forty-one years ago. In the early 1980s, sealants were recommended. Combined with fluorides, they offer the potential to prevent most decay.

In 1972, the Ten State Nutrition Survey reported higher caries scores for Hispanic children in Texas than for nine other states—Louisiana, South Carolina, Kentucky, West Virginia, New York, Massachusetts, Michigan, Washington, and California.[6] The 1984–1987 Texas Department of Health Prevalence Survey of caries in Texas adolescents showed Hispanics and blacks had higher mean caries scores than Anglos and a lower rate of treatment. This is a status of double jeopardy (Table 11.1).[7] Further analysis indicated a highly significant positive relationship between caries treat-

TABLE 11.2   Mean Caries Score for Deciduous Teeth of Convenience Samples
of Predominantly Mexican-American Head Start Children
from Low-Income Families, Aged 4-5 Years

Year	Location	defs[a]	Water Fluoride ppm[b]
1985	Eagle Pass, Texas	3.3	0.9
1988	San Elizario, Texas	4.6	0.7-1.2
1985	San Antonio, Texas	7.9	0.3

[a]defs = decayed, extracted and filled surfaces of deciduous teeth.
[b]Optimal fluoride level is 0.7-0.8 ppm.

Source: Brown JP, Baez MX. 1989. The Surface Distribution of Caries in Deciduous
Teeth of a High Risk Group of Children. *Journal of Dental Research* 68:941.

TABLE 11.3   Mean Caries Score for Deciduous Teeth of Convenience Samples
of Predominantly Mexican-American Children from Low-Income Families,
Aged 7-9 Years

Year	Location	dfs + S.D.[a]	Water Fluoride ppm[b]
1988	San Elizario, Texas (77)	4.1 ± 5.0	0.7-1.2
1987-88	San Antonio, Texas (302)	10.4 ± 11.9	0.3

[a]dfs = decayed and filled surfaces of deciduous teeth.
[b]Optimal fluoride level is 0.7-0.8 ppm.

*Source: Brown JP, Baez MX. 1989. The Surface Distribution of Caries in Deciduous
Teeth of a High Risk Group of Children. Journal of Dental Research, 68:941.*

ment rate and both educational attainment and economic status within representative counties of Texas.[8]

Even greater deviations from national data are apparent from studies of convenience samples of children in San Antonio, which is not fluoridated, and other Texas communities with largely Hispanic populations (Tables 11.2 and 11.3). Caries in deciduous primary teeth of Mexican–American children from families disadvantaged in regard to education and income are double those of groups of similar ethnic and socioeconomic status in fluoridated cities of this state.[9] There is a similar relationship for permanent teeth favoring largely non-Hispanic groups of children using fluoridated water, when compared with Mexican Americans in San Antonio (Table 11.4). This is so despite the national decline in caries prevalence over the past two decades. This decrease is attributed largely to water fluoridation and other topically used fluorides, especially toothpastes. It has not resulted in loss of the caries differential that disadvantages certain cultural, ethnic, socioeconomic, and educationally deprived groups, including many Hispanics.

TABLE 11.4   Mean Caries Scores for Permanent Teeth of Convenience Samples
of Life Residents Aged 12-14 Years,
Selected Texas Cities, 1985

Location	DMFS[a]	Water Fluoride ppm[b]
Port Arthur	2.7	0.9
Sweetwater	2.9	0.8
San Antonio	5.1	0.3

[a]DMFS = Decayed missing and filled surfaces for permanent teeth.
[b]Optimal fluoride level is 0.8 ppm.

Source: Stiles, M. NIH-NIDR 1985.

Caries in Adults

The prevalence of caries in Mexican–American adults in the H–HANES study is quite different from that reported by the National Health and Nutrition Examination Survey I (N–HANES I) general-population results ten years earlier. Decayed-, missing-, and filled-teeth scores (DMFT) were lower. Caries prevalence did not relate to poverty status, but less dental treatment was evident for Mexican Americans. Total tooth loss increased with age to 37 percent of people ages 65 to 74. There is evidence in these adults that caries activity continues through the adult years, and thus its prevention should not be directed solely to children.

Of particular interest is the concept of acculturation, which attempts to measure the process of adoption of the culture in a host country. Several acculturation scales have been proposed, mostly for Mexican Americans. Some of these scales include factors best considered as discrete social and demographic indicators and factors that are unchangeable and so inappropriate to a construct measuring a process of change. Low acculturation has been shown to relate to heart disease and diabetes in Mexican Americans.[10]

The formal use of language was critically important in one of Hazuda et al.'s validated scales, but their scales based on cultural identification, family, and sex roles were less health related. Formal language skills in English or Spanish are highly desirable in negotiating a path through service agencies so that the client is confident, unthreatened by other possible consequences whether real or not, and, thus, open to information, education, and follow-up.[11]

Periodontal Disease in Children and Adolescents

A very high proportion—76.9 percent—of Mexican Americans ages 5 to 17 in the Southwest, as represented in the H–HANES study, had gingivitis or gum inflammation. Periodontal pocketing, due to the loss of attachment of the tooth to soft tissue and bone, was not a feature (four children of 7,240 examined). Oral hygiene status was assessed by measuring soft-and hard-tooth deposits. The soft deposits consist of dentobacterial plaque and food residues. The hard deposits are calculus, which basically is calcified plaque above and below the gingival margin. Debris and calculus indices were higher in Mexican–American children in 1982–1984 than generally in Southwestern children who were examined ten years before (N–HANES I, 1971–1974), even after adjusting for income. Higher family income was associated with improved oral hygiene status.[12]

Periodontal Disease in Adults

A significantly higher percentage of adult Mexican Americans had gingivitis than did Southwestern residents a decade before. Oral hygiene status was generally poorer, based on this same comparison.[13] The percentage with periodontal pockets was higher with older age but lower than in N–HANES I.

The H–HANES revealed that gingivitis and periodontal pocketing were of significantly higher level with low acculturation, even after accounting for effects of age, sex, debris, calculus, income, education, and design.[14] All Hispanics had high prevalence of gingivitis.[15]

Two studies in New Mexico of predominantly Mexican–American populations have raised important questions regarding our understanding of the natural history of periodontal disease and long-held views of the inevitability of periodontal destruction and loss of teeth. The lack of consistent or joint association of risk factors that presently are considered important, and the failure of those risk factors to explain the variability in presence of advanced periodontal disease, has also caused conventional ideas of etiology to be questioned.[16] Even allowing for a possible underestimate, deep periodontal pocketing was found in only a quarter of these persons. Nevertheless, plaque score and educational status, but not sex or ethnicity, were associated with advanced loss of periodontal attachment in both reports.

Adult onset diabetes, which is of increased prevalence in Mexican Americans,[17] is associated with severity of periodontal disease. The Centers for Disease Control has indicated that periodontal disease is a likely complication in diabetics. This provides additional urgency for a better understanding of the epidemiology and nature of periodontal disease, especially in Mexican Americans.

Oral manifestations of HIV infection, oral, facial, and dental trauma, malocclusion, oral cancer and its association with various tobacco products and alcohol have not been reported specifically for Hispanics. In view of intense marketing of these products to minority populations, such information is highly desirable. Low acculturation also was associated with low usage of dental insurance and infrequent visits to the dentist, involving toothache and extraction more than prevention and treatment.[18]

Mexican Americans tend to have higher caries prevalence and lower rates of treatment. Gingivitis is also of higher prevalence than in the population at large but is not necessarily associated with excess periodontal disease. Multivariate analysis of socioeconomic and etiologic (relating to the causes of disease) variables with caries is incomplete. Consequently, data analysis from the H–HANES should be completed so the status of other Hispanics can be known and the association of oral disease fully explored from this benchmark study.

For planning oral health services at the community level, detailed local information is essential and can be obtained by simple pathfinder studies, as prescribed by the World Health Organization. This method also involves the local community in the study, ensuring its utilization.[19]

Specific sociodemographic, nutritional, and behavioral risk factors in oral disease should be studied, leading to risk-assessment studies and demonstration projects. Ultimately oral health must be addressed under a national health policy for the United States. One recent initiative in policy and advocacy was the U.S. Public Health Service Workshop on Oral Health of Mothers and Children.[20] Hispanics as a group present a clear instance of lack of utilization of existing preventive knowledge and technology. Apart from the obvious impact of pain, suffering, and infection, oral disease is now recognized to have a negative impact on self-image and quality of life. These in turn affect education, self-realization, employment, family finances, and the economy in general.[21]

Conclusions

Participants of the Workshop on Oral Health posed four broad solutions:

- Public education for improved knowledge and attitude about oral prevention must be developed in the public at large as well as among providers, health administrators, policymakers, and consumer advocates.
- National and local public coalitions must be set up to promote oral health. (There are numerous successful models for this, such as the American Heart Association and the American Cancer Society.)
- Legislative and regulatory initiatives, as well as the maximizing of existing policies, are needed to bolster oral health.
- The interaction of behavioral, psychosocial, and biological factors must be studied and outcomes monitored to provide feedback and achieve better oral health.

The background to oral health policy has been reviewed in detail and strategies of integration and collaboration between services proposed in a volume on equity and access to oral health care for mothers and children.[22] Present signs of opportunity and change include the high levels of public interest in a national health care system, whether insurance or service based. Also potentially beneficial to low-income, Medicaid-eligible persons are the Maternal and Child Health provisions of the Omnibus Budget Reconciliation Act of 1989. In addition to increasing age and family income eligibility levels, it provides health services more fully for pregnant women, children, and the disabled, requires integration of social and health services, and addresses issues of quality, effectiveness, and appropriateness of care. Oral health services are included in this legislation which, if effectively used at the state and health-service provider levels, will have a growing impact for lower income Hispanics and other minorities.

Preschool Hispanic children and parents need to have oral prevention integrated into existing education and health care networks. High-risk Hispanic children not in contact with health care services[23] can be successfully identified and reached through school-based preventive programs involving sealants and topical fluorides for caries prevention, oral hygiene instruction for gingivitis prevention, and education about risks to oral health. Risk assessment is essential for program efficiency. Unfortunately, in the past decade, many community and school-based programs have been discontinued by federal, state, and local health agencies. Because of the overall caries decline, oral health was no longer perceived to be a priority. The continuing problems of minorities and the high preventive potential for oral diseases were ignored.[24]

Lack of oral health in Mexican Americans is associated with disadvantages of education and income as well as unavailability, inaccessibility, and inappropriateness of education, prevention, and treatment services. Because of these disadvantages, dental caries prevalence appears to be higher in Mexican Americans and Puerto Ricans. Overall treatment rate of decay is lower. Gingivitis is more prevalent in Hispanic children and adults, and periodontal disease more advanced in adults. Given the predisposition to adult onset diabetes in Hispanics and the association of severe periodontal disease with diabetes, the link between these two conditions merits the close preventive attention of dentists and patients.

Many Hispanics are at greater risk of oral disease and its consequences for speech, nutrition, appearance, and quality of life because of disadvantages in education and employment, as well as lack of access to culturally sensitive oral health services. These problems of equity and access are solvable, but the collective will and effort required to do so have been lacking in the past decade as evidenced by the discontinuance of successful programs. Because baby bottle tooth decay has been found to be a particular problem, oral health education of mothers and children should be conducted through existing well-baby and nutrition programs. Health education and promotion efforts in preschools and elementary and junior schools, involving fluorides, toothbrushing, and sealants for high-risk groups, plus effective referral for treatment must be instituted on a wide scale. Parental and teacher involvement is essential. Finally, innovative oral health programs for Hispanic senior citizens must be developed.

Notes

1. National Center for Health Statistics. 1985. Plan and Operation of the Hispanic Health and Nutrition Examination Survey 1982–84. *Vital and Health Statistics*. Series 1, No. 19. Hyattsville, MD; and National Center for Health Statistics. 1979. *Basic Data on Dental Examination Findings of Persons 1–74 Years. United States 1971–74*. Series 11, No. 214. Washington, DC.

2. Ismail AI, Szpunar SM. 1990. Oral Health Status of Mexican–Americans with Low and High Acculturation Status: Findings from Southwestern H–HANES, 1982–84. *Journal of Public Health Dentistry* 50:24–31; and Ismail AI, Szpunar SM. In press. Oral Health Status of Puerto Ricans, Cubans and Mexican Americans. H–HANES 1982–84. *American Journal of Public Health* 49:111.

3. Ismail AI, et al. 1988. Dental Caries and Periodontal Disease Among Mexican–American Children from Five Southwestern States, 1982–1983. *Morbidity and Mortality Weekly Reports* 37:33–45; and Ismail AI, et al. 1987. Prevalence of Dental Caries and Periodontal Disease in Mexican American Children Aged 5 to 17 Years: Results from Southwestern H–HANES, 1982–83. *American Journal of Public Health* 77:967–70.

4. National Institute of Dental Research. 1982. National Caries Program. The Prevalence of Dental Caries in the United States. *The National Dental Caries Prevalence Survey, 1979–80*. Bethesda, MD: National Institute of Health, pp. 93–107.

5. Ismail AI, et al. 1987, 1988.

6. Centers for Diseases Control. 1972. *Ten State Nutrition Survey, 1968–1970. III: Clinical, Anthropometry and Dental*. Atlanta, GA.

7. Killian K, Crow D, Kapadia A, Brown JP. 1988. The Prevalence of Dental Caries in Texas Adolescents Grade 6 & 12 (1984–87). *Texas Preventable Disease News* 49(5); and Killian K, Crow D, Kapadia AS, Brown JP. 1989. *The Prevalence of Dental Caries in Texas Adolescents. 1984–87*. Texas Department of Health, Bureau of Dental and Chronic Disease Prevention.

8. Tucker-Englert M, Brown JP, Dodds AP. 1990. Socio-economic Indicators of Caries Treatment Rate in Texas Adolescents. *Journal of Dental Research* 69:259.

9. Baez MX, Brown JP. 1988. Elementary School Oral Prevention Program for Dental Students. *American Association of Public Health Dentistry*. Abstract 41. Washington, DC; Brown JP, Baez MX. 1989. The Surface Distribution of Caries in Deciduous Teeth of a High Risk Group of Children. *Journal of Dental Research* 68:941; Brown JP. 1988. Dental Health Status and Treatment Needs Among Mexican Americans. Hispanic Health Status Symposium, Proceedings. Center for Health Policy Development, San Antonio, TX, pp. 74–84; Folke L, Brown JP, Catalanotto F, Sawyer J. 1988. Oral Health of Children in San Elizario Texas, on the U.S. Mexico Border. *American Association of Public Health Dentistry*. Abstract 41. Washington, DC; and Folke L. 1989. *San Elizario Health Survey 1988. Oral Health in Adults Born 1954–73*. University of Texas Health Science Center at San Antonio and Thomason General Hospital, El Paso. May.

10. Hazuda HP, Stern MP, Haffner S. 1988. Acculturation and Assimilation Among Mexican–Americans: Scales and Population Based Data. *Social Science Quarterly* 69(3):687–706.

11. The H–HANES provided an opportunity for assessment of a modification of the acculturation scale of Cuellar, Harris, and Jasso in relation to caries and periodontal disease in teenage and adult Mexican Americans. Cuellar I, Harris LC,

Jasso R. 1980. An Acculturation Scale for Mexican–American Normal and Clinical Populations. *Hispanic Journal of Behavioral Science* 2(3):199–217.

Decayed and missing teeth were positively associated with low acculturation, but the difference was explicable in terms of the confounding effects of age, sex, education, and income. See Ismail AI, Szpunar SM. 1990. Caries prevalence of low-income Mexican–American children in San Antonio also has not been associated with language-related items from Hazuda's scale. See Brown JP, Baez MX. 1989.

Preliminary results of the H–HANES indicated that Puerto Ricans ages 5 to 44 have a higher number of decayed teeth than Cuban Americans but not more than Mexican Americans, and the difference can be accounted for by age, sex, income, and education status. Older Mexican Americans, 45–76 years, had a higher mean number of decayed teeth than the other two Hispanic subgroups of that age. When compared with the NIDR 1985–1986 survey, Puerto Rican and Mexican–American adults had more decayed teeth than Anglos, but not blacks. See Ismail AI, Szpunar SM. 1989.

12. Ismail AI, et al. 1987, 1988.

13. Ismail AI, Burt BA, Brunelle JA. 1987. Prevalence of Total Tooth Loss, Dental Caries, and Periodontal Disease in Mexican–American Adults: Results from the Southwestern H–HANES. *Journal of Dental Research* 66(6):1183–88.

14. Ismail AI, Szpunar SM. 1990.

15. Ismail AI, Szpunar SM. 1989.

16. Ismail AI, Eklund SA, Burt BA, Calderon JJ. 1986. Prevalence of Deep Periodontal Pockets in New Mexico Adults Aged 27–74 Years. *Journal of Public Health Dentistry* 46:199–206; and Ismail AI, Elkund SA, Striffler DF, Szpunar SM. 1987. The Prevalence of Advanced Loss of Periodontal Attachment in Two New Mexico Populations. *Journal of Periodontal Research* 22:119–24.

17. Gardner LI, Stern MP, et al. 1984. Prevalence of Diabetes in Mexican Americans. *Diabetes* 33:86–92.

18. Ismail AI, Szpunar SM. 1990.

19. Multivariate analysis controlling for variation in important socioeconomic characteristics indicates that single social variables may not be true health indicators. See Stein RE, Jessop DJ. 1989. Measuring Health Variables Among Hispanics and Non-Hispanic Children with Chronic Conditions. *Public Health Reports* 104:377–84. However, univariate analysis in local surveys can be a useful indicator of particular groups at high risk of disease and, therefore, in particular need of education, prevention, and treatment.

20. Steffensen JEM, Brown JP (eds.). 1990a. *Equity and Access for Mothers and Children. Strategies from the Public Health Service Workshop on Oral Health of Mothers and Children.* September 9–12, 1989. Washington, DC: Maternal and Child Health Bureau, US Department of Health and Human Services; and Steffensen JEM, Brown JP (eds.). 1990b. Public Health Service Workshop on Oral Health of Mothers and Children. September 9–12, 1989. Background Issue Papers. *Journal of Public Health Dentistry* 50:355–472. Single copies of these publications are available without charge from the National Maternal and Child Health Clearinghouse, 38th and R Streets NW, Washington, DC 20057.

21. Nikias M. 1985. Oral Disease and Quality of Life. *American Journal of Public Health* 75(1):11–12.

22. Steffensen JEM, Brown JP. 1990a, 1990b.

23. Trevino FM, Moss AJ. 1984. Health Indicators for Hispanic, Black and White Americans. *Vital and Health Statistics.* Series 10, No. 148. Hyattsville, MD: National Center for Health Statistics.

24. The basis of caries prevention is community water fluoridation. It is striking that of the eight of the fifty largest U.S. cities that lack this public health measure, six have substantial Hispanic populations: Los Angeles, San Diego, San Jose, Tucson, San Antonio, and Newark. The others are Honolulu and Seattle. National Hispanic leadership, such as the League of United Latin American Citizens and La Raza Unida, might consider addressing this health policy issue. They would have the full support of the U.S. Public Health Service, health professional associations, and Hispanic and other health care providers.

Bibliography Relevant to the Oral Health of Hispanics

Oral Status

DiAngelis AJ, Katz RV, Jensen ME, Pintado M, Johnson B. 1981. Dental Needs in Children of Mexican–American Migrant Workers. *Journal of School Health* August:395–99.

Markides KS, Coreil J. 1986. The Health of Hispanics in the Southwestern United States: An Epidemiologic Paradox. *Public Health Reports* 101(3):253–65.

Thomas DB. 1973. Epidemiologic Studies of Cancer in Minority Groups in the Western United States. *National Cancer Institute Monograph* 53:103–13.

US Department of Health and Human Services. *Oral Health of U.S. Adults. The National Survey of Oral Health in U.S. Employed Adults and Seniors 1985–1986. National Findings August 1987, Regional Findings May 1988.* National Institute of Dental Research, National Institute of Health.

Weintraub JA, Burt BA. 1987. Periodontal Effects and Dental Caries Associated with Smokeless Tobacco Use. *Public Health Reports* 102(1):30–35.

Woolfolk M, Hamard M, Bagramian RA, Sgan-Cohen H. 1984. Oral Health of Children of Migrant Farm Workers in Northwest Michigan. *Journal of Public Health Dentistry* 44(3):101–05.

Nutrition

Haffner SM, Knapp JA, Hazuda HP, Stern MP, Young EA. 1985. Dietary Intakes of Macronutrients Among Mexican–Americans and Anglos Americans: The San Antonio Heart Study. *American Journal of Clinical Nutrition* 42:1266–75.

Kerr GR, Amante P, Decker M, Callen PW. 1983. Supermarket Sales of High-Sugar Products in Predominantly Black, Hispanic, and White Census Tracts of Houston, Texas. *American Journal of Clinical Nutrition* 37:622–31.

Knapp JA, Haffner SM, Young EA, Hazuda HP, Gardner L, Stern MP. 1985. Dietary Intakes of Essential Nutrients Among Mexican–Americans and Anglo–Americans: The San Antonio Heart Study. *American Journal of Clinical Nutrition* 42:307–16.

Lowenstein FW. 1981. Review of the Nutritional Status of Spanish Americans Based on Published and Unpublished Reports Between 1968–1978. *World Reviews of Nutrition and Diet* 37:1–37.

Health Services Research

Andersen RM, Giachello AL, Aday LA. 1986. Access of Hispanics to Health Care and Cuts in Services: A State-of-the-Art Overview. *Public Health Reports* 101(3):238–52.

Chesney AP, Chavira JA, Hall RP, Gary HE. 1982. Barriers to Medical Care of Mexican–Americans: The Role of Social Class, Acculturation and Social Isolation. *Medical Care* 20(9):883–91.

Garcia JA, Juarez RZ. 1978. Utilization of Dental Health Services by Chicanos and Anglos. *Journal of Health and Social Behavior* 19:428–36.

Melgare R. 1975. Overcoming Barriers Associated with Increasing the Number of Mexican–American Dentists. In Sumnicht RW, Anderson CF (eds.). *Proceedings of the Workshop on Minority Dental Students Recruitment, Retention, and Education.* Kansas City, MO. April 24–26, pp. 67–73.

US Department of Health and Human Services. 1985. *Location Pattern of Minority and Other Health Professionals.* Public Health Service, H.R. and S.A. Bureau of Health Professions.

Waldman HB. 1987. Increasing Use of Dental Services by Very Young Children. *Journal of Dentistry of Children* July–August:248–250.

Waldman HB. 1987. Increasing Numbers of Minority Group Dentists. *Annals of Dentistry* 46(2):3–4.

Health Behavior

Caetano R. 1983. Drinking Patterns and Alcohol Problems Among Hispanics in the U.S.: A Review. *Drug and Alcohol Dependence* 12(1):37–59.

Coreil J. 1984. Ethnicity and Cancer Prevention in a Tri-Ethnic Urban Community. *Journal of the National Medical Association* 76(10):1013–19.

Elder JP, Molgaard CA, Gresham L. 1988. Predicators of Chewing Tobacco and Cigarette Use in a Multiethnic Public School Population. *Adolescence* 23(91):691–702.

Gombeski WR, Ramirez AG, Kautz JA, Farge EJ, Moore TJ, Weaver FJ. 1982. Communicating Health Information to Urban Mexican Americans: Sources of Health Information. *Health Education Quarterly* 9(4):293–309.

Marks G, Solis J, Richardson JL, Collins LM, Birba L, Hisserich JC. 1987. Health Behavior of Elderly Hispanic Women: Does Cultural Assimilation Make a Difference?. *American Journal of Public Health* 77(10):1315–19.

Ricer RE, Custer RM. 1989. Prevalence of All Types of Tobacco Use in the State of Ohio. *Ohio Medicine* March:214–17.

Schur CL, Bernstein AB, Berk ML. 1987. The Importance of Distinguishing Hispanic Subpopulations in the Use of Medical Care. *Medical Care* 25:627–41.

US Department of Health and Human Services. 1990. *Healthy People 2000. National Health Promotion and Disease Prevention Objectives. Objectives Targeting Hispanics.* Washington, DC: Public Health Service, pp. 599-601.

Weisenberg M, Kreindler BA, Schachat R, Werboff J. 1975. Pain: Anxiety and Attitudes in Black White and Puerto Rican Patients. *Psychosomatic Medicine* 37(2):123–35.

Woolfolk MP, Sgan-Cohen HD, Bagramian RA, Gunn SM. 1985. Self-reported Health Behavior and Dental Knowledge of a Migrant Worker Population. *Community Dentistry and Oral Epidemiology* 13:140–42. 1985.

Part Three

Economic and Social Considerations

12

Formulating Health Policy in a Multicultural Society

David E. Hayes-Bautista

The realm of health policy is, ultimately, the realm of values, ethics, and moral choice.[1] Even when policy is presented in strictly economic, clinical, or administrative terms, decisions that have to be made are undergirded by notions of desirable and undesirable conditions, the good and the bad, the right and the wrong.[2]

Health policy is—perhaps of all policy areas—the most visibly linked to societal values, for the provision or denial of health services greatly determines who shall live and who shall die.[3] And, within health policy, the current AIDS epidemic forces the consideration of the greatest extent of value issues: the "morality" of contagion, social worth, sexuality, costs of care, and near-certain death.

In a relatively homogeneous society, where there is a generalized consensus on the underlying values, ethics, and moral choices,[4] health policy decisions may be made with a minimum of dissent. Thus, in the California of 1940, when 89.9 percent of the population was Anglo, one might be excused for presuming that the value systems of the overwhelming majority were the "natural basis."[5]

However, in the 1990s, states such as California will, as a result of rapid and unprecedented demographic changes, reverse the traditional demographic structure and have a minority Anglo population.[6] In light of this type of change—which also is occurring in Texas, New York, Arizona, New Mexico, Florida, and the Chicago area, one has to at least question the assumption that the Anglo–Protestant value system as described by analysts, such as Parsons, is applicable to non-Anglo populations such as Latinos, Asians, and blacks.[7]

Currently, health policy addressing the needs of non-Anglo population groups is handled under the rubric of "minority health" and is often viewed as only a variant (usually pathological) of a cultural or economic sort of Anglo health policy.

However, just as these groups can no longer be called "minority groups," their health policy needs cannot be formulated as mere variations on a traditional theme. (The use of the term "minority groups" already is a statistical misnomer in the California population age 17 and younger of which more than 54 percent is already Latino, Asian, and black; henceforth, the collective term used to refer to these groups will be "emergent majority".)

In this chapter, we focus on the body of knowledge and experiences of Latinos—which we label the Latino discourse—and its significance in tracing the contours of a probable health policy process within a multicultural society with an "emergent majority."

The Assimilationist Assumption and the Latino Discourse

In California and in other key regions, the population can be characterized as heterogeneous and diversified. By the year 2000, however, California's population easily will be about 35 to 40 percent Latino, 10 to 15 percent Asian, and 9 percent black. This diversification means that in ten years, Anglos will be a minority population—from 36 to 46 percent of the total.[8]

How can policy be formulated in such a multicultural society? Previous social policy was based upon the assumption that immigrants and other new entrants to society were to become assimilated into the larger society and its discourse, thereby providing an intellectual basis for policy agreement.

Given the number of the emergent majority population, one must question whether this assimilationist assumption provides an adequate base for policymaking in a diversified population. Not only will agreement be hard to find, but it is unclear that there is any shared process for managing the inevitable differences of opinion.

Let us begin an examination of this assimilationist assumption by examining first the case of Latino social dialogue and then its application to Latino AIDS issues.

All human beings are involved in some form of discourse and its reproductions. This includes Latinos, who are faced with the all-too-human problem of taking meaningful action in the world. In order to better understand the contours of the Latino discourse, it is necessary to change the analytic stance taken vis-à-vis Latinos in society.

Latinos should not be seen as faceless, anonymous, unthinking, uncreative entities who merely "cling to their cultural heritage" but rather should be seen as subjects attempting to take meaningful action in the world, who have the capacity to create new categories of concepts, new courses of action, and create new meanings.

The analytic focus needs to change, from that of elucidating static categories of traditions, values, and belief systems, to a more dynamic view of Latinos as cultural creators, and to an understanding of the process by which Latinos continue to create meaningful actions.

In short, we need to see Latinos as full human beings leading lives in a complex, rapidly changing world. In order to make sense of it and to take some meaningful action upon it, Latinos draw upon a body of knowledge to guide their many decisions on questions as simple as, "What shall I eat for lunch?" to as complex as, "What is my individual and professional responsibility to a Latino person with AIDS?"

This body of knowledge, this sedimented mental experience we may call in its most comprehensive sense the "Latino discourse." To better understand the full complexity of this Latino discourse, let us consider a major portion of it: The Mexican intellectual construct.

With a human presence in the Valley of Mexico (now the environs of Mexico City) for at least 10,000 years, one may appreciate that for millennia there has been a mental framework guiding a wide variety of human activity.

The particular situation may have changed from the food-gathering lore of nomadic tribes to issues of public health in urbanized Aztec society to the response to Catholic doctrine as preached in Colonial New Spain to contemporary decisions of whether to vacation in Puerto Vallarta or Disneyland. During all this time, Mexicans, performing as subjects, have learned the earlier discourse, reproduced it, and created new frontiers for it as they have constantly attempted to take meaningful action in the world.

An individual's store of knowledge does not necessarily tell him or her what to do in "situation X," but rather provides a quarry of material to be used to fashion a response. In any given situation X, there is no single "real Mexican" response. A Mexican faced with situation X must craft a response, using as basic material the responses of other Mexicans as presented by family lore, neighborly gossip, novels, plays, tomes of jurisprudence and philosophy, and the previous evening's television fare. These and other inputs guide the crafting of the response, but in all cases the final form is the production of the Mexican individual, attempting to make sense out of the world and take some meaningful action.

The mental experience in Mexico is not uniform; nor is it static. Since the Spanish discovery and conquest 500 years ago, it has accommodated new languages, religion, governing structures, and economic activities. There are contradictions, discontinuities, and cleavages within it, yet its reproduction continues, binding a Spanish-speaking businessman (driving his Mercedes Benz to the airport for a business trip to Paris) to the lone Indian Nahuatl-speaking vendor he passes on a street corner.

This creation and reproduction of a social dialogue was carried out in other regions—Argentina, Brazil, Chile, Puerto Rico, Cuba—in a variety of languages, responding to a variety of local situations. And this discourse has been reproduced in what is now the United States before the Mayflower set sail.

Since 1591, settlements building on this mental experience fanned out into northern Mexico, founding now-important cities: Los Angeles, San Francisco, Albuquerque, San Antonio, El Paso, and hundreds of others. Along with the names, there was developed a social-intellectual construct.

Although virtually ignored by U.S. domestic policy, the Latino population, reproducing and re-creating its own variants of the larger Mexican and Latin American discourse, has been building its local worlds for over 400 years.

Health Policy and the Latino Discourse

A major theme in the Mexican and Latin American discourse has been health and health policy. The very definitions of death, life, wellness, illness, causation, and intervention have been the topic of much thought and discussion. Again, a focus on Mexico helps us outline some of its contours: Bernardino de Sahagun collected an extensive corpus of the Aztec roots of this discourse in his monumental work, *Historia General de las Cosas de Nueva Espana*, which was completed in 1577.[9] Martin de la Cruz in 1552 captured other indigenous elements in his *Libellus de Medicinalibus indorum Herbis*, as did Hernando Ruiz de Alarcon's *Tratado de las Idolatrias in 1629* and Francisco Hernandez' in his monumental work of epidemiology and medical discourse compiled in 1615, *Cuatro Libros de la Naturaleza*.[10] Modern analysts, such as Lopez Austin, Schendel, Somolinos D'Ardois, and Aguirre Beltran have traced the outlines of the pre-Columbian mental experience of health and public health policy.[11]

Certainly, well-developed bodies of anatomical and botanical knowledge existed and were transmitted in a formalized fashion to a wide variety of specialized practitioners[12] whose behavior, together with hygiene and sanitation measures, was defined, if not regulated, also by public policy.[13]

The Indian health discourse was radically altered after the conquest. Not only was the Spanish health discourse grafted onto the Indian one, the post-conquest epidemics ravaged the population, requiring a concerted public policy response in an environment of extreme discourse clash. The population was nearly exterminated, falling from 25.2 million in 1518 to 1.1 million by 1590.[14] Health policy issues were among the first tackled by Spain's vice-regal government. A number of publicly funded hospitals were established—secular and ecclesiastic[15]—and sanitation measures adopted. Licensure and regulation of medical providers was an early effort. Epidemiological surveillance was provided by a newly established office, the Protomedicato, which functioned much as a modern health officer.[16]

Formal medical education was continued with the establishment of chairs in medicine, surgery, and anatomy in 1578 at the Real y Pontificia University in Mexico City. A lively publishing industry sprang up, producing classics such as Francisco Bravo's *Opera Medicinali* in 1570, Agustin

Farfan's *Tractado Breve de Anatomia y Cirugia* in 1579, and Lopez de Hinojosos' *Suma y Recopilacion de Cirugia* in 1595, among others.

All these policy efforts were embedded in a dynamic, rapidly developing discourse about values, ethics, and identity: The social worth of Indians, the responsibility of the crown to its subjects, the relation between "immoral behavior" and disease, the value of a mother over a fetus, and other topics.

An examination of the Latino AIDS experience will highlight the notion that to be effective, health policy must include the Latino discourse in is formulation.

AIDS is more than an epidemiological phenomenon or a clinical issue. It is a very human issue, which touches upon the deepest chords of individual and social identity. In dealing with Latino AIDS and to develop policy that will be consistent and resonate with the way in which Latinos define self and society, right and wrong, moral and immoral one has to understand Latino individual and social identity.

In Los Angeles County, a Latino who is diagnosed as having AIDS, statistically speaking, will be dead in eight months.[17] (This short life expectancy has more to do with lack of access to care than virulence and the human immunodeficiency virus [HIV] infection.) AIDS prevention, treatment, surveillance, and other efforts in the Latino community must take into account this swift mortality: Death is a constant. And one must take into account the social construction of death, and the mental experience of death in the Latino population.

The basic framework for death in this population stems from the Latino–Catholic discourse on death. This mental experience is quite different from the Anglo–Protestant discourse on the same topic. One has only to contrast the difference between Halloween in the Anglo–Protestant experience, and the Day of the Dead in the Latino–Catholic mental construct. Many Anglos experiencing the Day of the Dead in Mexico are put off by the different imagery, the ceremonies, the altars, and the depiction of the role of death, the dead, and the dying. The Mexican variety of the Latino–Catholic social dialogue on death builds upon pre-Columbian philosophies, in which death was an omnipresent, central feature of philosophy. The lamentations of the Aztec poet-philosophers expressed this mental experience of death:

> It is not true
> That we come to this earth to live
> We come only to sleep, only to dream
> . . . The time of life is borrowed
> In an instant it must be left behind[18]

The Spanish Catholic discourse, introduced into Mexico via the conquest, resonated quite well with this perspective on death. The syncretism that followed, by which many preexisting Indian belief elements were incorporated into the Catholic tradition, preserved these ideas and emotions about death.

Today, some Anglos seem to feel that Mexicans are morbidly preoccupied with the image and notion of death.[19] Yet, in exchange, some Mexican-origin Latinos feel that Anglos are disrespectful towards death and the dead.

In a thumbnail sketch, one can point out some of these differences: In the Anglo–Protestant Halloween, the dead—via ghosts, spirits, goblins, and other such creatures—return anonymously to bother the living. If they are propitiated, they will go away without further bother. (The "trick or treat" demand of young children reenacts this mental construct.) In the Mexican–Latino social memory, the Day of the Dead is a time to welcome dead relatives and friends back into the family. Altars are built and food offered, not to "buy off" evil spirits but to welcome and nourish members of one's family and social networks.

Given the high mortality rate for AIDS cases, the Latino–Catholic mental experience of death must form the basis for prevention and education efforts. The images used to evoke emotional responses must resonate with the mental and social construct and experience of death in the Latino–Catholic social experience. This is rarely done.

As broad-level social policy is being developed in areas such as Southern California, in which more than one of three persons is Latino, the underlying discourse on the place and role of the dead and dying in society, the relation between society and the dying, the responsibility of society to the dead, and the soon-to-be-dead needs to form the basis for definition of services, control of access, financing, and the use of family and societal volunteer efforts.

The importance of the Latino–Catholic discourse in AIDS is quickly seen in another facet of AIDS. The major mode of transmission in the Latino population of Southern California is via sexual behavior, unlike Puerto Ricans in the Northeast for whom needle sharing via drug use is the common form of transmission. For persons of Mexican origin in the Southwest, 81 percent of cases are contracted through sexual transmission.[20]

Sexual behavior in the Latino population is made meaningful via the Latino–Catholic discourse on sex. Apart from the simple stereotypes so beloved of some researchers,[21] this discourse again extends backwards for thousands of years. All forms of sexual behavior—heterosexuality, bisexuality, homosexuality, lesbianism, interclass, interethnic, intergenerational—are constructed from this socially constructed storehouse of knowledge.

In a quick sketch, we may appreciate a variety of discourse on the man-woman relationship and its relation to "right" sexual behavior:

The first is the classic admonition given by an Aztec mother to her daughter about her relation to men in general, her future husband in particular, and her family. This admonition was transcribed by Sahagun in 1535, shortly after the conquest.

Hija mia muy amada, muy querida palomita, . . . este es el camino que has de llevar, porque de esta manera nos criarson tus sernoras antepasadas, las senoras nobles, ancianas y canas y abuelas . . . si viviereis sobre la tierra, mira hija mia, que no des tu cuerpo a alguno . . . si perdieres tu virginidad y te casares con (un hombre) nunca se llevara bien contigo . . . ni te tendra verdadero amor; siempre se acordara de que no te hallo virgen . . . de aqui sucedera infamia y deshonra a nuestros antepasados y senores y senadores, de donde vivimos, de donde naciste, y ensuciaras su ilustre fama y su gloria con la suciedad y polvo de tu pecado.

(Oh beloved daughter, my dear little dove. . . . This is the road you are to take, because in this fashion did your lady ancestors raise us, the noble lady ancestors, ancient and white-haired grandmothers. If you should live in this world, be careful, my daughter, that you do not give your body to anyone. If you should lose your virginity, and later marry (a man) he will never be happy with you; he will always remember that he did not find you a virgin. And from this (sin) will come about shame and dishonor upon our ancestors and lords and rulers, from which we come, from which you are born, and you will dirty their illustrious fame and glory with the filth and dust of your sin.)[22]

In the admonition, the mother locates her daughter within the historic discourse, reminding her of the social memory.

Post-conquest, there were major changes in society. These changes built upon, and influenced the formal and informal levels of Mexican discourse about the relation between man and woman. Three hundred years later, in 1859, Melchor Ocampo reflected upon the male-female relation and wrote his *Epistola de Melchor Ocampo*, which is read as part of the civil wedding ceremony, and is certainly part of the Mexican discourse:

Que el hombre cuyas dotes sexuales son principalmente el valor y la fuerza, debe dar, y dar a la mujer, proteccion, alimento y direccion . . . con la magnanimidad y benevolencia generosa que el fuerte debe al debil. . . . Que la mujer, cuyas principales does son la abnegacion, la belleza, la compasion, la persipicacia y la ternura, debe dar y dara al marido obediencia, agrado, consuelo, asistencia y consejo, tratandolo siempre con veneracion.

(That the man, whose sexual gifts are principally courage and strength, should always give to the wife, protection, food and direction, with the magnanimity and generous benevolence that the strong owes to the weak . . . That the woman, whose principal gifts are self-denial, beauty, compassion, insight and tenderness, should always give to the husband obedience, pleasure, consolation and advice, always treating him with veneration.)[23]

And yet, the Mexican discourse was not a straight line from Aztec times to the present. A nature of a storehouse of knowledge is that a Mexican individual not only receives it, but adds to it, providing new frontiers for it. Certainly in the man-woman relationship there was the woman's portion of the social experience that might see things a little differently from the man. One of the earliest formal examples of this was the seventeenth century poet, Sor Juana Ines de la Cruz, often referred to as the Tenth Muse. Upon contemplating the meaning for life for literary women in colonial New Spain, she offered a rather sharp rejoinder to the idyllic portrait given in other parts of the Mexican discourse:

Hombres necios que acusais
A la mujer sin razon
Sin ver que sois la ocasion
De lo mismo que culpais

Si quereis que obren bien
Por que las incitais al mal?

(Oh stupid, stubborn men,
Who blame the woman without reason
Not able to see that you are the source
Of that which you now blame
If you wish them to be chaste
Why do you incite them to sin?)[24]

Latinos are as sexually complex as any other population—but that sexuality is made meaningful within the context of the Latino–Catholic discourse on sex.

One final issue illustrates the linkage between the Latino social-intellectual construct and policy. In the eyes of some providers, an HIV-infected person is somehow "immoral," and might not deserve care. This attitude is expressed by some physicians of all ethnicities. Convincing a Latino physician to treat an HIV-positive person is most easily done by referring such a provider to his own discourse about social worth. Most FMG (Foreign Medical Graduate) providers are well-versed in the history of the Conquest, and are aware of the intense debate that took place about the question of whether or not Indians had souls.

This was a serious debate for if Indians had souls, the crown had certain responsibilities and obligations towards them. On the other hand, if Indians did not have souls, there were no obligations. The central argument was that of social worth. It would be a rare Latino physician who would argue that his ancestors did not possess souls. This internalized social dialogue on social worth can then be used to examine current attitudes and behavior toward another group with problematic social worth: The HIV-infected.

Towards Health Policy in Multicultural Society

Civilization . . . is society's vision of the world . . . its way of living and dying . . . dancing and burial; courtesy and curses; work and leisure; punishments and rewards; attitudes towards women and children, old people and strangers, enemies and allies; eternity and the present;[25]

Social policy requires the consent, support, and participation of significant portions of society. By drawing upon a social dialogue common to all, social memories are tapped to provide a coherence of vision and dream that allows for joint social action that is seen as meaningful.

As Latino society rapidly becomes one of the numerically largest elements in California, its consent, cooperation, and participation become a necessary condition for policy to be at all possible. As briefly illustrated above, there does exist a very rich, complex Latino discourse which has grappled with the basic issues of defining a meaningful life that must be used in the very human, sensitive area of Latino AIDS policy. To ignore that social memory will mean to create policies that will fail, because of their inability to elicit an active participation.

And if the Latino discourse is needed for Latino AIDS policy, it is also needed for Latino organ transplant policy, Latino substance-abuse policy, Latino maternal and child health policy, and all other facets of Latino health policy. And further, if needed for Latino health policy, it is also required for Latino policy in the areas of education, criminal justice, employment, housing, transportation, and immigration.

In sum, the Latino discourse should be used to frame any policy issue that will touch the Latino population. And, as Latinos will soon become one of California's largest populations, any policy issue that affects the state will affect Latinos. Hence, any policy issue that is of statewide importance should include the Latino discourse in its formulation.

Health policy can be possible in a multicultural society only when it builds upon the major discourses present in the population. This is the challenge for health policy research and medical education in the decade of the 1990s—to bring the Latino discourse to bear on health policy, so as to elucidate systematically its debate on values, ethics, morality, and identity in the health arena. In addition, the Asian and African discourses need to form part of the socially constructed mental experience of health in a multicultural society.

Although no such formal effort exists, there are blueprints for them.[26] Some preliminary work has been done codifying the Latino discourse.[27] Much more of the codification needs to take place, and then that storehouse of knowledge needs to be formally applied to research, clinical practice, and policy. These efforts need to be formally established, and U.S. health policy will be much the richer for their existence.

Notes

Reprinted with permission from David E. Hayes-Bautista, "The Intellectual Basis for a Latino AIDS Policy: Toward Health Policy in a Multi-Cultural Society," *Journal of Medical Humanities*, vol. XII. Copyright © by Human Science Press.

1. Menzel PT. 1983. *Medical Costs, Moral Choices: A Philosophy of Health Care Economics in America*. New Haven: Yale University Press; Purtell RL (ed.). 1985. *Moral Dilemmas: Readings in Ethics and Social Philosophy*. Belmont, CA: Wadsworth Publishing Co.; and Jennings B, Callahan D, Caplan AL. 1988. Ethical Challenges

of Chronic Illness. *Hastings Center Report.* Special Supplement. (February–March):1–16.

2. Rivlin AM, Wiener JM. 1988. *Caring for the Elderly: Who Will Pay?* Washington, DC: The Brookings Institution; Gutman RA. 1988. High-Cost Life Prolongation: The National Kidney Dialysis and Kidney Transplantation Study. *Annals of Internal Medicine* 108(June):899; and Harris L and Associates. 1987. *Making Difficult Health Care Decisions.* Cambridge, MA: The Loran Commission.

3. Fuchs VR. 1975. *Who Shall Live? Health, Economics, and Social Choice.* New York, NY: Basic Books.

4. Blank RH. 1988. *Rationing Medicine.* New York, NY: Columbia University Press; and Callahan D. 1990. *What Kind of Life: The Limits of Medical Progess.* New York, NY: Simon and Schuster, p. 87.

5. Caplan AL, Englehardt HT, Jr, McCartney JJ (eds.). 1981. *Concepts of Health and Disease: Interdisciplinary Perspectives.* Reading, MA: Addison-Wesley.

6. Hayes-Bautista DE, Schink W, Chapa J. 1988. *The Burden of Support: Young Latinos in an Aging Society.* Stanford, CA: Stanford University Press.

7. Parsons T. 1951. Social Structure and Dynamic Process: The Case of Modern Medical Practice. Chapter X in *The Social System.* New York, NY: The Free Press.

8. Hayes-Bautista DE, Schink W, Chapa J. 1988.

9. de Sahagun B. 1975. *Historia General de las Cosas de Nueva Espana.* Mexico: Editorial Porrua.

10. de la Cruz M. 1952. *Libellus de Medicinalibus Indorum Herbis.* El manuscrito pictorico mexico-latino de Martin de la Cruz y Juan Badiano de 1552. Mexico: Vargas Rea y El Diario Espanol; Ruiz de Alarcon H. 1953. *Tratado de las Idolatrias, Supersticiones, Dioses, Ritos, Hechicerias y Otras Costumbres en.* Mexico: Ediciones Fuente Cultural; and Hernandez F. 1888. *Cuatro Libros de la Naturaleza y Virtudes Medicinales de las Plantas y Animales de la Nueva Espana.* Morelia: Rosario Bravo.

11. Lopez Austin A. 1984. *Cuerpo Humano e Ideologia: Las Concepciones de los Antiguos Nahuas.* Vol. II. Mexico: Universidad Nacional Autonoma de Mexico, Instituto de Investigaciones Antropologicas; Schendel G. 1968. *Medicine in Mexico: From Aztec Herbs to Betatrons.* Austin, TX: University of Texas Press; Somolinos d'Ardois G. 1978. *Capitulos de Historia Medica Mexicana.* Mexico: Sociedad Mexicana de Historia y Filosofia de la Medicina; and Aguirre Beltran G. 1963. *Medicina y Magia: El Proceso de Aculturacion en la Estructura Colonial.* Mexico: Instituto Nacional Indigenista.

12. Lopez Austin A. 1980. *Cuerpo Humano e Ideologia: Las Concepciones de los Antiguos Nahuas.* Vol. 1. Mexico: Universidad Nacional Autonoma de Mexico, Instituto de Investigaciones Antropologicas; and Viesca C. 1984. El Medico Mexicano. In Cortes DM (ed.). *Historia General de la Medicina en Mexico.* Mexico: Universidad Nacional Autonoma de Mexico.

13. Lanning JT. 1985. *The Royal Protomedicato: The Regulation of the Medical Professions in the Spanish Empire.* Durham, NC: Duke University Press; and Bustamante ME. 1984. Saneamiento en los Pueblos Prehispanicos. In Cortes FM (ed.). *Historia General de la Medicina en Mexico.* Mexico: Universidad Nacional Autonoma de Mexico.

14. Cook SF, Borah W. 1971. *Essays in Population History: Mexico and the Caribbean.* Vol. I. Berkeley, CA: University of California, p. viii.

15. Venegas Ramirez C. 1973. *Regimen Hospitalario para Indios en la Nueva Espana.* Mexico: Instituto Nacional de Antropologia e Historia, Departamento de Investigaciones Historicas.

16. Lanning JT. 1985.

17. Chicano Studies Research Center. 1990. *AIDS, Education and the Latino Community Project*. Statistical Report #1. Los Angeles, CA: University of California.

18. Leon-Portilla M. 1971. *Aztec Thought and Culture*. Norman, OK: University of Oklahoma.

19. Heller CS. 1966. *Mexican American Youth: Forgotten Youth at the Crossroads*. Studies in Sociology Series. New York, NY: Random House.

20. Chicano Studies Research Center. 1990.

21. Heller CS. 1966.

22. de Sahagun B. 1975.

23. Ocampo M. 1948. Epistola, 1859. *La Religion, la Iglesia y el Clero*. Mexico: Empresas Editoriales, S.A.

24. Martinez JL. 1980. *Nuevo Declamador Mexicano*. Mexico: Libro-Mex.

25. Paz O. 1985. *The Labyrinth of Solitude*. New York, NY: Grove Press, p. 359.

26. Hayes-Bautista D. 1989. Intellectual Frameworks for a Multicultural Society. Los Angeles, CA: UCLA Chicano Studies Research Center.

27. Soldatenko-Gutierrez M. 1988. *The Mexican Medical Tradition: The Clash of Nahuatl and Spanish Medical Styles, A Bibliography*. Los Angeles, CA: Chicano Studies Research Center, University of California.

13

Health Insurance Coverage and Utilization of Health Services by Mexican Americans, Puerto Ricans, and Cuban Americans

Fernando M. Trevino, M. Eugene Moyer,
R. Burciaga Valdez, and Christine A. Stroup-Benham

The first national estimates of health care utilization among Hispanics by national origin was produced in 1984 from data gleaned in the National Health Interview Survey of 1978–1980.[1] The findings revealed that overall, non-Hispanic white, black, and Hispanic populations experienced an almost equal number of physician visits per person per year, 4.8, 4.6, and 4.4 visits, respectively.

When examined by national origin, however, Hispanic groups differed significantly in their use of physicians. Mexican Americans averaged fewer visits to a physician—3.7—than other whites and blacks, while Puerto Ricans and Cuban Americans averaged more visits—6.0 and 6.2 visits, respectively. These findings remained even after the data were adjusted for age.

A closer examination of the age-adjusted data revealed that Mexican Americans had lower overall utilization of physician services because about one-third of them did not visit a physician at all during the course of a year. Only one-fourth of non-Hispanics, Cuban Americans, and "other Hispanics" and one-fifth of Puerto Ricans had no physician visits during the year.

These variations in health care utilization may be due in part to differences in health insurance coverage among different ethnic groups. Researchers in 1984 examined the impact of health insurance coverage on use of medical care and found that persons without insurance were 50 percent more likely than insured persons not to have visited a physician in the previous year. Blacks, Puerto Ricans, and Cuban Americans under 65 years of age were found to be twice as likely as non-Hispanic whites to be uninsured for medical expenses. Among Mexican Americans, the noncoverage rate was 3.5 times greater than that of white non-Hispanics.[2]

Using data from the 1982 national survey conducted by Louis Harris and Associates,[3] a study in the Southwest revealed that Hispanics were more likely to be uninsured—16 percent—than blacks—11 percent—or whites—7 percent. Researchers said Hispanics found it more difficult than other whites to get medical help in 1982 than in earlier years; were more often refused care for financial reasons in 1982; and had less insurance coverage in 1982 than in earlier years.

Further, more Hispanics than non-Hispanic whites said they put off care in 1982 because they had less insurance; needed care in 1982 but did not get it; had a serious illness in the family that caused a financial problem; had medical emergencies; and were not at all satisfied with the care they received.

On the positive side, Hispanics were found to be as likely as other ethnic/racial groups to receive preventive services and, in fact, for certain procedures, such as Pap smears, were more likely to receive the service than were Anglos and blacks.

The most recent National Access Survey found that while the proportion of non-Hispanic whites and blacks who reported themselves in fair or poor health decreased from 1982 to 1986, the proportion of Hispanics who reported fair or poor health increased.[4] The National Access Survey further revealed that the percentage of uninsured Hispanics rose 50 percent from 1982 to 1986 to 21.7 percent—more than double the rate of blacks and Anglos. The percentage of Hispanics without a regular source of care was almost double that for non-Hispanic whites.

Unfortunately, previous surveys which examined access to medical care and health insurance coverage among Hispanic populations have been hampered by several limitations. A few studies, such as the 1976 National Survey on Access to Medical Care,[5] incorporated relatively small regional samples that were generalizable only to Mexican Americans and not to other Hispanics. Some studies, such as the 1986 National Access Survey, report findings for Hispanics as a whole but do not provide data specific to the Hispanic national origin groups. The 1984 data indicate that the health services utilization and health insurance coverage of Hispanics differs greatly among the different Hispanic national origin populations.[6] In addition, few of the previous surveys translated their questionnaires into Spanish and most of these surveys did not employ bilingual (English/ Spanish) interviewers. The validity and reliability of the findings from these surveys may be limited for Hispanics because their comprehension may have been overestimated. Differing survey methodologies—telephone vs. face-to-face interviews—limit the comparability of these studies and the ability to make generalizations about Hispanics. Lastly, the most recent national origin-specific estimates of health insurance coverage and use of medical care are ten years old.[7]

We designed an investigation to examine more recent indicators of health insurance coverage from the March 1989 *Current Population Survey*

(CPS) and to examine findings related to access to care and health insurance coverage from the Hispanic Health and Nutrition Examination Survey (H–HANES)—to date, the most culturally and linguistically sensitive. This investigation examined data from two cross-sectional population surveys so as to derive estimates of insurance coverage and use of services. It should be noted that the 1989 CPS and the H–HANES were conducted in different time periods and incorporated divergent sampling frames and methodology. As such, the 1989 CPS and the H–HANES are not directly comparable; therefore, results are presented separately for each survey. The rationale for examining data from two separate surveys is as follows: (1) The H–HANES is the most culturally and linguistically sensitive large-scale survey conducted to date of the U.S. Hispanic population. The H–HANES, however, did not sample non-Hispanics and, therefore, does not allow comparisons between Hispanics and non-Hispanics. Furthermore, the H–HANES data are almost six years old and the sampling frame used was regional in nature rather than national (although it had a net coverage rate of approximately 80 percent of the U.S. Hispanic population). (2) The 1989 CPS was a national survey which sampled white and black non-Hispanics as well as Hispanics, allowing for comparisons between Hispanics and non-Hispanics. In addition, the 1989 CPS affords the most recent data available on health insurance coverage. As detailed in the methods section, the 1989 CPS was not translated into Spanish and has other characteristics which may limit the validity and reliability of findings for Hispanics.

The purpose of the CPS is to collect statistics each month on the number of employed and unemployed U.S. residents. The current sample consists of about 60,000 households containing just under 145,000 individuals to represent the 243.7 million persons in the noninstitutionalized civilian population plus military personnel who live off-post or on-post with their families.

Each March, the Bureau of Labor Statistics (BLS) conducts a supplement to the CPS on family income and work experience during the previous year. Since March 1980, the supplement has included questions on the health insurance coverage of each adult family member. In March 1988, BLS made major changes in the CPS which included a reconstruction of the health insurance questions.[8]

The CPS did not use a translated Spanish-language questionnaire. If the CPS interviewer did not speak Spanish and no one in the household spoke English, the interviewer was instructed to contact a regional office. The office either attempted to send out a Spanish-speaking interviewer or would attempt to conduct a telephone interview using the best available translator. Even when a Spanish-speaking interviewer was available, the lack of a translated questionnaire meant that the translator had to translate freely the questionnaire as the interview was being conducted.

In the March 1989 survey, all adult respondents (15 years of age or older) were asked whether they and their children were covered by

TABLE 13.1   CPS Estimates of Health Insurance Coverage by Race and Ethnicity

Type of Insurance	Total U.S.	White Non-Hispanic	Black Non-Hispanic	Mexican American	Puerto Rican	Cuban American
For persons of all ages (percent coverage):						
Private	53.3	68.2	45.4	43.7	43.6	55.6
Medicare	10.8	12.5	7.0	2.9	3.9	10.0
Medicaid	8.3	5.0	23.3	13.7	32.5	11.9
Other Public	4.2	4.2	4.6	2.9	4.5	2.3
Uninsured	13.4	10.2	19.7	36.9	15.5	20.3
For persons under age 65 (percent coverage):						
Private	71.4	78.3	49.3	45.2	45.3	65.8
Medicare	1.0	0.9	1.5	0.5	1.8	1.3
Medicaid	8.4	4.9	23.3	13.5	32.2	6.6
Other Public	4.2	4.2	4.7	2.8	4.5	2.4
Uninsured	15.1	11.7	21.3	38.1	16.2	23.9

Source: U.S. Bureau of the Census, March 1989 Current Population Survey.

Medicare, by Medicaid, or, in a single question, by Champus, Veterans Administration medical programs, or Military Health Care. After responding to these questions about government-sponsored health insurance, all adults were asked a series of questions about their private health insurance coverage. (Because the number of persons who reported they were covered by Veterans Administration medical programs, Champus, or Military Health Care was relatively small, they were all collapsed into a category called "other public" health insurance for analytic purposes.) No questions were asked about the coverage of individual children under the age of 15 years.

Children were attributed coverage if their parents indicated that their private policy covered them or if their parents had Medicaid or were in the Armed Forces.

Data from the 1989 CPS reveal that approximately 13 percent of the entire U.S. population was uninsured for medical expenses during all of 1988. Only 10 percent of non-Hispanic whites, but 20 percent of non-Hispanic blacks, 37 percent of Mexican Americans, 16 percent of Puerto Ricans, 20 percent of Cuban Americans (32 percent for all Hispanics), and 18 percent of others (all other non-Hispanics—e.g., Asians, Native Americans, etc.) were found to be uninsured. See Table 13.1.

The country of origin of the Hispanic population made a major difference in their probability of being uninsured. Only 16 percent of Puerto Ricans and 20 percent of Cubans are uninsured for medical expenses compared with 37 percent of Mexican Americans.

TABLE 13.2   HHANES Estimates of Health Insurance Coverage
by Race and Ethnicity

Type of Insurance	Total U.S.	Ethnicity				
		White Non-Hispanic	Black Non-Hispanic	Mexican American	Puerto Rican	Cuban American
For persons ages 6 months to 74 years (percent coverage):						
Private	NA	NA	NA	53.7	39.8	58.8
Medicare	NA	NA	NA	3.0	2.8	5.1
Medicaid	NA	NA	NA	6.3	34.2	6.7
Other Public	NA	NA	NA	1.6	1.4	0.8
Uninsured	NA	NA	NA	35.4	21.9	28.6
For persons under age 65 (percent coverage):						
Private	NA	NA	NA	55.3	40.8	63.0
Medicare	NA	NA	NA	1.2	1.5	0.7
Medicaid	NA	NA	NA	5.7	34.1	5.4
Other Public	NA	NA	NA	1.6	1.4	0.7
Uninsured	NA	NA	NA	36.2	22.3	30.2

Source: National Center for Health Statistics, Hispanic Health and Nutrition Examination Survey, 1982-84.

Relative to other Hispanics, fewer Puerto Ricans were uninsured because almost one-third relied on the Medicaid program, compared with only 14 percent of Mexican Americans and 12 percent of Cuban Americans. Cuban Americans were less likely to be uninsured than were Mexican Americans—20 percent compared with 37 percent—because they were considerably more likely to have private health insurance (56 percent compared with 44 percent).

Since almost all persons aged 65 or older are insured under Medicare, analyses were included showing the insurance coverage of persons under the age of 65 years. In general, the ethnic/racial variations in insurance coverage found for the total population are very similar to those found for persons under the age of 65 years. See Table 13.1.

Data from the H–HANES revealed that 35 percent of the Mexican-American population was uninsured but yielded higher estimates of noncoverage among Puerto Ricans and Cuban Americans than the CPS. The H–HANES data reveal that approximately 29 percent of Cubans and 22 percent of Puerto Ricans are without public or private health insurance. See Table 13.2.

Puerto Ricans were the least likely of the three Hispanic populations to have private health insurance but were considerably more likely to have public health insurance coverage. Indeed, Puerto Ricans were found to be five-and-one-half times more likely to have Medicaid coverage than were

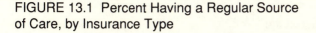

FIGURE 13.1 Percent Having a Regular Source
of Care, by Insurance Type

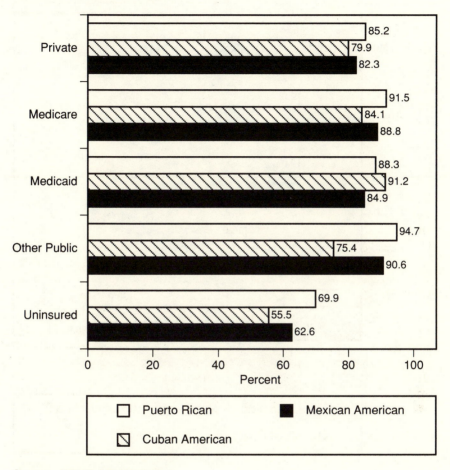

Source: NCHS–HHANES Data.

Mexican Americans—34.2 percent vs. 6.3 percent—and five times more likely than Cuban Americans—6.7 percent. Conversely, the Cuban population was found more likely to have Medicare coverage, reflecting an older age structure.

As seen in Figure 13.1, uninsured Hispanics were considerably less likely than Hispanics with health insurance to have a regular source of care. Not only were the uninsured less likely to have a regular source of care, they were also considerably less likely to have seen a physician within the past year. One-third of uninsured Puerto Ricans and almost 40

FIGURE 13.2 Percent Reporting No Physician Visit
in the Past Year, by Insurance Type

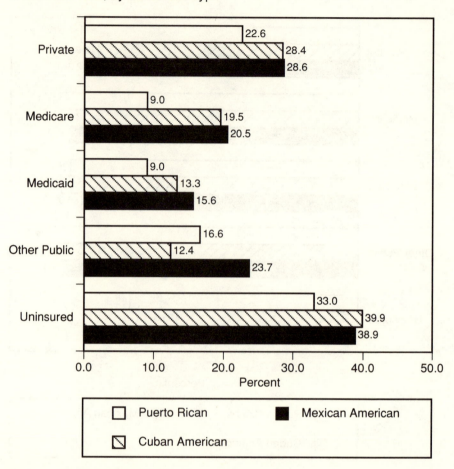

Source: NCHS-HHANES Data.

percent of Mexican and Cuban Americans reported that they had not
visited a physician within the previous year. Hispanics with Medicaid
coverage were the most likely to have seen a physician in the past year,
followed by those with Medicare and other public insurance coverage.
Hispanics with private insurance coverage were found to be less likely to
have seen a doctor in the past year than were those with public insurance
coverage but more likely to have seen a doctor than those without
insurance. See Figure 13.2.

Among the uninsured, Mexican Americans were three times more likely
than Cuban Americans and almost four times more likely than Puerto

FIGURE 13.3 Percent Reporting Never Had Routine
Physical Exam, by Insurance Type

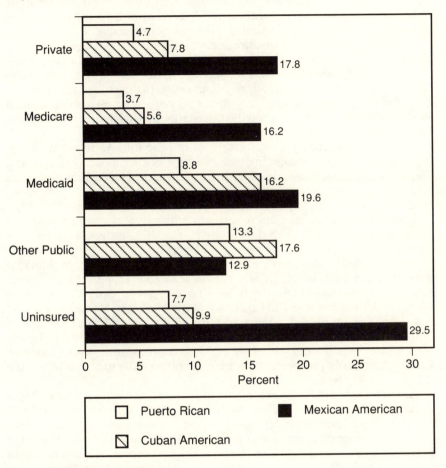

Source: NCHS–HHANES Data.

Ricans to have never had a routine physical examination—29.5 percent, 9.9 percent, and 7.7 percent respectively. See Figure 13.3.

With the exception of the relatively small number of persons who have public health insurance other than Medicare and Medicaid, Mexican Americans were found to be the least likely to have ever had a routine physical exam, followed by Cuban Americans and Puerto Ricans. Uninsured Mexican Americans were almost 70 percent more likely than those with private health insurance never to have had a routine physical exam. Age-specific analysis revealed Mexican Americans were consistently more likely to have never had a routine physical exam. For example, while almost one of every five (19.2 percent) Mexican Americans between the ages of 65 and 74 years had never had a routine physical examination, only 3.8 percent of Puerto Ricans and 5.9 percent of Cuban Americans of the same age had not had a similar physical examination.

Hispanics with private insurance coverage are much more likely than other Hispanics to report that their health status is excellent or very good. Hispanics with Medicare coverage were the least likely to rate their health status as excellent or very good, no doubt reflecting the older age structure of the Medicare population. Only about 30 percent of Hispanics without health insurance reported their health status as excellent or very good. See Figure 13.4.

Selected socioeconomic characteristics of Hispanics were examined by type of insurance coverage. Sixty-six percent of the Mexican Americans, 76 percent of the Cuban Americans, and 66 percent of the Puerto Ricans with private health insurance were found to be currently employed (includes children and spouses not employed outside of the household).

Seventy percent of Mexican Americans with private insurance coverage were interviewed in English during the H–HANES study, compared with 19 percent of Cubans and 54 percent of Puerto Ricans.

Among those with private insurance, only 13 percent of Mexican Americans, 6 percent of Cuban Americans, and 12 percent of Puerto Ricans had incomes below the federal poverty level. Only 11 percent of Mexican Americans and Puerto Ricans with Medicare coverage reported they were still employed, compared with 26 percent of Cuban–American enrollees. This is no doubt one of the major reasons that Mexican Americans and Puerto Ricans with Medicare coverage were twice as likely as Cuban Americans (53 percent vs. 25 percent) to have incomes below the federal poverty level.

Among Medicaid recipients, two-thirds were female and almost three-fourths had incomes below the federal poverty level. Sixteen percent of Mexican Americans with Medicaid coverage were employed, compared with 8.9 percent of Cubans and 8.3 percent of Puerto Ricans. Fifty-eight percent of uninsured Mexican Americans, 40 percent of the uninsured Cuban Americans, and 51 percent of the uninsured Puerto Ricans were found to be in poverty.

Among the uninsured, approximately one-half were male. Fifty-three percent of the uninsured Mexican-origin population was employed, compared with 60 percent of the Cuban Americans and 46 percent of the Puerto Ricans. Only one-fifth of the uninsured Cuban Americans were interviewed in English during the H–HANES, compared with 49 percent of the Mexican Americans and 43 percent of the Puerto Ricans.

Earlier research by Trevino and Moss revealed that in 1978–1980, 9.4 percent of non-Hispanic whites, 18.7 percent of non-Hispanic blacks, 29.2 percent of Mexican Americans, 18.8 percent of Puerto Ricans, and 15.4 percent of Cuban Americans were without health insurance in the United States.[9]

FIGURE 13.4 Percent Reporting Excellent
or Very Good Health, by Insurance Type

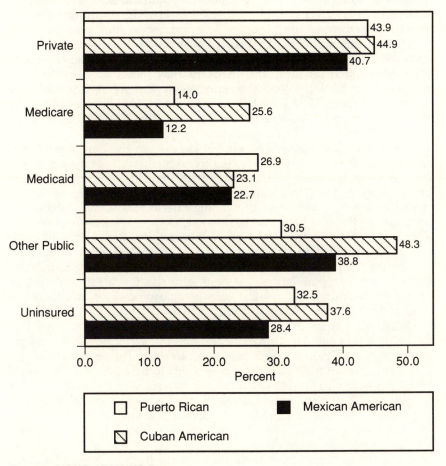

Source: NCHS-HHANES Data.

Data from the 1989 CPS estimated 10 percent of the white non-Hispanics, 20 percent of black non-Hispanics, 37 percent of Mexican Americans, 16 percent of Puerto Ricans, and 20 percent of Cuban Americans were uninsured in March 1988. H–HANES data further revealed that in 1982–1984, 35.4 percent of Mexican Americans, 21.9 percent of Puerto Ricans, and 28.6 percent of Cuban Americans were uninsured.

It is uncertain whether the increases in noncoverage among Hispanics are real and reflect changes over time, reflect divergent sampling and survey methodologies used, or whether the greater cultural and linguistic sensitivity of the H–HANES resulted in findings of higher noncoverage among these populations. This may well have been the case in particular for the Puerto Rican and Cuban–American populations.

Both the 1989 CPS and the 1982–1984 H–HANES found that approximately 35 percent of the Mexican–American population was uninsured for medical expenditures—an increase over the 29.2 percent found in the 1978–1980 National Health Interview Survey (NHIS). The higher noncoverage rates found for Mexican Americans may reflect changes that have occurred since the late 1970s. The estimates of noncoverage for the Puerto Rican and Cuban-origin populations from the H–HANES were considerably higher than the estimates provided by either the 1989 CPS or the 1978–1980 NHIS.

The H–HANES interviewed sample persons in the language of their choice while the other two surveys (CPS and NHIS) did not use a Spanish-language questionnaire and used bilingual interviewers only to a very limited degree. Thus, the higher rates of noncoverage (found by the H–HANES compared with the CPS) among Puerto Ricans and Cubans may have resulted from a better understanding of the questions because they were interviewed in the language of their choice. Regardless, it would appear that more than one-third of the Mexican–American population, one-fifth of the Puerto Rican population, and more than one-fourth of the Cuban–American population is at significant risk for catastrophic out-of-pocket expenditures for medical care or charity care or at risk of not receiving medical care when in need.

Uninsured Hispanics were considerably less likely than insured Hispanics to have a regular source of care. The impact of their not having a regular source of care on their access to care or to the continuity of care they receive when they do receive care needs to be examined. Uninsured Hispanics were also found to be less likely to have seen a physician within the past year. One-third of uninsured Puerto Ricans and almost 40 percent of Mexican and Cuban Americans reported that they had not visited a physician for over one year. Among those without health insurance, Mexican Americans were three times more likely than Cuban Americans and almost four times more likely than Puerto Ricans never to have had a routine physical examination. Furthermore, only about 30 percent of uninsured Hispanics rated their health status as excellent or very good.

The potential for a high prevalence of undiagnosed health needs among the uninsured Mexican Americans would appear to be great, given their limited contact with physicians and their extremely low rate of having received general preventive physical examinations. Additionally, the potential impact among Hispanics of preventive services provided by physicians, such as those recommended by the U.S. Preventive Services Task Force,[10] would appear limited, particularly among Mexican Americans.

Among the uninsured, 53 percent of Mexican Americans, 60 percent of Cuban Americans, and 46 percent of Puerto Ricans were found to be gainfully employed yet 53 percent of the Mexican Americans, 40 percent of the Cuban Americans, and 47 percent of the Puerto Ricans were living in poverty.

It appears that among employed Hispanics, low rates of insurance coverage may largely be the result of their low income and their employment in firms that do not provide private health insurance coverage as a fringe benefit.

Medicaid—the governmentally financed health insurance program designed to assist the medically indigent—does not appear to be providing proportionately comparable coverage to all Hispanic national origin groups. The Puerto Rican population was found to be five-and-one-half times more likely to receive Medicaid coverage than were Mexican Americans and five times more likely to receive it than were Cuban Americans. Since there are proportionately twice as many households headed by women with no husband present among Puerto Ricans as compared with Mexican Americans and Cuban Americans,[11] they may be more likely to qualify for Medicaid coverage under Aid for Families with Dependent Children (AFDC). In addition, Puerto Ricans may be more likely than other Hispanics to reside in states that provide greater optional coverage under Medicaid (e.g., New York) while Mexican and Cuban Americans may be more likely to reside in states with more restrictive Medicaid programs (e.g., Texas and Florida).

It may be time to undertake efforts to expand Medicaid coverage (particularly for states with more restrictive Medicaid programs) or to develop new private health insurance initiatives to cover the potential medical needs of the significant population of "working poor" Hispanics who are not eligible for government programs and cannot afford the rising cost of medical services.[12]

Notes

The material in this chapter has been updated and edited from an earlier version, "Health Insurance Coverage and Utilization of Health Services by Mexican Americans, Mainland Puerto Ricans, and Cuban Americans," *Journal of the American Medical Association* (January 9, 1991), vol. 265(2), pp. 233–237. Copyright © 1991 by the American Medical Association. Printed with permission from Fernando M. Trevino and the publisher.

1. Trevino FM, Moss AJ. 1984. Health Indicators for Hispanic, Black and White Americans. *Vital and Health Statistics.* Series 10, No. 148. Hyattsville, MD: National Center for Health Statistics.

2. Trevino FM, Moss AJ. 1983. Health Insurance Coverage and Physician Visits Among Hispanic and Non-Hispanic People. *Health—United States, 1983.* Washington, DC: U.S. Government Printing Office.

3. Andersen RM, Giachello AL, Aday LA. 1986. Access of Hispanics to Health Care and Cuts in Services: A State-of-the-Art Overview. *Public Health Reports* 101(3):238–52.

4. Robert Wood Johnson Foundation. 1987. *Access to Health Care in the United States: Results of a 1986 Survey.* Special Report Number Two. Princeton, NJ.

5. Andersen RM, et al. 1981. Access to Medical Care Among the Hispanic Population of the Southwestern United States. *Journal of Health and Social Behavior* 22:78–89.

6. Trevino FM, Moss AJ. 1984; and Trevino FM, Moss AJ. 1983.

7. Trevino FM, Moss AJ. 1984.

8. For a description of the changes in the questions and the methodology used to compute the number of uninsured from the *Current Populuation Survey*, see Moyer ME. 1989. A Revised Look at the Number of Uninsured Americans. *Health Affairs* 8(2):102–10. See also, Swartz K, Purcell PJ. 1989. *Health Affairs* 8(4):193–97 which disagrees with the methodology and suggests that the number of insured should be approximately 2 million smaller and the residual number of uninsured 2 million larger.

9. Trevino FM, Moss AJ. 1983.

10. US Preventive Services Task Force. 1989. *Guide to Clinical Preventive Services*. Baltimore, MD: Williams and Wilkins.

11. US Bureau of the Census. 1979. *Current Population Reports. Persons of Spanish Origin in the U.S.* Series P-20, No. 354. Washington, DC: US Government Printing Office, March.

12. Andersen RM, Giachello AL, Aday LA. 1986.

14

The Economic Costs of an Unhealthy Latino Population

Adela de la Torre and Refugio I. Rochin

The growth of Latino poverty has become increasingly evident during the post-Reagan years. Although this new social trend should not be surprising in light of the significant reductions in social programs during the Reagan administration, it does have implications for the scope of health problems faced by Latino workers and their families.

Because many Latino workers are disproportionately employed in low-wage, nonunionized, and limited fringe-benefit jobs, this population is primarily dependent on subsidized social and health services to meet both critical and routine health care needs.

Concurrent with the depletion of social services available to the poor, there has been a major change in immigration law resulting in more than 2 million—primarily Mexican-origin—applicants for legalization under the alien amnesty provision.[1] Most of these applicants are also working poor, who in addition to their income constraints, face limited access to need-based social and health service programs under the new agency restrictions imposed by the Immigration Reform and Control Act of 1989.

This chapter will identify the major health problems of Latinos, in light of both their economic and legal status. Specific questions of concern are: How is their health status linked to the Latino occupational distribution? What is the general level of third-party coverage for Latinos, and what are the implications of such coverage on the overall health of this population? And, given the data on health status and third-party coverage, what are the implications for the future productivity of this group?[2]

Latino men and women obtained some occupational upgrading during the 1980s. However, a relatively high proportion of Latino workers are employed in lower tiered, lower skilled, and lower paid occupations than the non-Latino work force.

A comparison of the occupational patterns for Latino and non-Latino men and women shows that in 1987, the majority of Latino men were employed disproportionately in occupations as operators, fabricators, la-

TABLE 14.1 Occupational Employment by Latino Origin and Sex,
Annual Averages, 1983-1987

	Latino		Non-Latino	
Occupation	Percent Distribution, 1987	Percent Change, 1983-1987	Percent Distribution, 1987	Percent Change, 1983-1987
Men, 16 yrs & older:	100.0	25.0	100.0	8.3
Managerial and professional specialty	12.0	30.0	25.9	10.3
Technical, sales, and administrative support	15.7	37.5	20.3	10.4
Service occupations	13.9	17.0	9.2	5.9
Precision production, craft, and repair	20.5	21.0	19.9	8.7
Operators, fabricators, and laborers	29.1	21.1	20.2	8.7
Farming, forestry, and fishing	8.9	33.2	4.4	-9.2
Women, 16 yrs & older:	100.0	33.7	100.0	13.2
Managerial and professional specialty	14.7	61.2	25.0	26.2
Technical, sales, and administrative support	39.9	27.4	45.5	11.7
Service occupations	23.3	40.1	17.8	7.7
Precision production, craft, and repair	3.7	22.3	2.2	14.6
Operators, fabricators, and laborers	16.9	27.5	8.4	2.9
Farming, forestry, and fishing	1.5	2.3	1.1	-7.1

Source: Cattan P. 1988. "The Growing Presence of Hispanics in the U.S. Workforce."
Monthly Labor Review, 111(8):13.

borers, and production, craft, and repair operators (Table 14.1). Relatively few were found in occupations with managerial or professional specialties. Women, in general, were employed disproportionately in positions providing technical, sales, and administrative support, but non-Latino women have much higher proportions in managerial and administrative occupations than Latino women.

The concentration of Latinos in primarily service, blue-collar, and agricultural jobs has considerable implications for the overall health status of this group and the overall direct and indirect labor market health costs. Direct and indirect costs are often estimated to assess the social costs of diseases. Direct costs estimate medical expenditures associated with treatment of disease. A major component of indirect costs are labor market

TABLE 14.2   Rank-Ordering of Highest Selected Occupational Injury and
Illness Incidence Rates by Industry, Total Cases and Lost Workday Cases, 1989

Industry	Total Cases	Lost Workday Cases
Durable goods:		
1. Lumber & Wood Products	18.9	9.6
Nondurable goods:		
2. Foods & Kindred Products	17.7	8.6
Durable goods:		
3. Primary Metal Industry	17.0	7.4
4. Fabricated Metal Products	17.0	7.2
Nondurable goods:		
5. Rubber & Misc. Plastics	15.9	7.6
6. Agriculture, Forestry, & Fishing	11.2	5.7

Source: Monthly Labor Review "Current Labor Statistics: Injury and Illness Data," June
1989:94, 95.

costs such as estimates of workdays lost and decreased income resulting
from disease. Although medical expenditures for specific illnesses and/or
diseases can be high, these expenditures do not capture the full impact
on worker productivity. Prolonged illness resulting from a chronic disease
such as asthma will have an impact not only on present but on future
employment choices available to an individual. When chronic disease
strikes, a person may stop working altogether or may continue working
but work fewer hours or switch to a less demanding job.[3] These labor
market costs are only indirectly related to disease but have significant
public policy implications. By estimating a disease's total impact on
individual worker productivity, critical information is provided for evaluating the cost effectiveness of programs aimed at prevention and containment of illness.

Using 1987 data, the occupations with the highest reported cases of
occupational illnesses were durable goods production (lumber and wood
products and primary and fabricated metals); nondurable goods production (food and kindred products and rubber and miscellaneous plastics
production); and construction and special trade contractors (Table 14.2).
Agriculture, forestry, and fishing had a lower number of occupational
injury cases but still were in the upper one-third of total cases reported.
More directly linked to measuring productivity losses due to occupational
injuries are the number of workdays lost as a result of these injuries. This
estimate reflects the lost workday cases that "involve days away from
work, or days of restricted work activity or both."[4] Here again, durable
goods construction industries, such as lumber and wood products, have
the highest rate of lost workday cases, followed by food and kindred

products, rubber and miscellaneous products production, and primary metal industries. The bulk of reported occupational injuries and illnesses and resulting lost or restricted workdays appears in primarily blue-collar durable, nondurable and, construction industries. With the exception of service occupations, which has approximately one-third of the reported total occupational injury and illness cases and lost workday cases, a relatively high proportion of Latinos fall within high-risk occupational injury and illness jobs.

Robinson, using California State Workers' Compensation data, highlighted that "Hispanic and black workers in California are exposed to higher risks of occupational injury and acute illness than are other white workers who are not Hispanic even after controlling for years of education and potential work experience."[5] One plausible reason Robinson gives for the higher relative risks of Latinos is differing job characteristics: Hispanics may be more likely to be employed in more hazardous occupations.

The direct and indirect costs of occupational injury/illness are often shifted to the employee and society if employers do not provide health insurance coverage. As long as employers can rely on an elastic labor supply in high health-risk occupations, and there is no public mandate to provide minimum health care coverage to employees, there will be little concern of employee turnover or exit resulting from an occupational injury/illness. In addition, productivity losses due to job-related health problems are difficult to measure under such labor market conditions as the relatively fluid points of anonymous entry and exit into these labor markets prevents accurate monitoring of the direct and indirect costs of occupationally related health care.

Indeed, in certain industries, such as agriculture, there may be no observable productivity impact from occupational injuries, particularly for those employed in agriculture where high elasticity of labor supply generally occurs. For example, a California study of agricultural migrants using time series data on occupational injuries of farm workers and productivity measures of selected crop outputs suggests that occupational injuries may have had minimal impact on production outcomes during the Bracero period, a seasonal guest worker program during the 1940s and 1950s.[6] Such outcomes call into question any causal inferences of productivity losses due to occupational injuries when conditions of high labor supply elasticity prevail.

The "right" to health care in the United States is clearly linked to employment status. Health insurance, a necessary condition for treatment by most private providers, has resulted in rationing both routine and critical care for the uninsured segments of the population.

As a large number of Latinos are members of the working poor and unemployed, access to health care for most Latinos is severely curtailed since employer-based health insurance is the major mechanism in the United States for financing private health care.

Employees in personal services, construction, entertainment, and agriculture have the highest rates of uninsured employees—31.5 percent, 30.6

percent, 30.2 percent, and 29.6 percent, respectively. Again, Latinos are disproportionately employed in three of these four occupational categories. Therefore, it is not surprising that a recent profile of the uninsured from the National Medical Expenditure Survey identified Hispanics at high risk of being uninsured—32.9 percent compared with 23.8 percent of black and 14.2 percent of non-Hispanic whites.[7] In states such as California, the uninsured tend to be young, Hispanic (40 percent), relatively low-wage earners in the service sector, and geographically concentrated in Southern California. A major problem in states such as California, where approximately 22 percent of the population is uninsured, is the lack of financial resources, particularly at the county and local health care agency levels, to adequately serve this growing, predominantly minority group of uninsured patients. Without adequate financing for emergency services for the uninsured, the emergency care system could collapse.[8]

Insurance status of Latinos is not the sole access constraint to health care services. An additional important factor is variation in citizenship status within the Latino community, which constrains institutional access to health care services. With the recent passage of the Immigration Reform and Control Act (IRCA), a resident's legal status has become a central factor in determining access to need-based programs such as Medicaid. By incorporating legal status as a criterion for access to public health and welfare services in the new law, this further segments the problems faced by the heterogeneous Latino population in the United States. Latino diversity not only makes it difficult to generalize about specific health problems facing Latinos, but also results in laws, such as the IRCA, having a disproportionate impact on newer Latino immigrants.

According to a 1989 report of the Bureau of the Census there were 20.1 million Hispanics in the civilian noninstitutional population—a 4.7 million increase from 1982.[9] The rates of change of this group and its component subgroups between 1982 and 1989 are shown in Table 14.3.

The Mexican-origin population during this period represented the largest proportion of the Latino population. In addition, this Latino subgroup became the most significant group during the first phase of the Alien Amnesty Program under IRCA. Seventy percent of the pre–1982 Alien Amnesty applicants were from Mexico, followed by applicants from El Salvador (8.3 percent) and Guatemala (2.9 percent). Within the Special Agricultural Workers Program (SAW), 83.4 percent were Mexican origin. Of deportable aliens located by the Immigration and Naturalization Service Border over 80 percent were Mexican-origin.[10] Facing limited access to need-based programs as they enter the legalization process under IRCA, the population groups most at-risk are those of Mexican, Salvadoran, and Guatemalan origins.

Although additional funds have been legislated to provide supplemental resources to local and state facilities for health, educational, and social welfare services to this new client population, these funds are to be parceled out over the five-year legalization period with an increasing

TABLE 14.3   Change in the Hispanic Origin Population, by Type of Origin:
March 1982 to 1989*
(Numbers in thousands)

Origin	March 1989	March 1982	Percent Change 1982 to 1989
Mexican origin	12,567	9,642	30.3
Puerto Rican origin	2,328	2,051	13.5
Cuban origin	1,068	950	12.4
Central and South American origin	2,545	1,523	67.1
Other Hispanic origin	1,567	1,198	30.8
Total Hispanic Population	20,075	15,364	30.7

*Data are from the civilian noninstitutional population of the United States.

Source: U.S. Bureau of the Census, *Commerce News*, CB89-158, October 12, 1989.

federal offset reducing the funding level towards the end of the five-year
funding cycle. Little thought was given in the IRCA legislation to the long-
run costs associated with the increased number of working poor admitted
under the amnesty program.

Prior to the passage of IRCA, need-based programs were primarily
linked to economic need. With the advent of the new goal to legalize
simultaneously formerly undocumented workers and control the tide of
new undocumented workers, the immigration law included in its targeted
reforms need-based programs that served these populations. One rationale
for including legal status in criteria for determining access to health care
services was to avoid legalizing individuals that may become "public
charges." If an individual becomes designated a "public charge" within
five years of entry, the law provides for deportation of the individual.
Access constraints to need-based programs provides one mechanism of
deterring potential public charges within the pool of eligible legalized
aliens.

Recent publication of the final eligibility rules for need-based programs
has resulted in providing some regulatory teeth to rationing health care
services and other need-based programs. For example, eligibility for
Medicaid will be limited for five years to those who have entered the
amnesty programs. Most newly legalized aliens will not be eligible for
such services until 1992 even during the period when they become
permanent residents. Exceptions to this new regulation are limited benefits
available to pregnant women and full Medicaid benefits for children under
the age of 18. Social Security Insurance (SSI) regulations for the aged,
blind, and disabled provide greater flexibility with respect to interpretation

of the new immigration law. Legalized aliens who apply for SSI are eligible if they are considered to be permanently residing in the United States under color of the law. This restriction requires verification that the INS will not enforce departure of the applicant for SSI benefits.[11]

The explicit and implicit pressure placed on eligible legalized aliens (ELAs) not to use federally subsidized health care programs places even greater strain on local health care delivery systems, such as county hospitals, which are the major providers of uninsured indigent care.

Finally, a potential problem that may occur as a result of a fear of the "public charge" designation is avoidance of preventative and routine health care by indigent Latino clients. Many of the relatively low-cost health care benefits from, say, routine health care screening and early prenatal care, may be lost if Latinos are not sure of their access rights to health care services. Ultimately, much of the final interpretation of these new regulations will depend on the eventual litigation that most certainly will ensue during the initial application of the immigration reform regulations.

There is little argument that Latinos face unique health care access problems because of their labor market positioning and, for some subgroups of this population, their legal status.

Intervention and treatment of specific injuries and illnesses will be severely constrained under such conditions. Moreover, the costs that result from employment-linked rationing of health care to this group is borne by the surrounding communities that serve the uninsured.

The cost of such care is not insignificant. For example, the California Medical Association estimated that each year in California, physicians each donate $25,000 to $50,000 of uncompensated care; private hospitals lose $2 billion for providing uncompensated care; and the public sector spends annually $1.3 billion on the county health care system. And, because of limited state dollars, greater pressure has been placed on the county level to absorb the increasing cost of indigent care.[12]

Several alternatives have been suggested at federal, state, and local levels to address the problem of indigent care (see Table 14.4). Given the high proportion of uninsured and working poor Latinos, a clear understanding of these suggested policies is critical.

The first plan—the Massachusetts model—has been heralded by many as an effective alternative to the problem of insuring the working poor: Building on the traditional employer-provided health insurance model, it "relies on tax incentives to encourage employers to offer insurance to full-time workers and sets up a fund financed by a payroll tax to help unemployed persons buy health insurance for themselves."[13] Reportedly, this approach not only builds on the traditional link of financing health care in the workplace, it also allows for pluralism in the selection of providers and private insurance, and the tax impact is somewhat hidden to the consumers. However, "mandated benefits are, in effect, a payroll tax," with the potential impact of increasing prices or affecting lowering

TABLE 14.4   Alternative Policies for Reducing the Number of Uninsured

Policies	Targeted Group	Advantages	Disadvantages
State Polices:			
Massachusetts model	Working poor not eligible for Medicare/caid	(1) Employer-based financing scheme (2) Pools risk for small employers	(1) Mandated benefits a form of payroll tax
Local Policies:			
School-district model	School age uninsured children and families	(1) "Employee type model" (2) Enhance private coverage	(1) Divert funds from county (2) Complicated market
Federal Policies:			
Medicaid expansion	Working poor pregnant women, infants, children, impoverished seniors	(1) No new bureaucracy	(1) Stress on state budgets (2) Shifts resources away from other social programs
Universal financing	Everyone	(1) Not piecemeal (2) Better coordination (3) Equitable	(1) Destroy private financing of care (2) Service rationing possible

Source: de la Torre A. 1990. Alternative Policies for Reducing the Number of Uninsured. Unpublished.

wages and other fringe benefits. An additional potential adverse impact would be its impact on employment of, in particular, small businesses that would be forced to dismiss or hire fewer employees.[14]

Unfortunately, for many Latinos who are service-sector employees in small- to medium-size businesses, the Massachusetts model may be a problem if the adverse employment impact is greater than the gains from mandated benefits. Shifting their status from working poor to nonworking poor, or reducing wages to offset the increased payroll tax, may not be the best solution. Finally, children, who in California compromise approximately 31 percent of the uninsured, may fall through the cracks with this type of coverage.

An innovative approach under consideration in Florida is the school district model for family health insurance based on school enrollment. The general idea is to mimic the private sector employer model of group coverage, but school districts would be used as a grouping mechanism for negotiating health insurance premiums, instead of private employers. Both family and individual student coverage would be made available and premiums would be based on a sliding scale similar to the fees set for school lunches. No new taxes would be necessary as the premium subsidies could be obtained from shifting funds from county indigent health care services to paying for the indigent care premiums.

The advantages of this plan are that (1) adverse selection is minimized given the age distribution of the insured population; (2) the Medicaid-eligible population would be excluded, thereby reducing the problem and cost of double coverage; and (3) greater portability of coverage for the family would be allowed if parents experience short-run work disruptions.[15] A demonstration project is currently under way in Florida, but is still in the developmental stage and potential problems may arise.

Shifting funds from financially strapped county facilities to subsidize premiums for working-poor families may not be viable in states such as California where undocumented Latinos still flow into the lowest occupations of the state. With the current refusal of the U.S. Senate to not include illegal aliens into the next census count and funding levels for state and local facilities often dependent on population counts, this may create unexpected overload of local facilities. A final point in assessing the economic viability of the school district model is whether this new insurance grouping will needlessly complicate the already cumbersome insurance market.

All of these issues should be of immediate concern to Latinos because the diversity of the subgroups within this population—both young and old, legal and undocumented—will be affected.

A third alternative that addresses the problem of the working poor and falls within the purview of a more traditional government intervention strategy is Medicaid expansion. Obviously, an immediate benefit of this approach is that it builds on an existing bureaucracy and is favored by the Bush administration. It targets a broad group of the needy, both working poor and indigent—pregnant women, infants and children, and impoverished seniors. However, some of this strategy's drawbacks have been voiced by the National Governors' Conference because its funding base is heavily linked to state budgets and would require funding shifts from other needy welfare and education programs.

For example, the current variation in Medicaid funding arrangements across states ranges from a federal share of 50 percent in 12 states to 79.8 percent in Mississippi to more than 70 percent in 13 other states.[16] The level of federal funding will critically influence these states' attitudes to any Medicaid expansion. Secondly, even with large federal funding in many states, Medicaid reimbursement rates are not perceived as competitive, particularly with respect to obstetric and gynecological services. Therefore, without increased reimbursement levels, many private doctors and hospitals will continue to avoid Medicaid patients.

Finally, given our current federal deficit problem, we must realize that expansion of Medicaid without expansion of revenue would increase expenses both at the state and federal level. This is not a pay-as-you-go program. The Congressional Budget Office says the federal share of the proposed expansion would be $60 million in fiscal 1990, rising to $140 million in fiscal 1991—a total of $1.2 billion over five years. The estimated five-year cost to states is $91.7 million.[17]

Although Medicaid expansion does not offer the direct impact on employment as does the Massachusetts model, there are other impacts on Latinos. Generally, as Medicaid recipients, working-poor Latinos will not have the degree of freedom in choosing physicians as those who are covered by private health insurance, unless reimbursement rates are competitive. Secondly, for the Latinos that fall within the immigration law category who are not pregnant or under 18, this type of coverage will not be available to them for five years, thereby effectively eliminating a substantial group in states such as California from health care coverage. Finally, Medicaid expansion is a zero-sum proposal to the states. They cannot increase benefits without reducing other social and welfare programs or without increasing substantially the state revenue base.

A final proposal to consider is universal financing of health care coverage. This model is patterned after the Canadian experience and provides universal reimbursement for health care services, subject to federal requirements.[18] The advantages of this approach are that it allows for complete portability of benefits across states. Funding need not be from general revenue but rather can be funded through a general payroll tax or can follow the general funding model of Social Security. This pay-as-you-go system also can save overhead expenses and may benefit from the economies of scales that have resulted in Social Security becoming more efficient than comparable private annuities. Finally, this approach would virtually eliminate rationing of health care on the basis of income and would end the two-tiered, private–public reimbursement scheme currently in place.

A major criticism against national financing of health care is that it would eliminate the private sector health insurance market which currently serves the majority of Americans. Government intervention in this model, it has also been argued, will reduce the autonomy of both patient and physician in determining proper care through increased regulation, and quality of care may be sacrificed. Finally, complete elimination of a two-tiered system of health care, where individuals with discretionary income will always be able to supplement health care with their own out-of-pocket expenditures, may not be viable in the long run.

Latinos, as a diverse group with varying health needs and employment status, should critically evaluate this final model. Although such an approach may destroy the pluralism enjoyed by many Americans in health care, it also provides a provocative alternative to piecemeal approaches that unintentionally disenfranchise Latino subgroups from health care services.

Notes

1. US Bureau of the Census. 1989. *Statistical Abstract of the United States 1989.* Washington, DC: US Government Printing Office.

2. Limited data on ethnicity and occupational injury/illnesses prevent direct causal inferences between Hispanic ethnicity and rates of occupational injury and illness.

3. Cooper ML, Krupnick AJ. 1989. Social Costs of Chronic Heart and Lung Disease. *Resources* 97(Fall).

4. *Monthly Labor Review.* 1989. Current Labor Statistics: Injury and Illness Data. June.

5. Robinson JC. 1989. Exposure to Occupational Hazards Among Hispanics, Blacks and Non-Hispanic Whites in California. *American Journal of Public Health* 79:5.

6. de la Torre A. 1982. Campesinos and the State: Control of the California Harvest Labor Market 1950–1970. Ph.D. dissertation. University of California: Berkeley.

7. Short PF, Monheit AC, Beuregard K. 1989. *A Profile of Uninsured Americans. Survey Research Findings 1.* DHHS Publication No. 89–3443. Washington, DC: Department of Health and Human Services.

8. Pischel ET. 1989. Who Will Pay for Their Care? Solving California's Unin-sured-Care Crisis. *California Physician.* March.

9. *Commerce News.* CB89-158. October 12, 1989. Washington, DC.

10. US Bureau of the Census. 1989.

11. de la Torre A. 1989. Immigration Reform: New Regulations for Need-Based Programs and the Impact on Agricultural Migrants. In ed. Thomas T. Williams, Walter A. Hill and Ralph D. Christy *Rural Development Issues of the Nineties: Perspectives from the Social Sciences.* Tuskegee University: Cooperative Extension Program. See also, de la Torre A, Rochin R. 1990. Hispanic Poor and the Effects of Immigration Reform. *Chicano Law Review* (UCLA School of Law) 10:1–13.

12. Pischel ET. 1989.

13. Hunter HR. 1989. State Health Insurance in Massachusetts–Implications for California. *California Physician* March.

14. Hunter HR. 1989.

15. Freedman SA, Klepper BR, Duncan RP, Bell SP. 1988. Coverage of the Uninsured and Underinsured: A Proposal for School Enrollment-Based Family Health Insurance. *New England Journal of Medicine* 318:13.

16. Health Care Information Center. 1989. *Medicine and Health.* Washington, DC. September 4.

17. Health Care Information Center. 1989.

18. Hatcher GH, Hatcher PR, Hatcher EC. 1985. Health Services in Canada. In Raffel MW (ed.). *Comparative Health Systems.* University Park: Pennsylvania State University Press.

15

Health Care on the U.S.-Mexico Border

David C. Warner

With rapid population growth, increasing manufacturing activity, and trade interdependence, health issues on the U.S.–Mexico border are demanding greater attention.[1]

Perhaps no other border in the world separates two nations with such variety in health status, entitlements, and health services utilization.

Binational initiatives in the areas of environmental health and sanitation are clearly needed. Further cooperation between the United States and Mexico in health services delivery is warranted and will probably require enhanced federal funding or subsidies to be successful.

The Hispanic population of the United States is increasingly from Mexico and Central America. In 1987, there were an estimated 11.8 million U.S. residents of Mexican origin.[1]

In 1519, when the Spanish arrived, it has been estimated that the population of Mexico was 25 million; by 1605, it had dropped to 1 million.[2] It is not until nearly 1940 that the population of Mexico returned to its level prior to the conquest. Current estimates of the population of Mexico approximate 88 million, and projections for 2010 range from 113 to 123 million, depending on the assumptions affecting demographic growth.[3]

The population of the six nations of Central America was 9.2 million in 1950 and is estimated to grow to 50.8 million by 2010.[4] Although fertility rates have fallen, these projections appear to be quite reasonable in the context of changing mortality rates and population age structure.

These larger populations will have diverse needs for health services. However, with increased integration of North American economies and interests, there will be greater motivation for both nations to improve health status in the region.

A correlate of the rapid population growth in Mexico and Central America and in the Mexican-origin population in the United States has been increased recognition for the importance of the border between the United States and Mexico. The rapidity of population growth and economic change, together with the border's traditional role as a staging area for new migrants to the United States, increase the importance of the border beyond mere population statistics. The growing numbers of U.S. citizens who retire on the border and of U.S.-owned companies locating on the Mexican side (*maquiladoras*) that employ over 250,000 Mexicans, contribute to the new socioeconomic dynamics of the region.[5]

An examination of border health issues illustrates how activities and services on one side of a border relate to and influence those living on the other side and, ultimately, the other nation as a whole. The U.S.–Mexico border is particularly appropriate for such an analysis.

Population, Economic, and Epidemiological Trends

Population growth on both sides of the U.S.–Mexico border has been rapid. Before 1900, there were fewer than 100,000 persons living in all of the towns and cities on the U.S. side,[6] while the population on the Mexican side was still smaller. Some observers believe that the total 1990 population of the border was approximately 10 million. In fact, the east side of Los Angeles, the west side of San Antonio, and much of Monterrey, Mexico, may be considered "border towns" in terms of trade, interaction, and consanguinity. Indeed, the border should be viewed as a number of trans-border metropolitan areas: The Tucson–Nogales region with a population of about 1 million and San Diego–Tijuana with a population probably in excess of 3.5 million are quite different from other border metropolitan areas because they both have more population on the U.S. side with a substantial non-Hispanic component. In contrast, El Paso–Juarez with well over a million persons, Laredo–Nuevo Laredo as a functional single city of 400,000, and Mexicali–Imperial County at more than 600,000 are all metropolitan areas far larger than most observers realize and have the preponderance of their population in Mexico.

While the Mexican border cities may be considered prosperous relative to other metropolitan areas of Mexico, the U.S. counties on the Texas border are some of the poorest in the United States.

Many border residents live in *colonias*—unincorporated settlements—on both sides of the border.[7] These communities frequently lack septic tanks, sewers, or running water, and outdoor privies not uncommonly abut water wells—making most of the water unfit for consumption.

On the U.S. side, most of the *colonias* are on the Texas border, where zoning and land-use covenants outside incorporated areas are far less restrictive than in Arizona and California. It is estimated that more than 110,000 persons live in approximately 600 of these *colonias* in Texas. Roughly 80 percent of them are located in the Lower Rio Grande Valley and about 20 percent in Webb (Laredo) and El Paso counties.[8] On the Mexican side, such settlements are very common and have expanded to accommodate the rapidly growing population.

TABLE 15.1 Death Rates by Age for the United States, Mexico, Mexico Border States, Texas and Border Area 1985-86, Death Rates per 100,000 Persons

	Age Groups			
	1-14 Years	15-44 Years	45-64 Years	65+ Years and Over
United States:				
All Races	33.8	137.3	897.3	5,153.3
Texas:				
All Races	35.8	154.0	846.7	4,749.6
Border Area:				
All Races	30.6	119.0	705.4	4,094.7
White	42.3	147.9	873.3	4,282.0
Hispanic	27.9	109.5	606.6	3,901.9

	Age Groups					
	1-4 Years	5-14 Years	15-24 Years	25-44 Years	45-64 Years	65+ Years and Over
Mexico	108.1	43.8	102.7	238.7	902.6	5144.9
Baja California	120.1	38.1	167.4	350.2	1102.0	5575.1
Chihuahua	165.1	33.4	144.6	241.5	785.3	4377.8
Tampaulipas	88.0	62.0	84.2	331.4	976.1	5084.3

Source: General Accounting Office. 1988. Health Care Availability in the Texas-Mexico Border Area. Washington, D.C. and Pan American Health Organization Field Office.

Mortality and Fertility Rates on the Border

Mortality rates by age for the Texas border counties are lower than those of the balance of Texas and the United States as a whole (see Table 15.1). In fact, mortality rates for Hispanics are lower in the Texas border counties than for whites alone in the United States for each age group. The substantially better mortality rates for the elderly can be explained in part by the relatively younger age distribution of permanent residents over age 65 in Texas border counties than in the United States as a whole.

These mortality rates do not reflect the health risks of a rapid increase in population accompanied by little change in public health infrastructure. Some of the more noteworthy issues regarding personal and environmental health on the border include high fertility rates; infant mortality; communicable diseases; water and air pollution; availability of water and indoor plumbing; and electricity. In each case, it is worthwhile to compare these health conditions on each side of the border to better identify potential improvements.

Fertility rates in the border area, while still well above U.S. rates,[9] have declined sharply during the last two decades.[10] Fertility rates in Mexico, which historically have been very high, also declined as a result of the General Population Law of 1974 aimed at managing Mexican population. Government and private programs[11] appear to have succeeded in improving access to contraceptives throughout Mexico and, generally, promoting family planning.[12]

Infant mortality and infants with low birthweights are often used as indicators of health status. Relatively few Mexican–American newborns, independently of location, are of low birthweight.[13] During the last decade, infant mortality rates on the U.S. side of the border have been at or below the rate for the non-Hispanic white population. This is not to say that all is well just because babies survive the first year. Poor nutrition and poverty can cause a number of health problems in children and later in adults not reflected in infant mortality statistics.[14] On the Mexican side of the border, infant mortality rates are significantly higher than in the United States. Nationally, they have declined from an estimated 84.7 deaths per 1,000 live births during the 1967–1971 period to 47 for the period between 1982 and 1987. A study conducted in Laredo and Nuevo Laredo between 1980 and 1982 illustrates some of the differences. There were 7,951 births by residence in Laredo, and 15,268 births in Nuevo Laredo by occurrence. Postneonatal deaths, occurring after thirty days of life, were seven times more common in Nuevo Laredo (see Table 15.2).

Bronchitis and pneumonia, noninfectious gastroenteritis, and intestinal infectious diseases accounted for 184 deaths in infants in the postneonatal period in Nuevo Laredo, while only two children in Laredo died of these causes. Differences between the two areas in sanitation, water quality, and availability of adequate pediatric care account for much of the variance.

Communicable diseases are a significant threat to the population on both sides of the border and shortcomings of immunization and treatment services need to be rectified. Drug-resistant tuberculosis remains a problem on the Mexican side, and it is vital that screening and treatment remain available to all persons on both sides of the border. Stray dogs are quite common on the Mexican side and canine rabies is more prevalent in that area. Sexually transmitted diseases on the border have long been a problem, not only due to the cross-border use of red-light districts, but also because contact tracing is much more difficult. Of the 1,502 cases of AIDS reported in Mexico through mid–1988, roughly 20 percent were thought to originate in the six Mexican border states.[15]

Another potential risk on the U.S.–Mexico border is dengue fever. Indigenous dengue transmission was documented in South Texas in 1980 and 1986. All other cases reported in the United States during the 1980s were imported cases. However, persistent outbreaks of dengue in Mexico make this area more at risk. The impact of a wide outbreak on the U.S.

TABLE 15.2   Causes of Post-neonatal Deaths Occurring in
Nuevo Laredo and Laredo, 1980-82

Case (ICD-9)[a]	Nuevo Laredo			Laredo		
	No.	%	Rank	No.	%	Rank
Bronchitis and pneumonia (485-486)	101	31.4	1	2	10.0	3.5
Respiratory distress syndrome (769)	6	1.9	9	1	5.0	7
Symptoms, signs, ill defined conditions (780-799)	48	14.9	2	3	15.0	1.5
Non-infectious gastroenteritis (558)	43	13.4	3	-	--	--
Intestinal infectious diseases (001-009)	40	12.4	4	-	--	--
Other causes originating in the perinatal period (760-764, 766-768, 770-779)[b]	5	1.6	10	3	15.0	1.5
Congenital Anomalies (740-759)	10	3.1	6	1	5.0	7
Immaturity (765)	2	0.6	16	-	--	--
Malnutrition of the third degree (262)	17	5.3	5	-	--	--
Other respiratory diseases (460-484, 487-519)[c]	8	2.5	7	2	10.0	3.5
Other endocrine, nutritional, metabolic diseases (240-261, 263-279)[d]	7	2.2	8	1	5.0	7
Burns (800-829)	3	0.9	12.5	-	--	--
Meningitis of unspecified cause (322)	3	0.9	12.5	1	5.0	7
Fractures (940-949)	3	0.9	12.5	-	--	--
Tuberculosis (010-018)	3	0.9	12.5	-	--	--
Other infectious and parasitic diseases (019-139)[e]	2	0.6	16	1	5.0	7
Bacterial Meningitis (320)	2	0.6	16	-	--	--
Other causes not listed above	19	5.9	-	5	25.0	--
TOTAL	322	100		20	100	

[a]Categories were selected prior to data collection. Categories were selected to focus on infant health issues.
[b]Excludes immaturity (765) and respiratory distress syndrome (769), which are presented separately.
[c]Excludes bronchitis and pneumonia (485-486), which is presented separately.
[d]Excludes malnutrition of third degree (262), which is presented separately.
[e]Excludes intestinal infectious diseases (001-009) and tuberculosis (010-018), which are presented separately.
Source: Alfonso Ortiz, Comparative Study of Infant Mortality in the Texas-Mexico Border Area of Laredo/Nuevo Laredo, Working Paper 29 (Austin: Lyndon B. Johnson School of Public Affairs, 1984).

side is now greater because the Aedes Aegypti mosquito is now found along the South Texas border, the far southeastern United States, and on the California–Mexico border.[16] In the absence of adequate protective measures and eradication programs, this condition produces significant health risks.

Environmental Issues

With regard to sanitation and water supply, the cities on the Mexican side have had to cope with particularly rapid growth. In Ciudad Juarez, for example, in 1981, roughly 67 percent of the 650,000 residents had private water taps inside their house; 23 percent had private outside taps; 5 percent depended on a communal tap; and 5 percent used water in street barrels delivered in city trucks.[17] On the U.S. side, some relief may come from $100 million in authority bonds to finance water supply, water quality, and flood control in the *colonias*, which was approved by Texas voters in November 1989.

Of broader concern is water and air pollution, which affects persons on both sides of the border. Daily, twelve million gallons of raw sewage flows into the Tijuana River, which flows into the United States from Mexico.[18] Well users in rural areas in San Diego County have noted increased contamination. Contaminants from the *maquiladora* plants in Mexico flow across the border in surface water or underground aquifers.[19] Also, Nuevo Laredo citizens are drawing their water downstream from raw sewage discharges.[20]

Air pollution in El Paso–Juarez has been a continuing problem with discharges from a smelter on the El Paso side previously generating high lead blood levels in both Juarez and El Paso.[21] More recently, El Paso has remained below EPA standards for ozone and carbon monoxide[22] due largely to the much older vehicular fleet in Juarez, the lack of emission controls, and the poor quality of gasoline used. El Paso and Juarez were also below EPA ambient air standards for total suspended particulates (TSPs). Unpaved streets and open burning of refuse appear to be the principal sources of suspended particulate matter in El Paso–Juarez.[23]

Illegal dumping of hazardous wastes from each country into the other country is also a concern. Any hazardous wastes generated from processing materials imported into Mexico must be returned to the country of origin. This policy was established by the passage of a comprehensive environmental and ecological protection law in Mexico in 1988 (Ley General del Equilibrio Ecologico y la Proteccion al Ambiente). This law, in conjunction with the third annex to the 1983 La Paz Agreement, obligates the two nations to work together to enforce their laws on transboundary hazardous waste shipments and appears to have created a very significant hazardous waste disposal problem for communities on the U.S. side of the border.[24]

In addition to these environmental issues, the adequacy of water remains a very serious problem for a region that is rapidly adding population while all of the available water has essentially been allocated.[25]

Several binational entities which address some of the environmental and public health issues on the U.S.–Mexico border are:

- The U.S.–Mexico Border Health Association is a membership organization whose secretariat is maintained by the El Paso office of the Pan American Health Organization. Participants include commissioners of health from the four U.S. and six Mexican border states and active binational health councils are in place for most of the major twin cities.
- The EPA and SEDUE (the Mexican Secretariat of Urban Development and Ecology) are obligated to cooperate as mandated by the August 1983 La Paz Agreement. The agreement will be carried out by subagreements to be negotiated by the two agencies, which have so far concluded four annexes.
- The International Boundary and Water Commission (IBWC), which has existed since 1889, has authority to mediate boundary and water conflicts along the U.S.–Mexico border. In the 1970s, IBWC Minute No. 261 was negotiated, which provided "bilateral procedures for dealing with border sanitation." In 1980, programs were concluded for Arizona and California border communities.[26] The Rio Grande Pollution Correction Act, signed in October 1988, gives the U.S. Secretary of State, through the IBWC, the authority to conclude agreements with the Mexican Ministry of Foreign Relations which will be advisory to their respective governments.[27]

A number of advocates believe that existing binational institutions are inadequate and that the United States and Mexico should establish a permanent U.S.–Mexico border environmental health commission. Advocates expect that such an organization could resolve environmental and water issues, provide rabies control and immunizations, and even help assure more comprehensive pediatric care.

Utilization of Health Care Systems on the Border

On both the U.S. and the Mexican sides of the border, there are several tiers of entitlement for care and there is a great deal of cross-border utilization of the health system for a variety of motives. These complex interactions will be best described by examining each system and its utilization.

On the U.S. side of the border, the medical care system has many of the characteristics of the national system with the exception that in most of the cities and several of the states, entitlements are quite seriously limited. The only large city on the U.S. side with a comprehensive public hospital—fully supported by public taxes and which serves as a hospital of last resort for the poor—is El Paso (R.C. Thomason Hospital).

One positive medical care development in Texas was the 1990 expansion of Medicaid coverage to pregnant women and children under age 6 up to 133 percent of poverty as required by the Omnibus Budget Reconciliation Act amendments of 1989. This provision should enhance the services available to many of the needy and reduce some of the fiscal strain faced by Texas hospitals and local governments.

While many of the poor in the Lower Rio Grande Valley have access to federally funded migrant health centers for ambulatory care, in-hospital care for the poor and near poor is limited. The executive director of a community health center recently stated: "There is no indigent facility (in Brownsville), which is another incomprehensible nightmare. We have only two for-profit hospitals in a town with such a high rate of poverty. But we haven't come up with a solution yet. It would take a whole lot of money and a commitment from the community, the counties and the state officials to get a city or county hospital. The county spent $2.3 million last year on the indigent, and that was just the tip of the iceberg."[28] In many cases, people without coverage seek alternatives. Of the 1980 births occurring in Texas border counties, 6,215 of the 28,645 births to persons giving a Texas residence were out of a hospital, while 2,660 of the 4,216 births of persons listing a Mexico residence were out of a hospital.[29]

A recent survey of poor residents of the Lower Rio Grande Valley showed that, annually, more than one-fourth of low-income respondents went to Mexico for pharmaceuticals, and that in the prior year 15 percent received medical services and 10 percent, dental services in Mexico.[30] The principal attraction appears to be lower cost rather than cultural appropriateness or exotic cures.[31] Also in some cases, physicians on the U.S. side will refer patients to Mexican labs, where an ultrasound may be $20 instead of $150 on the U.S. side.[32]

The Brownsville Community Health Center has developed a binational program called PROFAX to provide sterilizations in Mexico for American patients. The cost is from $3 to $5 in Mexico and is used by people who can not afford a hospital or clinic on the U.S. side and who do not qualify for Planned Parenthood programs.[33] A survey of 462 health-service providers in Hermosillo Sonora found that 40 percent of the dentists and 34.5 percent of the medical-care providers served some U.S. citizens annually.[34]

An irony related to the lack of a public hospital along much of the border is that State Legalization Impact Assistance Grants (SLIAGs) only reimburse public entities for health, education, and human services given to newly legalized immigrants under the Immigration Reform and Control Act of 1986 (IRCA). Consequently, most of the counties along the border may have limited claims on these funds, since the services are currently provided primarily by nonpublic entities.

Although, in theory, Mexico has a national health system, on the Mexican side of the border there are many gaps quite similar to those on the U.S. side. Within the broad middle class, government workers, employees of large firms, members of unions, and residents of certain communal agricultural communities generally have access to Social Security [Instituto Mexicano de Segura Social (IMSS)] or to the government employee insurance services—Instituto de Seguridad y Servicios Sociales para los Trabajadores del Estado (ISSSTE)—clinics and hospitals. It was estimated in 1980 that roughly 40 percent of the population in the twelve principal Mexican municipalities on the border were covered by ISSSTE or IMSS.[35]

The balance of the population is, in principle, covered by the Health and Welfare Ministry (SSA, or more specifically, Servicios Coordinado de Salud Publica en los Estados). In urban areas, SSA maintains health clinics often staffed by new medical school graduates providing a year of public service (pasante) as a prerequisite to entering a residency or becoming fully licensed. In some urban areas, the clinics may be quite distant from the newer poor barrios. In rural areas, smaller settlements are likely to be served by a promotora or a nurse. Hospital access for those who are poor and not covered by IMSS and ISSSTE is often limited to a civil hospital which may not be well staffed or funded.

Utilization by Mexicans of services in the United States takes place at least at three levels: there are the quite wealthy who pay in full on a fee-for-service basis for their physicians and hospital care; there is utilization by those who, although they live in Mexico, have some entitlement to care in the United States, whether by employment or other status; and finally, there are those who come to the United States in order to have a child who is a U.S. citizen, to find adequate care, or to respond to an emergency.

A recent study of 660 households in Tijuana found that during the prior six months, 40 percent used services in Mexico while 2.8 percent used services in the United States. About half of these users were lawful residents or citizens entitled to use public facilities or clinics.[36] Most of the visits to the U.S. health system—91 percent—were to private facilities.

Recent surveys of physicians on the Arizona and Texas borders have shown that Mexican nationals use many primary and specialist providers on the U.S. side of the border.[37] It does not appear that current residents of Mexico are a major burden to U.S. facilities although there are, of course, individual cases where, as a matter of decency, quite expensive courses of treatment have been provided.

Conclusions

Obviously, many of the problems on the border could be solved if both countries worked in a complementary fashion toward improving the environment, providing access to basic health care, and strengthening public health activities.

A barrier to cooperation is that while the problems are similar, if of a different magnitude, on both sides of the border, their solution through joint action implies administrative and technical changes in the delivery mechanisms of two different nations responding to different priorities and political stimuli.

A 1978 report by U.S. and Mexican public health officials spelled out potential joint programs in communicable disease control, health services delivery, sanitation, systems development, and planning and evaluation.[38] The Border Health Initiative that was to develop from this report was not forthcoming. This may have been partially due to the difficulty in coordination between the two nations. Also, a shift in the U.S. leadership in 1980 and the peso devaluation in Mexico beginning in 1982 may have blurred the focus.

A second binational initiative was that of the American Academy of Pediatrics, in which members of the Academy from Mexico and the United States worked with the Academy's Committee on Community Health Services to develop a study of maternal and child health on the U.S.–Mexico border. This study, which detailed conditions on both sides of the border, was published in 1987.[39] Although a number of dedicated pediatricians have instituted programs with Mexico and on the border, permanent nongovernmental, binational professional cooperation in developing a plan for providing adequate child care on both sides of the border has not emerged. The advantage of a nongovernmental, binational professional group in this kind of advocacy is that it can avoid many of the nationalistic and bureaucratic roadblocks to progress.

Other initiatives have been promoted by the Pan American Health Organization in El Paso, and especially by the binational councils, or local affiliates, of the U.S.–Mexico Border Health Association. These have proven to be very useful groups for the coordination of public health policy and for improved communication and standards between local health departments across the border.

A natural extension of some of these activities might be an exchange program of personnel between local health departments, perhaps with salaries supplemented by a foundation or other grant. In this way, U.S. workers could maintain their salaries and Mexican professionals could afford to live or work on the U.S. side. Improved immunization programs, collection of vital statistics, prenatal care, and well child care would be some reasonable short-term goals from such collaboration.

An emerging consideration is the potentially enhanced role of universities in providing health services on one or both sides of the border. Texas Tech, with its training program in El Paso at R.C. Thomason Hospital; the University of Arizona through its many border programs and student-exchange relationship with hospitals in Sonora; the University of California at San Diego Medical School and hospital; and the multitude of programs conducted by the University of Texas Medical Schools in the Lower Rio Grande Valley are all examples of institutional responses to some of the personal health-service needs on the border.[40] They represent foundation, state, and federal funds rather than simply local tax dollars.

There is little doubt that a great deal of charitable care can be funded under the mantle of medical education. There is even the possibility that high-quality services could be developed on the Mexican side of the border in conjunction with U.S. and Mexican medical schools. Collaborations between and among researchers has already begun and has increased the probability that productive binational clinical collaboration could now take place.

Policy formation and implementation on the U.S.–Mexico border with regard to health issues depends on national decisions and initiatives in each country as well as upon informal professional networks and initiatives at the local level.

Some of the national initiatives which may affect health status and health care delivery include the impetus towards free trade between the United States, Canada, and Mexico; a push to privatize much of the health care delivery in Mexico; the movement toward a more uniform national system in the United States; increased environmental standards; and the possible convergence in medical education and standards of care between the two nations.

One initiative that would also lead to further convergence of the two health care systems would be the increased portability of health care coverage across the border. On the Mexican side, with possible increased private insurance and the growing importance of the *maquiladora* industries on the border, it might lead to even more cross-border utilization. Similarly, if Medicare and Medicaid coverage were portable to Mexico, there would likely be a substantial increase in services on the Mexican side of the border as well as in areas where U.S. retirees choose to live.[41]

At the local level, the problems faced by border twin cities are international as well as regional. U.S. counties and cities often have more autonomy than their counterparts on the Mexico side, where in many cases permission for new programs must be received not only from the state government, but also from Mexico City. Consequently, common health issues are often left unresolved due to national differences in history, attitudes, and perspective.

An approach developed in San Diego and Tijuana incorporates a stepwise approach, which begins with framing the technical problem and depends upon consensus building between experts and professionals from both communities to articulate the proposed solution and to institutionalize the design of a cooperative arrangement between the necessary governments or institutions.[42]

Even with the development of these highly productive collaborative efforts, some extra-national entity probably will have to be developed to address environmental, sanitation, and water quality issues.

Because many of the solutions will be costly, the funding mechanisms will require sophistication and commitment on the part of the cooperating governments. Improvement of border health may be one of the preconditions for the further integration of the Mexican and United States economies. With the increasing importance of the border to both the United States and Mexico, it is likely that further initiatives will be undertaken.

Notes

The material in this chapter has been updated and edited from an earlier version, "Health Issues at the U.S.-Mexican Border," *Journal of the American Medical Association* (January 9, 1991), vol. 265(2), pp. 242–247. Copyright © 1991 by the American Medical Association. Printed with permission from David C. Warner and the publisher.

1. US Bureau of the Census. 1988. *Current Population Reports. US Population Characteristics. The Hispanic Population in the United States: March 1986 and 1987.* Series P-20, No. 416. Washington, DC: US Government Printing Office, pp. 7–8.

2. Semo E. 1987. *Historia del Capitalismo en Mexico.* Mexico DF: Consejo Nacional de Fomento, Educativo.

3. Alba F. 1989. The Mexican Demographic Situation. In Bean F, Schmandt J, Weintraub S (eds.). *Mexican and Central American Population and US Immigration Policy.* Austin, TX: Center for Mexican–American Studies, The University of Texas, pp. 5–32.

4. Diaz-Briquets S. 1989. The Central American Demographic Situation. In Bean F, Schmandt J, Weintraub S (eds.). *Mexican and Central American Population and US Immigration Policy.* Austin, TX: Center for Mexican–American Studies, The University of Texas, pp. 33–64.

5. Portes A. 1989. Unauthorized Immigration and Immigration Reform: Present Trends and Prospects. Working Paper No. 8. Washington, DC: Commission for the Study of International Migration and Cooperative Economic Development.

6. Hansen N. 1981. *The Border Economy: Regional Development in the Southwest.* Austin, TX: The University of Texas Press.

7. Holz R, Shane C, Davies CS. 1989. *Third World Texas: Colonias in the Lower Rio Grande Valley.* Austin, TX: Department of Geography, The University of Texas.

8. US General Accounting Office. 1988. *Health Care Availability in the Texas–Mexico Border Area.* Washington, DC.

9. Chan L, McCandless R, Portnoy B, Stolp C, Warner DC. 1987. *Maternal and Child Health on the US–Mexico Border.* Austin, TX: LBJ School of Public Affairs, The University of Texas.

10. Alba F. 1989, p. 15.

11. Alba F, Potter J. 1986. Population and Development in Mexico Since 1940: An Interpretation. *Population and Development Review* 12:47–75.

12. McDermott C. 1989. *Family Planning in Mexico: A Multi-Sectoral Approach.* Austin, TX: LBJ School of Public Affairs, The University of Texas.

13. Ventura S. 1989. Prenatal Care and Infant Health Characteristics for Mexican Americans. Paper presented at Conference on the Health and Nutritional Status of Mexican–American Children. Stanford University. April 14–15.

14. Malina RM, Zavaleta AN, Little BB. 1987. Body Size, Fatness and Leanness of Mexican–American Children in Brownsville, Texas: Changes Between 1972 and 1983. *American Journal of Public Health* 77(5):573–77.

15. Valdespino G, et al. 1989. AIDS in Mexico: Trends and Projections. *Pan American Health Organization Bulletin* 23(1-2):20–23; and Nichols A. 1989. AIDS Along the US–Mexico border (with emphasis on Mexico). *Border Health* (August):30–32.

16. Pinheiro F. 1989. Dengue in the Americas 1980–87. *Epidemiological Bulletin*. Pan American Health Organization. 10(1):1-8.

17. Lloyd W. 1984. Growth of the Municipal Water System in Ciudad Juarez, Mexico. In Sepulueda C, Utton U (eds.). *The US–Mexico Border Region: Anticipating Resource Needs and Issues to the Year 2000*. El Paso, TX: Texas Western Press.

18. American Medical Association. 1990. Report of the Council on Scientific Affairs. A Permanent United States–Mexico Environmental Health Commission. *Journal of the American Medical Association* 263:3319-21.

19. Collins H. 1989. Overview of Border Health in California. Texas Medical Association Border Health Conference. El Paso, TX. August 23–24.

20. American Medical Association. 1990.

21. Landrigan PJ, Gehlbach SH, Rosenblum BF. 1975. Epidemic Lead Absorption Near an Ore Smelter: The Role of Particulate Lead. *New England Journal of Medicine* 292:123–29.

22. Environmental Protection Agency. 1988. EPA Lists Areas Failing to Meet Ozone or Carbon Monoxide Standards. *EPA Environmental News* 3(May):1–8.

23. Appelgate HG, Bath CR, Brannon JT. 1989. Binational Emissions Trading in an International Air Shed: The Case of El Paso, Texas and Cuidad Juarez. *Journal of Borderland Studies* IV(2):1–25.

24. Bock K. 1989. Maquiladoras, Hazardous Substances and San Diego. Draft Report. San Diego County Department of Environmental Health. August.

25. Eaton D, Anderson J. 1987. *The State of the Rio Grande Rio Bravo*. Tucson, AZ: University of Arizona Press.

26. American Medical Association. 1990.

27. American Medical Association. 1990.

28. Lawrence A. 1989. Health Issues on the Texas–Mexico Border. Plan II, Senior Paper. Austin, TX: The University of Texas.

29. Powell-Griner E. 1983. Characteristics of Births in Two Areas of Texas: 1980. Working Paper No. 21. Austin, TX: LBJ School of Public Affairs, The University of Texas.

30. Indigent Health Care Review Committee of the Health Planning Advisory Committee of the Lower Rio Grande Development Council. 1989. Report. Houston, TX: The University of Texas Health Science Center, August.

31. Belkin L. 1988. Health Care on the Border: Poor Go to Mexico. *New York Times* October 17, pp. 1, 9.

32. Fowkes V, Fowkes W, Walters EG. 1989. *Assessment of Factors Which Impede Development of Area Health Education Centers in Medically Underserved Areas Along the US/Mexico Border in Texas*. United Management Systems of Arizona and Division of Family and Community Medicine. Stanford University. July.

33. Lawrence A. 1989.

34. Sosa FC, Soler MO. 1988. Utilization of Health Services in Hermosillo Sonora by United States Residents. *Border Health*. IV(2):27–35.

35. Chan L, McCandless R, Portnoy B, Stolp C, Warner DC. 1987.

36. Jasis M, Guendelman S. 1988. Measuring Tijuana Residents Choice of Mexican or US Health Care Services. *Public Health Reports* 106(6).

37. Nichols A, Estrada A, LaBrec P. 1990. *Border Health Utilization Study*. Tucson, AZ: Southwest Border Rural Health Research Center, University of Arizona; and Zinnecker AK. 1990. *The Use of US Health Services by Mexican Nationals Along the Texas–Mexico Border*. Austin, TX: LBJ School of Public Affairs, The University of Texas.

38. US Public Health Service. 1978. *Review of the Health Situation–United States–Mexico Border and Recommendations for Binational Cooperation.* Rockville, MD.

39. Chan L, McCandless R, Portnoy B, Stolp C, Warner DC. 1987.

40. The University of Texas System Valley Task Force. 1988. *Border Health Inventory.* Austin, TX; and The University of Texas System Valley/Border Health Symposium. 1990. Austin, TX. October 22–23.

41. Warner D. 1989. Mexican Provision of Health and Human Services to American Citizens: Barriers and Opportunities. *Public Affairs Comment* XXXVI(1). Austin, TX: LBJ School of Public Affairs, The University of Texas.

42. Guidotti TL, Conway JB. 1987. Cooperation in Health Affairs Between Adjacent International Communities: A Successful Model. *American Journal of Preventative Medicine* 3(5):287–92.

Part Four

Epilogue

16

Searching for Solutions

Antonio Furino and Ciro V. Sumaya

The Challenges

The preceding chapters reflect the multidisciplinary nature and the complexity of the challenges confronting policy designers as they address the health status of the Hispanic population.

There are many good reasons for seeking solutions to Hispanic health problems with determination and haste. Hispanics will soon represent the largest minority in American society. Twenty million persons with Latin American/Spanish origins contribute a large, youthful, and potentially very productive group of workers to our aging labor force. And, more importantly, the health of all Americans can be improved while containing costs only if we are successful in addressing, proactively, the special needs of our culturally diverse society.

Recent advances in science and technology, progress in understanding the linkages between health and socioeconomic status, and new knowledge about the cultural and environmental determinants of physical and mental disorders offer powerful tools to reach that goal. Unfortunately, as often is the case with rapid technological progress, the social maturity needed to resolve issues of equity and opportunity cost lags behind the rate at which new scientific achievements become available. And expensive, at times almost miraculous, clinical outcomes coexist with the national embarrassment of providing insufficient or no health insurance to almost forty million Americans.[1]

It was noted in the introductory chapter to this volume how unprecedented budget constraints will limit federal public health programs. This inevitable reality is aggravated by a national impatience with long-term commitments and delayed rewards. Improved health status and human resource development often require investments in physical and human capital whose returns do not become obvious for generations. But the national mood swings quickly from issue to issue, clamoring for rapid solutions to complex problems which can be only identified but not resolved by successful conferences or well-orchestrated political campaigns. These, at best, clarify the issues and prime the political machine. What needs to follow is steadfastness resulting from the conviction that incurring costs for improving the health status of our underserved citizens is the rational choice for improving the quality of life of all.

Solutions for the health problems of our underserved citizens require a critical mass of efforts capable of supporting an appropriate mix of complementary interventions. Allocating the necessary resources in spite of restrictive federal and state budgets necessitates public and private sector alliances and, most likely, major public policy reforms.[2] Unfortunately, reliable data on which to base alliances and propose reforms for improving the health status of Hispanics is not available.[3] With inadequate information, many myths and emotionally loaded preconceptions are able to survive and hinder adequate policy responses.

In the next sections, we will examine these intellectual barriers to better care for minorities, review present health policy options, and conclude with a possible agenda for action.

The Myths

A recent and lucid commentary about widespread myths and their impact on minority access to public services was articulated by the Action Council on Minority Education which, under the leadership of Ray Marshall (see Chapter 5), has drafted a plan for educating minorities.[4] Education and health status are closely and positively related[5] and most of the barriers that blur the vision of policy designers and stifle public support for the education of minorities have their counterpart in the health arena. Eight items of the list compiled by the council are relevant to this discussion.

The first myth has to do with the belief that minorities are less capable of being educated than the traditional population.[6] When the educational myth is transferred into the health arena, it becomes the perception that certain health problems among Hispanics are virtually unavoidable because of deep-seated barriers to learning appropriate health behavior. Or that the limited number of Hispanic health professionals is explained as the result of difficulties peculiar to Hispanic students in coping with demanding curricula.

The second myth identified by the council as having a negative impact on minority education is applicable to the health sector exactly as stated: "The problems minority youth face, including poverty, teenage pregnancy, unemployment, drug abuse, and high dropout rates, are so overwhelming that society is incapable of providing effective responses."[7] In the health sector, this fatalistic attitude undermines the resolve of providing quality interventions, promoting healthier behavior, or treating acute conditions peculiar to each minority group.

The third myth is that of considering education an expense rather than an investment, a faulty perception conducive to underestimating the indirect costs of the nation's dropouts in terms of increased crime and higher utilization of welfare, health care, and health services.[8] Similarly, the negative impact of inadequate access to health care on employment and productivity is seldom considered in decisions promoting economic development.

The fourth myth consists of the belief that equity and excellence in education are in conflict. So, it can be held that high-end medical treatment (the one utilizing high-cost medical technologies) is, "inevitably," not available to everyone. The council argues that quality intervention in education should be applied early to produce excellence at lower cost than possible with remedial work later in people's lives. In the health arena, early access to quality health care and health education not only saves money in reduced utilization of expensive acute care but, through its indirect impact on productivity and social harmony, contributes to the quality of life of all Americans—independently of their socioeconomic status or ethnic and social affiliation.

The fifth commonly held myth consists of the perception that all that is needed are marginal changes. The council states:

> For more than 100 years, this system has been unfair to minorities, and perpetuating that condition is both self-defeating and morally unacceptable. Our society cannot thrive in the 21st century with an educational system devised to meet the needs of the 19th. Marginal changes are insufficient; rigid school systems can neutralize marginal changes. Just as the requirements of flexibility, quality, and productivity demand a radical restructuring to create a growing economy, so too must our schools reject the status quo if they are to produce individuals with the creativity and problem-solving skills the nation needs.[9]

As American society will be poorly served in the 21st century by an educational system designed to address 19th century needs so the broader and more complex health needs of this decade and the next millennium require a new mix of services and new mechanisms of health care delivery. The present destabilization of the traditional system is an indication that the changes cannot be any longer just marginal. On the other end, change in itself may not provide the answer. The critical question asked by Eli Ginzberg[10] and other keen observers of our health institutions is whether the present winds of change are likely to produce more equitable and efficient mechanisms than those being abandoned. These authors believe that true improvements will be difficult to attain without visionary leadership from the health professions and some empowerment of the presently disenfranchised underserved groups to better articulate their needs and mold policy.

The sixth faulty perception identified in the council's report is that minorities do not really care about education. Combining this perception of carelessness with the American ideal of success as the inevitable outcome of individual determination and hard work brings about the seventh myth that educational achievement and failure are solely the result of individual choice.[11]

Similarly, the perception exists that conditions of poor health and poverty affecting minority groups are often due to personal neglect and that they could be avoided if there were a will to do so. Many health conditions are improved by appropriate behavioral changes, but economic, cultural, and social barriers frustrate personal initiative and decrease or annul the effectiveness of interventions independently of the preferences and commitments of individuals.

Finally, in education, a long-held and persistent myth views bilingualism as an hindrance to academic achievement and multicultural literacy unnecessary to those whose first language is English. The globalization of social and economic interactions are making fluency in a second language a necessary tool for national and international competitiveness. In the health arena, this myth has de-emphasized the use of the Spanish language and weakened the effectiveness of programs targeted to Hispanics. Also, it has discouraged initiatives for teaching foreign languages in professional or health science schools, and has decreased the motivation of physicians to acquire language skills. Because language is the mirror of the culture it defines, it remains the best key for unlocking many subtle clues that, beside clinical tests, guide physicians in the difficult art of diagnosing and treating diseases. The secondary importance given to bilingualism has seriously affected the quality of and the access to health care for Hispanics.

Eliminating myths and damaging preconceptions is neither easy nor likely to occur without deliberate action. But there are no federal offices for "myth abatement" and winning over those who hold them is far from being a clear-cut educational task. In fact, myths are overcome through a process of knowledge dissemination and social evolution that may span several generations. At least we must begin by acknowledging their existence and evaluating their impact when we promote, design, or implement health programs for minorities. With this in mind, let us now look at present health policy options that might improve the health status of Hispanics.

The Health Policy Options

Eli Ginzberg, in his recent book, *The Medical Triangle*, points out that lack of consensus on the many unsolved problems in the nation's health policy agenda makes their solutions next to impossible.[12] His warning reinforces a point we made earlier. Alliances among key power brokers (that is, the medical professions, the local, state, and federal governments, the hospitals, the insurance companies, the manufacturers of health products, the academic health centers, and the special interest groups), supported by a public willingness to sacrifice immediate limited rewards for a more durable but delayed general good, are necessary preconditions to a better but presently elusive future. These preconditions are not easily attained—strong leadership and many compromises are necessary—but, at the very least, they should be explicitly addressed in policy agendas. We discuss some of these key factors next.

Empowerment

In the area of Hispanic health, much of the stimulus and perseverance in promoting convergence of purposes must come from the Hispanic community. Unfortunately, large portions of the Hispanic population lack empowerment. The number of Hispanic health professionals in influential positions as hospital board members, as faculty of academic health institutions, as decisionmakers of federal agencies, such as the Department of Health and Human Services, National Institutes of Health, etc., or as heads of state health departments, is still insignificant. *The Health Policy Agenda for the American People,*[13] a report produced in 1987 by a decision-making body of representatives from state and national organizations listed no one person with a Hispanic surname among its 244 working group members and 171 advisory committee members. A similar lack of influence exists, to a lesser degree, in the business and political arenas.

Political Cohesion

The political effectiveness of an emerging minority group rests on its cohesion on major issues. However, socioeconomic and cultural differences in Hispanic population subgroups have created barriers to broad alliances and account for lack of consensus among Hispanic politicians on Capitol Hill.[14] Actually, not only consensus among Hispanics but alliances and cooperation with other minorities sharing their needs are required to insure progress in addressing Hispanic health challenges. Complementary goals need to be fostered and resources and benefits shared if substantial policy responses are expected in the short run. Among the power brokers in the health sector, an important role is to be played by local governments. As the federal supremacy of almost two decades is withering away, local governments are left with the task of using wisely scarce state and federal funds, promoting alliances with the private sector, and making full use of civic action.[15]

Adequate Information

We noted earlier that overcoming myths and building consensus toward a clear Hispanic health agenda are undermined by the scarcity of Hispanic health studies to date. Insufficient statistics about the Hispanic community and its demographic components provide a weak base for consensus on major health issues. National health assessments from the National Center for Health Statistics, the National Health and Nutrition Examination

Survey, or even national model death certificates did not have Hispanic identifiers until very recently. Other data sources, such as the Hispanic Health and Nutrition Examination Survey, the Epidemiologic Surveillance Project of the Centers for Disease Control, and even the *Report of the Secretary's Task Force on Black and Minority Health,* have brought new but still limited information on Hispanics and their subgroups (see Chapter 13).

Demographic growth and greater political clout may induce public and private investments in data collection and analysis to extend the comparability of demographic, socioeconomic, and epidemiologic information on non-Hispanic whites to major Hispanic subgroups and other minorities. Concurrently, clinical investigations about Hispanic health need to be systematically related to the larger issues of equity and socioeconomic deprivation.

A recent issue of the *Journal of the American Medical Association* totally dedicated to the medical care needs of Hispanics is a significant and symbolic event of progress toward these objectives.[16] But to trigger adequate policy responses, the emerging clinical evidence must be presented in the context of broad societal issues and disseminated through the media in a manner capable of capturing the interest of the general public.

Involvement of Health Professionals

In the short run, the needs of the underserved, and, among them, the Hispanic population, may be more effectively met through training and incentive programs for physicians and other health care providers. Medical practitioners, now facing competitive pressures from an increasing supply of physicians, are likely to be more receptive to locating in underserved areas. Additionally, it would be helpful if more Hispanics could find their way into the health professions since they may be more motivated to work with underserved Hispanic populations. Unfortunately, a sizable increase in the Hispanic health human resource pool is unlikely without drastic changes in the educational system. While health careers rank among the three top career choices among university-bound Hispanic high school students, their enrollment in science and mathematics courses is disproportionately low to adequately support their professional ambitions.[17] The educational myths discussed earlier play an important role in fostering this condition and besides long-term work to eradicate these myths, immediate interventions to increase science and math literacy of Hispanic students are needed at the middle and the elementary school levels and throughout secondary education. Inducing physicians and other health professionals to locate in underserved areas has been the goal of two major federal programs. The status of these and other public efforts to bring health care to the poor are discussed in the next section.

Past Solutions

In the past, national and state initiatives to improve the access and quality of health care for underserved populations have had limited impact on Hispanics. The National Health Service Corps program has placed physicians and other health professionals in public health facilities throughout the country, but participants have too frequently changed location after their obligatory payback time is fulfilled. Changes to increase retention have been slow due to serious funding setbacks. Only recently has the program been reconsidered favorably by Congress.[18]

Area Health Education Centers (AHECs) have almost two decades of tradition in increasing the number and improving the distribution and quality of health professionals to underserved areas.[19] However, AHECs and the parallel program, Health Education Training Centers (HETCs),[20] recently created to target more efforts in U.S.–Mexico border states, need stronger legislative support for bill reauthorization and larger appropriations if they are to address effectively health human resource deficiencies.

The Minority Health Improvement Act passed in 1990 is another vehicle for increasing health labor resources in deserving regions, but only $1.5 million of the $15.5 million for minority health professional manpower enhancement is targeted to "Hispanic Centers of Excellence"[21]—a designation created to identify and support institutions that foster health education and training for Hispanic students.

Since Hispanics are less likely to have private insurance than either white or blacks (see Chapter 13), they rely on public hospitals often affiliated with an academic institution, and, for primary care services, on community health centers (CHCs). CHCs were created in the 1960s as a viable alternative to municipal hospitals for ambulatory care of inner-city poor.[22] Stimulated in 1977 by the Robert Wood Johnson Foundation Municipal Health Services Program (MHSP) and the support of the U.S. Conference of Mayors, the American Medical Association and, later, the Health Care Financing Administration of the Department of Health and Human Services, the initiative confronted a host of difficulties ranging from unfavorable local politics to larger than expected funding needs.[23] After evaluating their performance, the Conservation of Human Resources at Columbia University considers CHCs a feasible and desirable alternative to the municipal hospital for ambulatory care. Also, it predicts that CHCs' limitations in treating trauma and complex medical cases and their inability of being financially self-sustaining—particularly when serving large groups of uninsured individuals—will make their existence questionable as federal, state, and local funds are cut back.[24]

The uncertain future and the predictable lack of growth of CHCs will have a negative impact on the delivery of health care to Hispanics. Community health centers—after some broadening of mission and appropriate alliances with schools and churches—if strategically located, are logical candidates for integrating primary health care and educational interventions in effective outreach programs within Hispanic neighborhoods. CHCs could be subsidized, through grants and expanded eligibility to Medicare and Medicaid payments, to continue providing accessible primary care to inner-city Hispanic communities and, therefore, to contain the cost of more expensive emergency and inpatient care.

Academic health centers recently confronted with the high cost of ambulatory care in teaching hospitals and the difficulties of adequately funding graduate medical education have been experimenting with programs that have public visibility and help demonstrate the value of biomedical research and education to the public at large. The trend is generally favorable to better minority health care and it is particularly advantageous to Hispanics who are in dire need of a strong scientific base for articulating more effectively their health care demands. Alliances or, at least, cooperation between Hispanic organizations and academic health centers can be mutually beneficial and have the potential of bringing about improvements in Hispanic health research, providing culturally sensitive care, and offering educational opportunities to Hispanics.

Clear Goals

To insure success, it is important that the opportunities and strategies just outlined be pursued in the context of clearly stated regional and national Hispanic health goals. A significant undertaking led by the Public Health Service of the Department of Health and Human Services has just produced, after three years of national hearings and the testimony of 750 individuals and organizations, a report—*Healthy People 2000*—that articulates health objectives for the nation. The report sets, as one of three major national goals, the reduction of health disparities among Americans and, for each adverse health condition, indicates improvements that may be achieved in this decade through health promotion, health protection, and preventive service strategies.[25]

Three essential premises to effective minority health care planning discussed in the report have been repeatedly emphasized in this book. They are, first, the recognition that "health care programs are characterized by unacceptable disparities linked to membership in certain racial and ethnic groups." Second, the observation that, "rather than amalgamating into one single group, we have come to recognize and even celebrate our diversity as a basis for national strength," and, third, the warning that "within each racial and ethnic category, significant subgroup differences exist" and that "differences within the principal population must always temper generalizations about their health needs."[26]

These statements are encouraging, but *Healthy People 2000*, due to lack of data, inadequately or, at best, partially describes Hispanic subgroups and their unique health difficulties. Nevertheless, it can be used as a point of departure for setting comparable, realistic, and measurable goals for the major Hispanic subgroups and the regions where Hispanic people concentrate.

Conclusion

In searching for solutions to the Hispanic health challenges, one quickly realizes that in spite of a more favorable environment for a national policy response, drastic federal budgetary constraints are likely to reduce the size and the effectiveness of the few programs that will survive austerity measures. To mention just one example, the whole budget of the Health Resources and Service Administration—responsible for such programs as the National Health Service Corps and the Community and Migrant Health Centers—already inadequate for fiscal year 1991 at the $2,097 million level—has been reduced $79 million in the Administration request for fiscal year 1992.

If immediate relief to the growing health needs of Hispanics is desired, local communities must find the political will to induce support from state governments and foster local alliances with employers, practicing health professionals, private foundations, religious and charitable institutions, and volunteer groups to enhance the effectiveness of scarce resources and extend the reach and scope of existing programs.

In summary, solutions to Hispanic health problems may be pursued on two parallel tracks. On one track, at the national level, long-term solutions may be sought by supporting health care legislation favorable to the poor and the underserved. Hispanic needs likely to be addressed first are those shared by other minorities and compatible with or, possibly, complementary to private sector and industry goals. The strategy suggested here is not to make Hispanic health priorities subservient to goals preferred by other interest groups but to exploit first those opportunities that will insure a rapid and effective policy response.

Also, at the national level, Hispanics should be recognized for their youth and their motivation to succeed—contrary to well-established stereotypes. They should be identified with their family orientation, with a willingness to make sacrifices for a better future for the children and a serene retirement of the elderly. Looking at the demand side of the economic equation, the growing buying power of the Hispanic community should be promoted. And, in the underserved regions of the U.S.–Mexico border, Hispanic health goals should be associated with the future of trade, manufacturing activities,[27] and the survival and growth of the entire North American hemisphere. These broader dimensions of Hispanic health problems are important to the business community and to the public at large and should be relentlessly underlined in national campaigns. Efforts such as those of the Pan American Health Organization (PAHO), presently leading a program of education and planning responsive to regional priorities on both sides of the U.S.–Mexico border, should be supported, kept independent from special interests, and their outcome integrated in documents such as *Healthy People 2000.*

Alliances and cooperation have become the essence of national and global strategies for success in the decade ahead and the next century. The Hispanic community is naturally fragmented because of cultural, geographic, and socioeconomic differences among component groups. While these differences are to be addressed and studied independently for program effectiveness, the political will of these groups and subgroups needs to converge into the national priorities compatible with the goals of other minority and majority groups. But a stronger case for Hispanic health needs must be securely anchored on objective knowledge. And this requires higher-than-current public and private investments in data collection and analysis, standardization of methodologies to increase data comparability, and continuous efforts to relate clinical research to the larger issues of inequity and socioeconomic deprivation. Private foundations can provide needed leadership in this area of applied research whose payoff is too far in the future for attracting traditional sources of federal funds or business support.

The other parallel track of action should, in our view, be aimed at "immediate" solutions for Hispanic health needs. As discussed earlier, this involves regional and statewide strategies relying on local empowerment and regional interests. At the local level, the role of practicing physicians is crucial. Special agreements among municipalities, Medicaid administrators, and medical and dental schools with the support of federal programs, such as AHECs, may create the necessary mix of continuing education opportunities and economic incentives to induce the location of medical practices in underserved areas and effectively expand access to care for Hispanics. Other local and immediately available mechanisms to improve Hispanics' access to care are the sharing of functions and sources of funds among community health centers and municipal hospitals—a difficult but not impossible objective (see Chapter 2)—municipal transportation to clinics and hospitals, coordination of clinical and hospital health improvement programs with schools and churches to insure continuity of care, and the availability of tertiary care from public hospitals and academic health centers. The empowerment of local communities and their participation in policy-making is an essential element of this track of actions.

Is anything happening now that offers hope for the future? The answer is a cautious yes. We have mentioned the favorable changes in the national political environment fueled by the demographic explosion of the Hispanic people. But the political interest of many Hispanic politicians remains fragmented.

There are creative, capable, and dedicated scientists knowledgeable of Hispanic health problems throughout the country. Their number, however, is barely sufficient to provide some policy guidance and totally inadequate to produce the needed data base.

There are effective local and national organizations dedicated to Hispanic health problems. Their work is admirable but usually limited by

Hispanic subgroup loyalties or the political isolation often accompanying militant agendas. Their role is an important one, indispensable to unveil forgotten problems and issues. Yet these endeavors must be complemented with broader cooperative efforts where Hispanic and non-Hispanic intellectuals and decisionmakers work together and educate one another.

Some states and municipalities have articulated Hispanic health objectives, but the good intentions are rarely adequately expressed in budget allocations, partially because sufficient documentation cannot be found to support drastic legislative departures from traditional programs.

In this uncertain future, perhaps we should be guided by the essential vision of the Hispanic culture exposed earlier in this volume by David Hayes-Bautista. Then, we should cautiously look at the limitations identified by Eli Ginzberg and Ray Marshall. And, following the path shown by Henry Cisneros, find inspiration and strength in the American credo for moving forward with deliberate haste to address the needs and barriers that research sampled in this volume has identified.

Notes

1. Wilensky GR. 1988. Filling the Gaps on Health Insurance. *Health Affairs* (7):133–49; Walker B Jr. 1989. Public Health and the New National Effort. The 1988 Presidential Address. *American Journal of Public Health* 79:419–23.

2. Furino A, Munoz E. 1991. Health Status Among Hispanics: Major Themes and New Priorities. *Journal of the American Medical Association* 265:255–57.

3. Walker B Jr. 1989; Novello AC, Wise PW, Kleinman DV. 1991. Hispanic Health: Time for Action. *Journal of the American Medical Association* 265:253–55; and Valdez A. In press. Health Information Resources and Latinos: Some Implications for Health Policy. In Furino A (ed.). *Hispanic Health Policy Issues from Recent Research*. San Antonio, TX: Center for Health Economics and Policy and South Texas Health Research Center, The University of Texas Health Science Center.

4. Action Council on Minority Education. 1990. *Education That Works: An Action Plan for the Education of Minorities*. Cambridge, MA: Massachusetts Institute of Technology. January, pp. 37–44.

5. Lefcowitz MJ. 1982. Poverty and Health: A Re-examination. In Luke RD, Bauer JC (eds.). *Issues in Health Economics*. Rockville, MD: Aspen Systems Corp.

6. Action Council on Minority Education. 1990, p. 37.

7. Action Council on Minority Education. 1990, p. 37.

8. Committee for Economic Development. 1987. *Children in Need*. New York.

9. Action Council on Minority Education. 1990, p. 39.

10. Ginzberg E. 1990. *The Medical Triangle: Physicians, Politicians, and the Public*. Cambridge, MA: Harvard University Press, pp. 3–11.

11. Committee for Economic Development. 1987, p. 40.

12. Ginzberg E. 1990, pp. 276–83.

13. Hirt EJ (ed.). 1987. *The Health Policy Agenda for the American People*. Washington, DC, pp. 251–253.

14. Parker R. 1990. All Over the Map. *Hispanic Business*. March.

15. Cisneros HG. 1990. Health Policy at the Local Level: Improving Access to Affordable Health Care. The Richard and Hinda Rosenthal Lectures, 1990. Washington, DC: Institute of Medicine.

16. *Journal of the American Medical Association.* 1991. January 9.

17. Medina MA. 1989. Health Human Resources and the Hispanic. Paper presented at the National Action Forum on Health Policy and the Hispanic. San Antonio, TX. October 6–7.

18. US Public Health Service. 1990. *Proposed Strategies for Fulfilling Primary Care Manpower Needs.* National Health Service Corps. National Advisory Council. Washington, DC: US Department of Health and Human Services; and US House of Representatives. 1990. *National Health Service Corps Revitalization Amendment of 1990.* Report 101–945. Washington, DC: House of Representatives, October 25.

19. Area Health Education Center Programs: Final Regulations 1983. *Federal Register* 48(36):7443–51.

20. Health Education and Training Centers: Final Regulations. 1990. *Federal Register* 55(148):31237–39.

21. Centers for Excellence in Minority Health Professions Education: Program Announcement. 1990. *Federal Register.* 56(45):9705–07.

22. Anderson RM, Giachello AL, Aday LV. 1986. Access of Hispanics to Health Care and Cuts in Services: A State-of-the-Art Overview. *Public Health Reports* 101(3):238–52.

23. Ginzberg E. 1990, p. 95.

24. Ginzberg E. 1990, pp. 96–110; Ginzberg E, Davis E, Ostow M. 1985. *Local Health Policy in Action: The Municipal Health Services Program.* Totowa, NJ: Rowman and Allanheld.

25. US Public Health Service. 1990. *Healthy People 2000: National Health Promotion and Disease Prevention Objective.* Washington, DC: Department of Health and Human Services, p. 6.

26. US Public Health Service. 1990, p. 31.

27. *Business Week.* 1990. November 12. Cover story.

Appendix
Additional Contributions to the Debate:
Abstracts from Recent Research

Following are abstracts of papers presented at the National Action Forum on Health Policy and the Hispanic held in San Antonio, Texas, on October 6 and 7, 1989. The papers offer a rich view of the variety and complexity of issues related to Hispanic health. Requests for copies of the papers should be directed to the authors.

Accessing Oral Health Care:
The Case of the US/Mexico Border
Ramon Baez

Several variables have been identified that influence the oral health status of a population. Among these, sociodemographic characteristics, socioeconomic status, educational level, dietary patterns, and adequacy of oral services are the most significant and influence the prevalence of dental and oral diseases. The relation of these factors and their degree of influence on the oral health status of the population inhabiting the U.S.-Mexico border is not exactly known; however, populations of low socioeconomic status are more severely affected. Part of the population living along the border fall into the latter category. Hispanics comprise about 80 percent of the border population living on the U.S. side of the border, but this percentage is higher if both sides are considered. Although some Hispanics are wealthy, others live in conditions void of the most basic sanitary elements. Obviously this group faces many barriers to accessing oral services provided by private practitioners. While accessibility obviously is a very important factor in evaluating adequacy of oral health care, it should not be considered alone but in combination with acceptability of providers. Eight counties on the border have been designated "dentists shortage areas." Studies have shown that Hispanics are least likely to go for regular dental care compared to whites, and only seek dentists when an emergency arises, usually when pain becomes intolerable. This indicates that community educational programs to increase awareness and perception of need for regular care should be implemented. Incomplete data on the accessibility, availability, and acceptability of oral health status of the community living in the border region document the need for developing epidemiological studies. The constant flow of people between the United States and Mexico suggests the inclusion in these studies of people from both sides of the border if adequate strategies are to be developed to improve oral health conditions on the U.S.-Mexico border region.

Ramon J. Baez, D.D.S., The University of Texas Health Science Center at San Antonio, 7703 Floyd Curl Drive, San Antonio, TX 78284

The Increasing Significance of Class:
Class, Culture and Mexican American Assimilation
Jorge Chapa

In contrast to the view that assimilation is an endogenous, progressive process which occurs with the mere passage of time, this research suggests that assimilation occurs only under certain economic, political, and social circumstances. Furthermore, the circumstances faced by many Mexican Americans have precluded equitable economic assimilation. Educational and occupational attainment measures obtained from 1940–1970 Census microdata and November 1979 CPA files are compared for third and third-plus generation California Asians, blacks, Anglos, and Mexican Americans. The educational attainment of Mexican Americans relative to Anglo levels indicates very little increase from 1950 through 1979.

There is no significant change in the occupational attainment of Mexican American males as measured by Duncan Socio-economic Index from 1940–1979. Mexican Americans have thus experienced a large relative decrease in occupational attainment when compared to Anglo males. The disaggregation of occupational attainment into class categories shows that third-generation Mexican–American males have become highly concentrated in blue-collar occupations. The analysis of earnings by educational level suggests that much of the inequality between Anglo and Mexican–American earnings is due to lower wages earned by Mexican Americans who have not finished high school and the fact that proportionately many more Mexican Americans have not completed high school than Anglos. Additional analysis of data from the 1979 National Chicano Survey for third and third-plus generation Mexican Americans in California shows that there are marked differences in each of the several different groups of Mexican Americans. Middle-class and white-collar Mexican Americans are much more assimilated than are blue-collar or lower class Mexican Americans. Similarly, Mexican Americans who have finished high school are more assimilated than those who have not. These findings suggest that a large proportion of Mexican Americans may become part of a politically alienated and marginalized lower class with a distinct and disaffected culture and social structure.

Jorge Chapa, Ph.D., The University of Texas at Austin, LBJ School of Public Affairs, Drawer Y, University Station, Austin, TX 78713

Etiology of Non-Insulin Dependent Diabetes Mellitus:
Implications for Therapy
Ralph A. DeFronzo

Non-insulin dependent diabetes mellitus (NIDDM) is a common disorder that affects approximately 5 percent of the U.S. population. In certain subgroups, however, the incidence is much higher and in Mexican Americans it approaches 15–20 percent. The pathogenesis of abnormal glucose tolerance in NIDDM involves defects in both insulin action and insulin secretion. Insulin resistance is a characteristic and universal finding in type II diabetic patients and involves both peripheral (muscle) and hepatic tissues. Augmented glucose production by the liver accounts for fasting hyperglycemia while diminished muscle glucose uptake is responsible for the excessive rise in plasma glucose concentration above baseline following glucose ingestion. Early in the natural history of NIDDM, insulin secretion is enhanced. Yet this increase is not sufficient to offset the presence of insulin resistance. As the diabetic state worsens, there is a progressive decline in insulin secretion and in patients with severe fasting hyperglycemia ($>180-200$ mg/dl) insulin secretion is diminished in absolute terms.

Patients with NIDDM have a markedly increased incidence of hypertension, hyperlipidemia, atherosclerotic cardiovascular disease (myocardial infarction, stroke), and microvascular (nephropathy, retinopathy) complications. There is compelling evidence, in both man and animals, that the microvascular complications are related directly to the degree of hyperglycemia and that tight glycemic control can prevent, or at least ameliorate, the development of diabetic retinopathy and nephropathy. Hypertension also markedly accelerates the progression of diabetic eye and kidney disease. It follows logically, therefore, that control of glycemia and blood pressure are worthy goals in the NIDDM population. There also is irrefutable evidence that both hypertension and hyperlipidemia (which occur with increased frequency in the diabetic patient) contribute to the high incidence of atheroscleriotic cardiovascular complications. Furthermore, there is a compelling body of data suggesting that hyperinsulinemia (which is characteristic of the early stages of NIDDM and occurs as a compensatory response to the insulin resistance) is responsible, at least in part, for the development of hypertension and the abnormal lipid profile (increased LDL cholesterol, decreased HDL cholesterol, elevated VLDL). Thus, insulin resistance, with secondary hyperinsulinemia, can readily explain the frequent occurrence of hyperglycemia, hypertension, and hyperlipidemia in NIDDM; these complicating metabolic disturbances, in turn, can largely account for both macrovascular and microvascular complications in the diabetic patient. From the preceding discussion of the pathogenesis of NIDDM it is easy to understand the high incidence of both macrovascular (heart attack, stroke) and microvascular (kidney and eye disease) complications in this insulin-resistant state. Because hyperglycemia, hyperlipidemia, and hypertension occur in concert in the diabetic patient a comprehensive approach to therapy is indicated. Such an approach would be expected to significantly reduce morbidity and mortality in the diabetic population and prove to be cost effective.

Ralph A. DeFronzo, M.D., The University of Texas Health Science Center at San Antonio, 7703 Floyd Curl Drive, San Antonio, TX 78284

Substance Abuse Prevention in Hispanic Communities: National Perspectives and Regional Comparisons

Sylvia Rodriguez-Andrew

During the past three decades, considerable attention has focused on the prevention of alcohol and other drug abuse. Historically, prevention efforts were primarily school-based programs for youth between the ages of 12 and 18. While studies on alcohol and other drug use have proliferated, little is known about the extent of substance abuse and prevention intervention strategies in Hispanic communities. Data suggest Hispanics are overrepresented among the victims of alcohol and other drug abuse, including drug-related deaths and homicides. (Hispanics are 2.7 times more likely to be in treatment for a drug abuse problem than are whites, and their average age of admission at age 25 suggests early onset of use for heroin, cocaine, marijuana, PCP, and inhalants, usually in combination with alcohol.)

In 1986, the Office of Substance Abuse Prevention (OSAP) was created as a result of the Anti-Drug Abuse Act to develop multidimensional prevention programs to focus on high-risk youth. A total of 130 grants were funded in fiscal year 1987. These programs located in thirty-nine states, target youth in diverse locations, ethnic groups, and high-risk characteristics. Twelve percent (N=16) of the funded OSAP projects target a predominantly Hispanic population.

This report includes an analysis of existing data on alcohol and other drug use among Hispanics and describes emerging characteristics of Hispanic high-risk target populations. The role of culture in prevention intervention strategies and general recommendations for continuing and expanding current prevention, intervention, and treatment efforts with Hispanic populations are also described.

Sylvia Rodriguez-Andrew, Texas Lutheran College, 1000 West Court Street, Seguin, TX 78155

AIDS Risk-Reduction Among Hispanic Intravenous Drug Users

Antonio L. Estrada, Julie Erickson, Peggy Glider, Sally Stevens, Maria Eugenia Fernandez, and C. Phil

Recent evidence documents a critical need to provide culturally relevant risk-reduction interventions for IV drug users in general, and Hispanic IVDUs specifically.

As of August 30, 1989, 6,234 Hispanic cases of AIDS had been diagnosed in persons who reported IV drug use (CDC, 1989). Another 1,050 Hispanic AIDS cases had been diagnosed in homosexual/bisexual men who reported IV drug use. Moreover, of the 353 Hispanic pediatric AIDS cases, 85 percent have IV drug use of parents as a cofactor in HIV transmission.

This paper documents the extent of risk behaviors among a sample of Hispanic IVDUs in Tucson and Nogales, Arizona. These risk behaviors include multiple sexual partners, unsafe sexual practices, needle-sharing patterns, and frequency of injection. Another purpose of this paper is to present a prevention or risk-reduction model that appears relevant to AIDS risk among this population.

Pender's Health-Protecting Model is a modification of Becker's Health Belief Model based on research to date concerning the determinants of preventive behavior. Pender's Prevention Model offers an organizing framework for research efforts and for health-promoting interventions related to the risk for AIDS among Hispanic IV drug users. Variables in the model and their hypothesized relationships are consistent with recent work on AIDS including Emmons et al.'s (1986) psychological predictors of behavior change among homosexual men, Joseph et al.'s (1984) approach to assessment of coping with the AIDS threat, and William's (1986) community intervention project.

Antonio L. Estrada, Ph.D., M.S.P.H., University of Arizona College of Medicine, 3131 E. Second Street, Tucson, AZ 85716

Assessing Needs and Developing Treatment Strategies for Service Deprived Populations

Lars Folke

The ultimate challenge facing the health sciences is to prevent and intercept diseases early on in the process by simple, comfortable, and cost-effective methods. Such strategies become particularly beneficial to populations of low socioeconomic status and devoid of appropriate health services. Many Mexican–Americans living in *colonias* meet these conditions and needs.

To address these problems, the emerging interdisciplinary science of health care assessment should be employed to integrate both epidemiological and socio-economical surveys, strategic health care planning, health care delivery, and subsequent assessment of cost-effectiveness, cost-utility, and patient satisfaction.

This approach was initiated in 1988 at San Elizario, Texas, a small town of 3,000 residents, located twenty miles southeast of El Paso. The prime concern was to establish medical and dental health needs in preselected family units. Subjects (N=394) between 4–34 years of age were surveyed as to health habits, prior illnesses, socioeconomic information as well as clinically examined to determine medical and oral conditions and needs. This report will focus on individuals (N=182) 15–34 years of age.

The average family income was $7,500 with a median household size of 4.2 subjects. Forty-five percent of the households received food stamps. Self-reported health status indicated that 28 percent experienced excellent to very good health while 34 percent expressed fair to poor health. No hypertension was detected in this age group while approximately 25 percent had a body mass index greater than the 85th percentile. Six percent of the individuals examined had elevated cholesterol levels. Antibody to hepatitis B was found in 1 percent of the subjects while the corresponding prevalence of antibody to hepatitis A surpassed 90 percent in individuals 23–34 years of age. The majority of these infections were reported as asymptomatic.

The oral status of this sample provides interesting comparisons with recently published data presented in "The National Survey of Oral Health in Adults, 1985–1986." Among the San Elizario residents, age 15–34, none were edentulous. Existing tooth loss was almost exclusively related to the molar teeth. This was primarily due to occlusal decay (dental caries). Insufficient financial means and lack of local access to preventive health services were the main barriers to proper conservative care. The San Elizario residents had twice the prevalence of decayed surfaces compared to the national average, which in turn revealed five times as many filled surfaces. Whether excessive treatment explains the greater number of filled surfaces, a comparison of data clearly supported the observations that caries prevalence is much less among 15–34-year-old subjects in San Elizario. Yet, these residents had more active dental decay due to unmet preventive care. Periodontal disease was a very frequent observation. The mean number of bleeding gingival sites ranged from 50 to 60 percent which corresponded well with the presence of subgingival calculus. In contrast, the mean number of sites with probing pocket depth (.3mm) was less than 17 percent which seemed remarkably low, especially since many were pseudo-pockets, considering the extensive distribution of subgingival calculus. In comparison, the San Elizario residents revealed far more incipient signs of periodontal disease than reported in the national survey. Yet, attachment loss, based on clinical and radiographic examinations, seemed much contained indicating an unexpected individual resistance to the etiological insults present.

Studies on cost-effectiveness have so far been carried out in reference to dental decay and periodontal disease. Initial data indicate that restorative care of all established lesions in an estimated population of 1,068 subjects, age 14–34, would amount to $326,000 excluding yearly follow-ups. On the other hand, a preventive, early interceptive approach involving sealant therapy and dental hygiene care would be estimated at $54,000 per year.

Regarding general health patterns in San Elizario, it would be essential to focus on the environmental factors and, in view of oral diseases, it would be particularly cost-effective to practice preventive care.

Lars E. A. Folke, D.D.S., Ph.D., The Center for Medicine and Dentistry, 301 85 Halmstad Sweden

Acculturation, Access, and Utilization of Health Services by Hispanics

Helen P. Hazuda

Since Mexican Americans are becoming more culturally and socioeconomically diverse, an important consideration in targeting public health interventions for this group is whether Mexican Americans at different levels of acculturation (i.e., adoption of mainstream, non-Hispanic white attitudes, values, and behavior) and socioeconomic status (SES) differ significantly in their health care needs, access, and utilization of services. To answer this question, data were obtained on a community-based, random sample of Mexican Americans, 839 men and 1,169 women. Commonly used indicators of health care need, access, and utilization of services were regressed on age, SES, and three separate dimensions of adult acculturation: functional integration with mainstream society (Functional Integration), value placed on preserving Mexican cultural origins (Cultural Value), and attitude toward traditional family structure and sex-role organization (Family Attitude). Analyses were performed separately for men and women, applying a test for trend in the effects of each separate acculturation dimension and SES.

As the level of Functional Integration and SES increased, the proportion of both men and women who perceived their physical health as fair or poor progressively decreased. Neither acculturation nor SES were significantly associated with the presence of major health problems in men, but as the level of acculturation on Family Attitude increased, the proportion of women with major health problems decreased steadily. Interestingly, as the level of Functional Integration increased, the proportion of men and women who reported any disability days became progressively larger, and, for women, increased SES was also associated with an increase in any disability days.

Access to health care was strongly related to both acculturation and SES in men. At each higher level of Functional Integration and SES, an increasingly greater proportion of men had a regular source of care and private health insurance; acculturation of Family Attitude was also associated with an increase in private health insurance. In addition, a progressively greater proportion of women at each higher level of Functional Integration, had a regular source of care and private health insurance; increased SES was also associated with increased private health insurance.

Utilization of health services, as measured by physician visits and hospitalization during the previous year, was not related to either acculturation or SES in men. In women, however, an increasingly greater proportion had visited a physician within the previous year at each higher level of Functional Integration. Cultural Values had no significant effect on health care needs, access, or utilization of services in either sex group.

These results indicate the need to target specific Mexican–American subgroups for various public health interventions and to use specific dimensions of acculturation as well as SES in identifying the subgroups most in need of intervention.

Helen P. Hazuda, Ph.D., The University of Texas Health Science Center at San Antonio, 7703 Floyd Curl Drive, San Antonio, TX 78284

Unemployment and Mental Health: Mexican American and Anglo Workers and Their Wives

Sue Keir Hoppe

Increasing research attention is being given to the mental health costs of unemployment. Studies have shown increased depression and anxiety following job separation, but not all individuals are affected equally by the experience. Identification of individuals and groups psychologically vulnerable to job loss is needed to formulate responsive public policy and effective intervention strategies. There are no available data on the mental health effects of job loss for Mexican Americans, a group for whom the unemployment rate is higher and more sensitive to economic downturns than that for Anglos. This paper reports results of a study designed to address this knowledge gap.

The primary purpose of the paper is to assess ethnic differences in psychological response to job loss and to reemployment or continued unemployment among male breadwinners and their wives. Specifically, sex and ethnic differences in levels of depression are examined at two time points—at or near the time of the male's job loss (Time 1) and four months later (Time 2). In addition, the paper examines: (1) work and job loss context (occupation, industry, union membership, job satisfaction, prior unemployment, reason for job loss, anticipation of job loss, reemployment prospects) as correlates of or "risk factors" for initial (Time 1) depressive reactions of men to job loss; (2) the effect of change in work context on depression levels in reemployed men at Time 2; and (3) effects of unemployment benefits and job-seeking assistance on depression among continuously unemployed men at Time 2.

Method. In 1987, 1,016 men were interviewed in the San Antonio Work and Health Study, a panel study designed to investigate ethnic differences in responses to job loss. Men who had recently experienced job loss were identified through the Texas Employment Commission (TEC) at the time of application for benefits. A control group of stably employed men was selected with multistage probability sampling procedures in census tracts in which high densities of unemployed respondents lived. Study subjects were married, 20–45 years of age, and employed or formerly employed in selected industries. An extensive work history and information on health and resources used to cope with job loss were obtained. Four months later, 856 of the men were re-interviewed to determine changes in employment status and health. A subsample of 220 wives was also studied at both times to assess the effects of job loss on the families of unemployed breadwinners. The primary dependent variable employed in these analyses, depression, was measured by the 20–item Center for Epidemiologic Studies–Depression Scale (CES–D). CES–D scores range from 0 to 60; scores of 16 or greater indicate clinically significant depression.

Initial Reaction to Job Loss. At Time 1, mean depression levels were significantly higher among unemployed than employed men (9.8 versus 5.3, respectively). Levels of depression were somewhat higher for Anglo than for Mexican–American men in both employment status groups, but the differences were not significant. About 20 percent of the unemployed men in both ethnic groups were experiencing depressive symptoms at levels indicative of clinical impairment (CES–D > 16).

Among unemployed men at Time 1, there were no ethnic differences in depression levels among those who had been in skilled occupations, worked in trade, construction, or government industries, or had been laid-off. However, levels of depression were significantly higher among Anglos than among Mexican Americans who had been in semiskilled or unskilled jobs, or in manufacturing. For unemployed Mexican–American men, there was an inverse relationship between depression and job satisfaction—i.e., men who reported low job satisfaction were most likely to react to job loss by becoming depressed; there was no relationship between job satisfaction and depression among unemployed Anglo men. Union membership, prior unemployment experience, and anticipation of job loss did not affect depression levels among unemployed men. Perceived difficulty of finding a new job was strongly related to depression among unemployed men in both ethnic groups.

At Time 1, there were no significant differences in levels of depression among Anglo wives by employment status of husband. However, Mexican–American women whose husbands were unemployed reported significantly higher mean levels of depression than those with employed husbands (11.1 versus 7.8, respectively). Levels of clinically significant depression for both Mexican–American and Anglo women with unemployed husbands were about 20 percent.

Effects of Reemployment and Continued Unemployment. From Time 1 to Time 2, mean depression levels decreased among men who became reemployed (10.6 to 6.3 for Anglos, 9.1 and 5.2 for Mexican Americans), but the mean Time 2 depression levels for Anglo men remained above those for their continuously employed controls (5.4). Rates of clinically significant depression also declined among reemployed men (to 10 percent for Anglos and 5 percent for Mexican Americans). A change in occupation or industry to obtain reemployment did not significantly increase depression.

Mean depression levels also decreased somewhat from Time 1 to Time 2 for men who did not return to work (9.6 to 7.9 for Anglos, 9.2 to 8.0 for Mexican Americans), but remained higher than those for reemployed or stably employed men. Continuously unemployed Mexican Americans experienced a higher rate of clinically significant depression than Anglos at Time 2 (14 versus 10 percent). Use of TEC placement services did not affect depression levels among continuously unemployed men; unemployment insurance benefits buffered the impact of unemployment for these men, especially for Mexican Americans.

Mean depression levels for wives whose husbands were reemployed by Time 2 decreased from 10.2 to 6.8 for Anglos and from 13.8 to 11.4 for Mexican Americans. However, depression levels for the latter remained dramatically high, with 32 percent of these Mexican–American women experiencing symptoms of clinical significance. For wives whose husbands did not return to work, depression levels decreased from 9.4 to 7.9 for Mexican Americans but increased somewhat for Anglos (7.3 to 8.1). About 15 percent of the latter experienced clinically significant symptomatology, compared to 13 percent for Mexican Americans.

Summary and Discussion. The findings indicate significant initial depressive reactions to job loss among both Mexican–American and Anglo men. Over time, depression decreased among these men, more so for those who became reemployed than for those who did not return to work. Reactions of wives to husband's job loss were more variable. Anglo women showed less initial reactivity to husband's job loss than Mexican–American women, but their levels of depression tended to increase if husbands did not gain reemployment. These findings are discussed with respect to: (1) the contribution of work context to explaining reactions to job loss; (2) ethnic and sex differentials in vulnerability and resilience to stress associated with job loss; (3) the health care needs of unemployed men and their wives; and (4) the quality and productivity of the labor force.

Sue Keir Hoppe, Ph.D., The University of Texas Health Science Center at San Antonio, 7703 Floyd Curl Drive, San Antonio, TX 78284

AIDS and the Mexican Americans:
Comparisons with National Data

Cervando Martinez, Jr.

On a national level, AIDS is affecting blacks and Hispanics at disproportionately high rates. The principal reason for this is the higher representation of blacks and Hispanics among intravenous drug users (IVDU). Hispanics make up 13.1 percent of AIDS cases nationally but represent only 6.4 percent of the 1980 U.S. population. Also, Hispanics are culturally unique and many speak primarily Spanish, thus making prevention and education efforts more complicated and challenging. Finally, the treatment of AIDS is now moving in the direction of earlier, and perhaps more hopeful, intervention. However, blacks and Hispanics are underrepresented in National Institute of Health AIDS treatment trials, again, presenting a major challenge and issue.

This report presents national data in three areas (epidemiology, education/prevention, and treatment) focusing on Hispanics and presents data about Mexican Americans for comparison. The similarities and differences are highlighted and policy implications discussed.

Cervando Martinez, Jr., Ph.D., The University of Texas Health Science Center at San Antonio, 7703 Floyd Curl Drive, San Antonio, TX 78284

Health Human Resources and the Hispanic

Miguel A. Medina and Pedro J. Lecca

Despite the millions of dollars spent to increase the number of minorities in health professions schools, gains have been meager. Even with the unprecedented explosion in scientific knowledge and the capacity of medicine to diagnose, treat, and cure disease, Hispanics have not benefited fully from the fruits of science.

We know that health professions schools need a minority student pool on which to base any successful recruitment effort, yet the size and quality of that pool has been determined by many factors, many of them negative, that occur as early as the elementary grades. One-third of the Hispanic high school students in the nation indicate a desire to pursue a professional career which requires a university degree and within this group a health career ranks among the top three career choices. Yet the number of Hispanics enrolled in science and mathematic courses in high school is substantially lower than that of Anglo students. Somehow the information regarding the academic background required to enter this professional area has not been communicated to these students.

There are a large number of health professions schools which have initiated programs to increase minority access to a health career, however, the literature on minority participation in these schools reveals a paucity of research. There have been reports on individual programs, but few evaluations on the success of the programs or their individual components. Most of the programs focus on activities primarily designed for juniors and seniors in colleges and universities. Although it has been demonstrated that early intervention is required to prepare them for a health career and to stem the high dropout rate, programs at the middle and early high school years are few in number.

The number of college-level Hispanic students who indicate a professional health career as their goal is greatly diminished by the time they become seniors. One strategy to increase the number of upper classmen who will be viable applicants is to broaden the base of this pool. This base could be greatly amplified by the expansion and intensification of efforts directed at the middle school or the elementary school level.

Intervention programs must be rigorous and challenging. They must make the students aware of the level of academic difficulty which awaits them in their future studies and also must prepare them to succeed in these courses. Three important components that could compose the core of any model designed to increase the participation of minorities in the health professions will be presented.

Recommendations to increase minority participation must also involve the health professions schools. They must demonstrate a strong commitment to increasing minority admissions and retention. Elitism must be replaced with community involvement. The health professions schools must become more actively involved in the minority community, maintaining close contact with high schools, teachers, principals, and parent and youth groups. A similar interaction should exist at the college and university level. One question which the health professional schools must address is whether it is part of their responsibility as educational institutions to become involved with these types of activities in the community. Many of them provide low-cost or free medical services to the underserved and poor minority population. Should they not also use their resources to enhance the educational status of this same population?

Miguel A. Medina, Ph.D., The University of Texas Health Science Center at San Antonio, 7703 Floyd Curl Drive, San Antonio, TX 78284

The Economics of Health Care Among the Latinos of South Florida

Raul Moncarz

With the influx of political refugees in the 1960s, and with the increasing participation of Hispanics in the total population, the health system experimented a process of cultural adaptation. Cuban clinics were established to provide family-oriented health services for low- and middle-income Cuban families, initially, as a prepaid cooperative practice operation, which experimented with a process of "market concentration", in the 1980s, and now work on a base of payment of fee for services. In spite of the critics of the "Cuban clinics," these health care facilities are appreciated by the Hispanics they serve. The recent influx of refugees put pressure on the health system, especially in emergency and prenatal care, where health services for indigent persons was overburdened. It is estimated that of 406,600 medically indigent in district XI, in 1987, 173,600 were Hispanics, there is a significant number of Hispanics, under 65, uninsured or partly insured who do not meet medicaid eligibility. A 1986 sample shows that 25 percent of the Hispanics considered cost a serious problem for access to health services. The price index for medical services has increased at a higher rate than global inflation, and the influx of immigrants has increased the labor supply for low-income jobs, and, therefore, has put pressure on real wages. As a result, many Hispanics with low income, do not have the financial capacity to pay insurance premiums, and use medical assistance almost only in emergency cases. The growing and relatively old Hispanic population would require in the future an increase in the financial resources needed to provide health services to this segment of the population. Particularly, different policies will need to be implemented or expanded, regarding the low-income segment of the consumers of health services, and for the elderly population.

Raul Moncarz, Ph.D., Florida International University, University Park Campus, Miami, FL 33199

Epidemiology of Diabetes Complications in Mexican Americans: Implications for Health Care Access and Utilization

Michael P. Stern and Jacqueline A. Pugh

The prevalence and incidence of type II diabetes (non-insulin dependent diabetes) is substantially higher in Mexican Americans than in non-Hispanic whites. This, combined with its earlier age of onset and the younger age structure of the Mexican–American population, makes diabetes a major public health problem in this ethnic group and one which to a greater extent than in non-Hispanics strikes people in the prime of life. Both genetic and environmental factors undoubtedly contribute to this epidemic. The environmental factors would appear to be those commonly associated with the phenomenon of "modernization" or "westernization," namely, dietary change, and adoption of sedentary life-styles. As such, they are potentially modifiable and amenable to clinical and public health action. There is as yet no proof from clinical trials that modification of any or all of these environmental factors will in fact prevent diabetes. When clinical trials are performed, high-risk population such as Mexican Americans should be considered as potential target populations, both because of the public health relevance and the lower sample size requirements in such populations. Further advances in identifying genetic susceptibles would also facilitate the design and execution of such trials.

The increased risk of microvascular complications in Mexican–American diabetics puts this population in "double jeopardy," i.e., they have a greater risk of acquiring diabetes in the first instance, and, once having acquired it, they have a greater risk of suffering from its complications. It is still not clear whether the increased risk of complications in this ethnic group stems from an intrinsically more severe biological process or barriers to adequate medical care and/or poor compliance. Prospective data currently being gathered should help resolve this issue. Assuming that medical care plays a role, a major opportunity—and challenge—exists to reduce substantially the morbidity, mortality, and economic burden associated with type II diabetes and its complications in the Mexican–American population.

Mexican Americans with non-insulin dependent diabetes have higher rates of microvascular complications than non-Hispanic whites. One mediator of this difference may be poorer health care access. Data were obtained for 349 Mexican Americans and 76 non-Hispanic whites with non-insulin dependent diabetes identified in the San Antonio Heart Study, a population-based study of diabetes and cardiovascular risk factors. More Mexican Americans than non-Hispanic whites had no form of health insurance (30 vs. 4 percent; $p < .001$) and relied on clinics rather than private doctors as their primary source of care (21 vs. 12 percent; $p = .05$). Among those with health insurance, fewer Mexican Americans than non-Hispanic whites had private health insurance (71 vs. 92 percent; $p = .001$), and those Mexican Americans that were privately insured had less comprehensive coverage than did non-Hispanic whites. Mexican Americans were less likely than non-Hispanic whites to receive reimbursement for outpatient doctor visits (69 vs. 89 percent; $p = .06$) or for medications (56 vs. 85 percent; $p = .01$). Among Mexican Americans who had been previously diagnosed with non-insulin dependent diabetes, those with microvascular complications defined as proteinuria $1+$ or greater by dipstick, albuminuria of 30mg/1, or retinopathy had a consistent pattern of poorer health care access than did those without microvascular complications. Associations between microvascular complications and indicators of health care access were statistically significant for albuminuria and receiving care from a clinic vs. private doctor; for proteinuria and lack of health insurance coverage for outpatient doctor visits; and for retinopathy and lack of health insurance coverage for medications. Since all associations between albuminuria, proteinuria, and retinopathy were in the expected direction even though not all were statistically significant, these results suggest that poorer health care access may at least partially explain the higher than expected rates of microvascular complications in Mexican Americans.

Michael P. Stern, M.D., The University of Texas Health Science Center at San Antonio, 7703 Floyd Curl Drive, San Antonio, TX 78284

Hispanic Mental Health: A Family Affair

Jose Szapocznik

The demographics of Hispanics, a young and fast-growing population, have important implications for both present and future mental health needs of this ethnic group. Both Hispanic culture and Hispanic demographics point to the central role of the family in planning mental health programs. It is for this reason that this paper presents a mental health strategy that builds on the crucial role of the Hispanic family.

The family is of paramount importance to the mental health of its members. This is particularly true because the family is both the buffer for environmental stressors as well as the context within which Hispanic children learn to cope with the environmental stressors that will confront them throughout their lives.

Research on high-risk families has indicated a relationship between family functioning and sociodemographic variables such as race, poverty, and unemployment. These factors may contribute to family disruption or dysfunction. However, reviews of family factors show that the final pathway through which family factors influence delinquency in the child is the way the family functions, rather than external demographic variables. Family and parental variables affect the adjustment outcome of children and adolescents. There is some evidence that the family may play a more important role in the adjustment of children among Hispanics than among non-Hispanics.

We recognize that the mental health needs of Hispanics are broad and far reaching, including, among others, the needs of infants, the developmentally disabled and the elderly. However, in this paper we focus on a specific issue, behavioral problems among Hispanic youths, that has become urgent because of its epidemic proportions in Hispanic communities throughout the United States.

The literature has shown a close link between family functioning and adjustment of its members. Research on the adjustment of the Hispanic children, adolescents, and their families has generally focused on high-risk factors associated with the development of behavioral problems among Hispanic youth. The "behavioral problem" literature has focused on adolescent substance abuse, delinquency, gang membership/violence, and teenage pregnancy. More recently, interest can be found in protective factors contributing to adjustment. This paper looks into the family to determine which family interactional characteristics mediate to make families most vulnerable to these stressors and which family interactional characteristics serve as a protective factor that attenuate environmental stressors and promote adjustment.

The psychological literature has identified a long list of antecedent, moderator, and outcome variables of family and child adjustment. Research has shown that behavior problems in children and adolescents are generally a symptom of a broader, more complex syndrome of acting-out behaviors. Problem behaviors tend to coexist as a syndrome and have antecedents. Adolescent acting-out behaviors such as substance abuse, delinquency, and teenage pregnancy are part of this more general "behavior problem syndrome."

The behavior problem syndrome is hypothesized to be the result of a set of underlying antecedent factors, among the most important of which is maladjustive family organization or interactional patterns. Differences in acculturation levels between Hispanic parents and their more Americanized children often contribute toward behavioral dysfunction in families. Among Hispanics, problems in acculturation affect family functioning and increase the risk of adjustment problems of its members.

Families who show maladaptive patterns of interaction are often unable to successfully deal with conflicts that emerge within the family and family members become more vulnerable to environmental stressors. From a preventive perspective the goal is to improve family functioning in order to prepare the family to handle current and future stressors.

Much work remains to be done in the conceptualization and testing of intervention specifically aimed at the Hispanic family. Nevertheless, already available are a number of effective prevention and intervention approaches which target maladaptive patterns of family functioning in Hispanic families. Research efforts must continue to shed light on the protective and high-risk factors affecting Hispanic families. Preventive and treatment family-oriented mental health models based on suitability and effectiveness are required for meeting the mental health needs of Hispanic youths and families of the 1990s.

Jose Szapocznik, Ph.D., University of Miami School of Medicine, 1425 N.W. 10th Avenue, Suite 302, Miami, FL 33136

Information—Poor Health Policy:
The Case of Latinos

Armando Valdez

Contemporary society is characterized by an information-rich environment in which the volume of printed matter has been increasing exponentially every year in the past two decades. In the 1980s, the advent of the high-density, integrated circuits ushered in an era of innovation in information processing and storage technology. With the introduction of microcomputers—desktop personal computers—this decade has magnified our power to access, control, and manipulate information of all types. The prognosis for the information society is for an increased tempo in the production of information paralleled by an expansion of the capacity and power of the tools we use for processing this information.

Advances in information technology enable us to manage this abundance of information. Our ability to organize, catalog, store, search, and retrieve information tames the passive information in our environments and puts it at our disposal in the form of computerized databases, both desktop and online databases. This abundance of seemingly disparate information now becomes a valuable and useful information resource.

There are numerous online public databases in the United States on a wide range of topics, including health. Among these, the best known and more widely used of the health databases is Medline/Medlars. There is only one public online database focused on Hispanic health, the Hispanic Health Database developed at Stanford in the mid–1980s. Given the increasing numbers and diversity of online health databases and the pressing need for current and accurate information on the health of Latinos, it is apparent that the development of information resources on Latino health has not kept pace with the field. But in fact the situation is worse than a mere lag in development. The nation's health information resources on Latinos are seriously underdeveloped. This condition is not the result of a conscious national policy. Quite the contrary, it is the result of an unconscious absence of a coherent policy. This information underdevelopment is largely due to the same structural, systemic factors that account for the marginalization of Latinos in our society.

The underdevelopment of Latino health information resources has serious complications for health policy. There is general consensus that Latinos comprise a significant segment of the nation's at-risk population. Current and accurate information are essential to the formulation of public policy.

The principal factors that place Latinos at risk—demographic growth and increasing poverty—create a sense of urgency for policies that address the needs of this population. Latinos are among the fastest growing segments of the nation's population, increasing at five times the national rate. An estimated one-fourth of Latinos in the United States live below the poverty line. The number of Latinos living in poverty is increasing by an estimated 400,000 persons annually. The Latino poor are beset by all the difficulties of poverty, not the least of which is limited access to adequate health care.

In spite of the absence of adequate and comprehensive data on the health status of Latinos and the myriad health problems faced by this community, the segment of this population that is at risk will continue to grow. Given the paradigm that research precedes public policy, the development of information resources on Latino health is a critical adjunct to addressing the health issues of that community.

Information resources on Latinos are in an underdeveloped state. It wasn't until the mid–1980s that the Hispanic HANES data began to provide us with an accurate and current profile of the health and nutritional status of Latinos in the nation. Prior to this, we had only an incomplete glimpse at health and nutritional status of Latinos. Research can provide vital information on which health policy can be based. So too can an integrated, online database on Latino health.

An integrated online database on Latino health would serve two critical functions. It would serve as a research tool to provide a detailed view of the state of knowledge (epidemiology, incidence, treatments, etc.) in any given health area or specialty and thus inform and guide researchers and other scholars about gaps in research that need to be addressed. Moreover, an integrated database would provide policymakers a comprehensive view of specific areas of concern and suggest areas that require additional research as well as indicate aggregate progress in addressing specific health issues.

Armando Valdez, Ph.D., Valdez and Associates, 10 Jordan Avenue, Los Altos, CA 94022

About the Book and Editor

Exploring the many dimensions of Hispanic health issues, this book updates interested readers with recent information and offers a view of the depth, scope, and complementarity of the challenges of providing adequate health care. Accordingly, the book is organized in four sections addressing, first, the conceptual, institutional, and policy elements of the problems and their solutions; second, the clinical evidence about diseases for which Hispanics are disproportionally at risk; third, social and economic factors that have an impact on the health status of Hispanics; and, fourth, future policy options that could improve the health conditions of this increasingly large and underserved group of Americans.

While clarifying the issues, the book documents the importance of seeking solutions to Hispanic health problems with determination and haste. Hispanics will soon represent the largest minority in American society. And, 20 million people with Latin American and Spanish origins contribute a large, youthful, and potentially very productive group of workers to our aging labor force.

Finally, in searching for solutions to Hispanic health challenges, we learn that in order to improve the health of all Americans, while containing costs, it is necessary to address, proactively, the special needs of our culturally diverse society.

Antonio Furino is professor of economics and director of the Center for Health Economics and Policy at The University of Texas Health Science Center at San Antonio, where he is teaching and heading research on the economic, entrepreneurial, and policy aspects of health professions and health care services. He is a senior research fellow at the IC² Institute of The University of Texas at Austin, where he is engaged in studies of human resource development and productivity. His writings are multidisciplinary with a focus on the policy implications of health and human resources problems.

About the Contributors

Katherine Baisden, M.A., Stanford Center for Chicano Research, Stanford University, Stanford, California

John P. Brown, B.D.Sc., M.S., Ph.D., Professor and Chairman, Department of Community Dentistry, The University of Texas Health Science Center at San Antonio, Texas

Henry G. Cisneros, Ph.D., former Mayor of the City of San Antonio, Deputy Chairman of the Federal Reserve Bank of Dallas, and Chairman, Cisneros Asset Management Co., San Antonio, Texas

Adela de la Torre, Ph.D., Associate Professor and Chair of the Chicano and Latino Studies Department, California State University, Long Beach, California

David V. Espino, M.D., Assistant Professor and Director, Division of Geriatrics, Department of Family Practice, The University of Texas Health Science Center at San Antonio, Texas

Antonio Furino, Ph.D., Professor of Economics and Director, Center for Health Economics and Policy, The University of Texas Health Science Center at San Antonio, Texas

Eli Ginzberg, Ph.D., Professor Emeritus and Director, The Eisenhower Center for the Conservation of Human Resources, Columbia University, New York, New York

Fernando A. Guerra, M.D., M.P.H., Director of the San Antonio Metropolitan Health District, Practicing Pediatrician, former Kellogg Fellow at the Harvard School of Public Health, and Founder and Medical Director of the Barrio Comprehensive Health Care Center, San Antonio, Texas

Steven M. Haffner, M.D., Associate Professor, Division of Clinical Epidemiology, Department of Medicine, The University of Texas Health Science Center at San Antonio, Texas

David E. Hayes-Bautista, Ph.D., Professor, School of Medicine, and Director, Chicano Studies Research Center, University of California, Los Angeles, California

Douglas S. Livornese, Resident of Internal Medicine, Medical College of Pennsylvania, Philadelphia, Pennsylvania

Ray Marshall, Ph.D., former U.S. Secretary of Labor, Professor and Audre and Bernard Rapoport Centennial Chair in Economics and Public Affairs, LBJ School of Public Affairs, The University of Texas at Austin, Texas

Reynaldo Martorell, Ph.D., Professor of Nutrition, Food Research Institute, Stanford University, Stanford, California

Maureen McCormac, Director of Nursing Systems, Robert Wood Johnson Hospital, New Brunswick, New Jersey

Fernando S. Mendoza, M.D., M.P.H., Associate Professor of Pediatrics and Director, Stanford Center for Chicano Research, Stanford University, Stanford, California

M. Eugene Moyer, Ph.D., Senior Economist, Office of the Assistant Secretary for Planning and Evaluation, U.S. Department of Health and Human Services, Washington, D.C.

Eric Munoz, M.D., M.B.A., F.A.C.S., Medical Director, University Hospital, Associate Professor of Surgery and Associate Dean for Clinical Affairs, Medical School, University of Medicine and Dentistry of New Jersey, Newark, New Jersey

John W. Odom, M.D., Attending Surgeon, Memorial Medical Center, Savannah, Georgia

Refugio I. Rochin, Ph.D., Professor, Department of Agricultural Economics, and Director of Chicano Studies, University of California, Davis, California

Mary Ann Sakmyster, Ph.D., Data Analyst, Quality Assessment, University of Medicine and Dentistry of New Jersey–University Hospital, Newark, New Jersey

Laura Saldivar, M.D., Resident, Department of Pediatrics, Stanford University School of Medicine, Stanford, California

Marta Sotomayor, Ph.D., President, National Hispanic Council on Aging, Washington, D.C.

Michael P. Stern, M.D., Professor and Chief, Division of Clinical Epidemiology, Department of Medicine, The University of Texas Health Science Center at San Antonio, Texas

Christine A. Stroup-Benham, M.A., Research Associate, Center for Cross-Cultural Research, The University of Texas Medical Branch at Galveston, Texas

Ciro V. Sumaya, M.D., M.P.H.T.M., Professor of Pediatrics (infectious diseases) and Associate Dean for Affiliated Programs and Continuing Medical Education, Director, South Texas Health Research Center and Area Health Education Center, The University of Texas Health Science Center at San Antonio, Texas

Ramon Torres, M.A., Medical Student, University of Medicine and Dentistry of New Jersey–New Jersey Medical School, Newark, New Jersey

Bartholomew J. Tortella, M.D., Assistant Professor of Surgery and Acting Director of Emergency Services, University of Medicine and Dentistry of New Jersey–University Hospital and New Jersey Medical School, Newark, New Jersey

Fernando M. Trevino, Ph.D., M.P.H., Professor and Dean, School of Health Professions, Southwest Texas State University, San Marcos, Texas

R. Burciaga Valdez, Ph.D., M.H.S.A., Assistant Professor, School of Public Health, University of California, Los Angeles, California, Health Services Researcher, RAND Corporation

Stephanie J. Ventura, A.B., M.A., Statistician, National Center for Health Statistics, Rockville, Maryland

David C. Warner, Ph.D., Professor of Public Affairs, LBJ School of Public Affairs, The University of Texas at Austin, Texas

Index